Macro Magic
with
Turbo Assembler®

Macro Magic
with
Turbo Assembler®

Jim Mischel

Edited by Jeff Duntemann

John Wiley & Sons, Inc.
New York • Chichester • Brisbane • Toronto • Singapore

Library of Congress Cataloging-in-Publication Data

Mischel, Jim
    Macro magic with Turbo Assembler / Jim Mischel ; edited by Jeff Duntemann.
    p.   cm.
    Includes index.
    ISBN 0-471-57815-0 (acid free paper)
    1. Assembler language (Computer program language) 2. Turbo assembler (Computer program) I. Duntemann, Jeff. II. Title.
    QA76.73.A8M57 1992
    005.265--dc20

Printed in the United States of America

10 9 8 7 6 5 4 3 2 1

To Debra, with love.

And in memory of my father, Jerome J. Mischel. I miss you, Dad.

Contents

Foreword

by Jeff Duntemann

Assembly language seems to be a popular sort of secret vice, judging by the mail we get every day at *PC TECHNIQUES* magazine. People apologize for loving it, giving a variety of reasons for their shame (it's difficult, it's obscure, it's culturally backward) and then demand MORE MORE MORE!

Hey, the customer is always right.

Why It Feels Good

Some years back, I began work on a series of books for Scott, Foresman & Co. that was intended to be the end-all series of works on assembly coding. We got three titles into print before the company got engulfed, devoured, and dismantled in a corporate takeover. They were good titles, and at least one of them, Michael Abrash's *Zen of Assembly Language*, has become a legend among legends in the programming book field, especially now that it is out of print. (One of the other two, my own *Assembly Language From Square One*, has been rewritten, enlarged, and recently re-issued as *Assembly Language Step By Step*.)

The point is, I knew back then and I know now that assembly will always be popular, because within an unswervingly loyal audience it just *feels* good. It feels good, I think, because with no other tool at your fingertips do you feel quite as in touch with the machine that you're controlling. There are no curtains, no guardrails, no unbreakable safety rules, nothing to dull your grip on the naked silicon.

You might be tempted to call this pure programmer machismo, until you remember that without that assembly language fever, 1-2-3, Turbo Pascal, and Sidekick could never have happened. Assembly language, then and now, is the racer's edge.

The Little Book That Wasn't There

There's been no shortage of assembly language books in the past, most of them appallingly bad. I learned from several of them, none of which I truly liked. Most remarkably, none of those books ever even *tried* to do justice to the topic of assembly macros, even though the concept was built right into the name of the best-selling assembler of all time: Microsoft's Macro Assembler, MASM.

Macros fascinated me, and I looked around for a book that treated them thoroughly, or (best of all) an entire book on the craft of macros. Nothing. To the best of my knowledge, there has never in history been a book written entirely about assembly macros for the PC.

Now there is—and a good one.

Getting a Little High When You Need To

I'll let Jim explain to you what macros actually are and how they work. He knows the subject far better than I. What I want to emphasize here is that, like everything else in the craft of assembly coding, macros are an instrument of choice. The choice involved is choosing how much to "run on automatic" when running on automatic makes sense.

The core value of assembly is the ability to control an instruction sequence individually, instruction by instruction, for the purpose of producing the fastest and most compact code possible. A macro, on the other hand, automatically expands itself into an instruction sequence so that you don't have to hand-code it yourself. This is great in many circumstances, most obviously when you find yourself coding the same general sort of instruction sequence again and again and again. As Jim mentions late in the book, working extensively with macros is a lot like working with a high-level language. In fact, early in my career as a programmer with Xerox, I learned and used a language for two years without ever understanding that it was, in fact, nothing more than a sackful of macros feeding into an 8080 assembler.

A macro is very much like a high-level language statement stuck into the middle of an assembly program—with the added benefit that you the programmer get to define the nature of this high-level "language." Just as modern C or Pascal compilers allow programmers to "drop down into assembly" when necessary, macros allow assembly programmers to "drop up into" a high-level construct when they need to—or when they can get away with it.

So you can get a little high when you need to—and better still, you can control the nature of this "high" going into the game. Like everything else in assembly, writing macros is a matter of choice. Down to the very last bit, all choices are yours. Understand the nature of your choices, and learn to use them well: That's the way to become a master assembly language programmer.

This book is one more step along the path. Good luck.

Introduction

I n high school Biology class, we examined cells under the microscope. On one of its settings, the microscope showed me all of the detail inside a cell, but it wasn't until I backed off on the magnification that I saw the overall structure of whatever I was examining. The detail was meaningless unless I had some idea of what I was looking at.

Programming with a Microscope

More than with any other language, assembly language programming is done at a microscopic level. At this level, you're responsible for everything that goes on in the machine. And if you're like most of us, you find that programming at this level is darned difficult because there are just too many things to remember. It's too easy to get bogged down by little details and lose sight of the big picture.

What I want to show you is how macros help adjust the magnification so that you can keep the big picture in sight. That way, you'll spend less time worrying about minute details that are best left up to the assembler, and you'll have more time to spend on the important parts of your program.

What You'll Need

First of all, you'll need to be at least passingly familiar with the basics of assembly language programming. We won't be touring the instruction set much, and some of the code examples get quite involved. If you're new to assembly language programming or need a quick refresher course, I suggest that you pick up one of the fine introductory texts that are available. In order to assemble the programs that come on the listings diskette, you'll need a copy of Borland International's Turbo Assembler. Any version will do, although I recommend that you upgrade if you're still using version 1.0.

If you don't have Turbo Assembler, there is still plenty of information in this book for you. All of the concepts presented in this book are applicable to any of the Microsoft MASM- compatible assemblers, and the code examples require only slight modifications in order to work with MASM.

Although it's not absolutely necessary, you may find it useful to have a good DOS programmer's reference close at hand.

Most importantly, you need an interest in learning and a willingness to try new things.

Acknowledgments

Special thanks to Jeff Duntemann, who gave me the push to get started, and the regular encouragement to get it finished. Thanks also to Debra, who never complained about the late nights, and to Sandy the dog and Kameeke the cat, whose antics kept me laughing when things were looking grim.

An Introduction to Macros

I always dreaded the first few weeks of a new school year. It wasn't going to school that bothered me—I was genuinely interested in learning—but the weeks of reviewing the material that we'd gone over the previous year. I always thought, "I already know this!" It wasn't until I entered second year algebra that I realized something: although I was somewhat familiar with the information we were reviewing, I obviously hadn't grasped it fully or I would have aced the review quiz that the sadistic instructor gave on the first day of class.

As I began writing this book, I actually started with Chapter 2, figuring anybody who read the book would already be familiar with the fundamentals of assembly language macros. How wrong I was! When I showed an early draft of Chapter 2 to a friend, he didn't get much past the first example before he started asking questions that I had assumed he already knew the answers to.

So, we have to start at the beginning. What are macros, what can they do and how are they used in our programs?

If you're an old hand with macros, please take the time to go over this chapter anyway. We'll get to the fancy stuff soon enough, but first you have to build a foundation. In the process, this chapter develops a small set of macros that we will be using in the following chapters.

1.1 The Nature of the Beast

Simply put, a *macro* is a label that stands for some sequence of code in your program. Macros are commonly used to reduce repetition by enabling you to use a single command that instructs the assembler to produce several (or several hundred!) lines of code.

The details of *how* the assembler accomplishes this bit of magic are best left to the assembler's authors, but a conceptual idea of what is going on within the assembler will help explain how macros work. Let's take a look at a very simple macro and examine how it is used in an assembly language program.

Following is the definition of a macro called **MultiplyBy16** that multiplies the AX register by 16 using 4 left shifts.

```
; MultiplyBy16--A macro to shift AX left 4 times
Macro MultiplyBy16
  shl ax,1      ;; *2
  shl ax,1      ;; *4
  shl ax,1      ;; *8
  shl ax,1      ;; *16
Endm MultiplyBy16
```

When the assembler encounters this macro definition, it stores the macro name, **MultiplyBy16**, and the macro's definition in its internal symbol table for later reference. *No code is generated from the macro definition.*

After this definition, the assembler replaces any occurrence of **MultiplyBy16** with the four **shl ax,1** instructions that make up the macro text. For example, when the assembler encounters

```
MultiplyBy16
```

somewhere in the program, it looks in the symbol table, determines that **MultiplyBy16** is a macro, and then *expands* the macro to

```
shl ax,1
shl ax,1
shl ax,1
shl ax,1
```

Figure 1.1 illustrates this concept.

Figure 1.1. Defining and expanding a macro

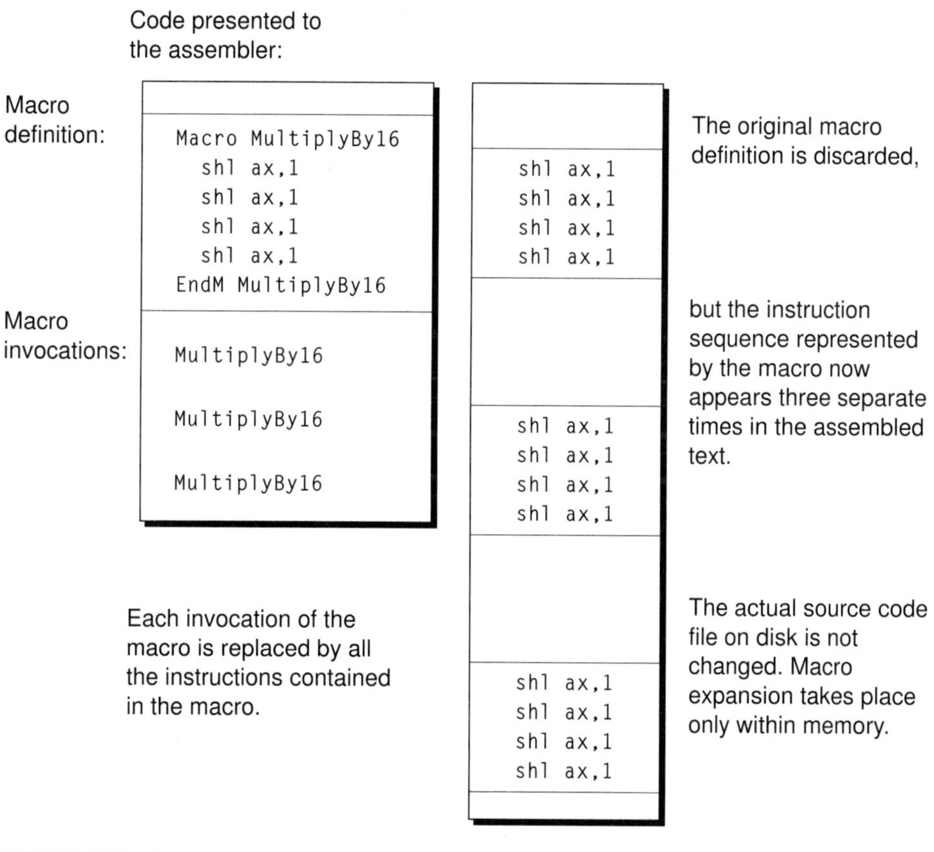

Code presented to
the assembler:

Macro
definition:

```
Macro MultiplyBy16
    shl ax,1
    shl ax,1
    shl ax,1
    shl ax,1
EndM MultiplyBy16
```

Macro
invocations:

```
MultiplyBy16

MultiplyBy16

MultiplyBy16
```

```
shl ax,1
shl ax,1
shl ax,1
shl ax,1



shl ax,1
shl ax,1
shl ax,1
shl ax,1



shl ax,1
shl ax,1
shl ax,1
shl ax,1
```

The original macro definition is discarded,

but the instruction sequence represented by the macro now appears three separate times in the assembled text.

Each invocation of the macro is replaced by all the instructions contained in the macro.

The actual source code file on disk is not changed. Macro expansion takes place only within memory.

There are three parts to a macro definition: the *macro header*, the *macro body*, and the **EndM** directive. In the **MultiplyBy16** macro given earlier, the macro header consists of the **Macro** directive followed by the macro's name. Macros that accept parameters include a parameter list after the macro name. We will take a look at macro parameters in the next section.

The macro body contains the assembler instructions that will be substituted when the macro is invoked. The body of our **MultiplyBy16** consists of the four **shl ax,1** instructions. Any valid assembler instructions or directives may be placed within a macro body.

The **EndM** directive denotes the end of a macro definition. In Turbo Assembler, the macro name after the **EndM** directive is optional.

Macros of this type—those that expand to several lines of code—are sometimes referred to as *macro procedures*. The name *procedure*, however, is rather misleading if you have any experience with high-level language procedures, which behave like assembly language subroutines. In order to avoid confusion, I will use the short form, *macro*, to refer to macro procedures, except when I must distinguish macro procedures from *text macros*, which will be discussed in a later section.

As a further attempt at avoiding confusion, I have been very careful to use the term *macro invocation* to refer to the use of an assembly language macro. Remember: Macros are invoked; subroutines are called.

Comment Suppression

You probably noticed that the comments in **MultiplyBy16** start with two semicolons rather than one. It's not a typographical error and I haven't gone mad. The **;;** is a special *comment-suppression operator* that prevents the comments inside of macros from being placed in the listing when the macro is expanded. There are two very good reasons to use the comment-suppression operator in macros.

Suppose you use single-semicolon comments in **MultiplyBy16** and your program reuses the macro many times. Every time you use the macro, the assembler expands it to

```
shl  ax,1    ; *2
shl  ax,1    ; *4
shl  ax,1    ; *8
shl  ax,1    ; *16
```

in the listing. Whenever you look through the listing, you're going to see those comments cluttering up the code and distracting you from what you're really looking for. The comment-suppression operator prevents these comments from being placed in the listing file.

The second and more compelling reason for using comment suppression is memory conservation. Whenever a macro is defined, the assembler stores the entire macro definition—*including comments*—in memory. The only comments that are not included are those that begin with the comment-suppression operator. If you have a large number of macros that contain lots of comments, you're going to run out of space in short order, unless you use the comment suppression operator rather than single-semicolon comments.

1.2 Repeat Blocks and Macro Parameters

Multiplying by powers of 2 consists of *repeated* left shifts. It just so happens that the assembler provides a directive that makes typing repetitive instruction sequences easier. The **rept** directive tells the assembler to repeat a set of instructions a given number of times. Our **MultiplyBy16** macro, for example, can be rewritten using **rept** as shown here:

```
; MultiplyBy16--A macro to shift AX left 4 times
Macro MultiplyBy16
  rept 4
    shl ax,1
  endm
Endm MultiplyBy16
```

The assembler repeats the instructions between **rept** and **EndM** the number of times specified—4 in this case.

Repeat blocks are treated as macros, which explains the use of the **EndM** directive to terminate the repeat block. The version of **MultiplyBy16** just shown is a simple example of a *nested macro*—a macro within a macro.

Macro Parameters

So what happens if we want to multiply by 4 or 8, rather than 16? We could define separate **MultiplyBy4** and **MultiplyBy8** macros, but that seems a bit cumbersome. If our macro invocation could tell the macro how many **shl ax,1** instructions to generate, we could create a single **LShift** macro that will multiply AX by any given power of 2.

We use *parameters* to pass information to a macro. The **LShift** macro shown next generates code to shift the AX register left the number of times specified by the **Count** parameter.

```
; LShift--shift AX left a specified number of times
Macro LShift Count
  rept Count
    shl ax,1
```

```
    endm
Endm LShift
```

When this macro runs it replaces every occurrence of **Count** within the macro body with the value that is passed in the parameter. To multiply by 16, for example, the assembler expands this statement:

```
LShift 4     ; multiply AX by 16 using 4 left shifts
```

to this assembly language code:

```
rept 4
  shl ax,1
endm
```

and then further expands the repeat block to this:

```
shl ax,1
shl ax,1
shl ax,1
shl ax,1
```

Similarly, to multiply AX by 8, we would simply write:

```
LShift 3     ; multiply AX by 8 using 3 left shifts
```

and the assembler will expand the macro to 3 occurrences of **shl ax,1**.

Macros can accept any number of parameters; the only restriction being that all the parameters must fit on a single line in the macro's definition. Because the maximum line length that Turbo Assembler will accept is 255 characters, this sets a rather arbitrary (albeit large) limit on the number of parameters that a macro can have. Most macros won't need to accept more than a half-dozen or so parameters, so this limit shouldn't present a problem.

Optional Parameters, IFB, and the Literal Text String Operator

All macro parameters are optional to the assembler. If you define a macro that accepts a parameter, the assembler will not flag an error if that parameter is not specified. **LShift**, for example, accepts a single parameter, but the assembler will not signal an error about a missing parameter if you were to write this:

```
LShift ; shift AX left
```

Missing parameters are blank, and any use of the parameter within the macro produces blank space. In the previous example, the expanded macro code would be

```
rept
  shl ax,1
endm
```

which the assembler is sure to reject because there is nothing to tell it how many times to repeat the **shl** instruction. So, although the assembler doesn't reject a line that lacks a parameter to the **LShift** macro, it will flag you about the missing **Rept** count. There is, fortunately, a way to prevent this error. While there is no way we can force the assembler to insist on a parameter, we can determine whether a parameter was passed by using the **ifb** (if blank) and **ifnb** (if not blank) directives, as shown in Listing 1.1.

```
 1:   ; Listing 1.1--LShift
 2:   ;
 3:   ; LShift--Shift AX left a specified number of times.
 4:   ;
 5:   Macro LShift Count
 6:   ;;
 7:   ;; If no Count is given, produce an error message.
 8:   ;;
 9:     ifb <Count>
10:       Err           ;; produces an error message
11:       Display "Count parameter to LShift required"
12:     else
13:     ;;
14:     ;; Generate the requested number of left shifts.
15:     ;;
16:       rept Count
17:         shl ax,1
18:       endm
19:     endif
20:   Endm LShift
```

The **ifb** directive examines the text that is enclosed in the angle brackets and, if the text is blank, an error message is displayed. If the text between the brackets is not blank, the assembler will process the repeat block. The **ifnb** directive is the mirror image of **ifb**. We will see uses of both directives throughout this book.

Angle Brackets

Arguments to **ifb** and **ifnb** must be surrounded by < and >, which together are called the *literal text string operator*. The term *operator* for this construct is confusing—I find it much more instructive to use the term *literal text string brackets* or simply *angle brackets*, which is the term that the *Turbo Assembler Reference Guide* employs.

In short, the assembler treats everything enclosed within angle brackets as a single item, even if it contains commas, spaces, or other characters to which the assembler normally attaches special meaning. You will see more uses of angle brackets as you explore more of the macro operators.

Commenting Macros

This is as good a time as any to plan how you will document your macros. As the next chapter demonstrates, macros have a habit of growing very quickly and, unless you're very careful, they can become almost incomprehensible. The only solution to this potential problem is to document—heavily and accurately—the macros that you create. And therein lies the problem.

A macro of any complexity that generates more than a few instructions requires documentation not only of the code but also the larger picture of how the macro works. Unless you use some standard of documentation, mixing comments on how the macro works with comments on how the generated code works is going to confuse you and anybody else who looks at it.

After quite a lot of experimentation, I have settled on a standard of macro documentation that works for me and provides a separation of the *how* from the *what*. Comments that document the generated code are placed to the right of the instruction—as is normally done in assembly language programming. Comments that document how the macro goes about generating the code are placed above the block of code in question and indented to show the macro's structure.

In cases that require longer descriptions of the code that the macro is generating, the descriptions are prefaced with "Generate code to, . . ." "The generated code, . . ." or similar phrases. "How" comments, on the other hand, are *never* placed to the right of the code.

All macros in this book are documented using this scheme. You are free, of course, to develop your own commenting style.

Testing Parameters with IFDIF and IFIDN

In addition to the **ifb** and **ifnb** directives, macro parameters can also be tested to determine whether their value is the same as or different than a given text string or another macro parameter. The directives that make this possible, **ifdif** (If Different) and **ifidn** (If Identical), work in much the same way as **ifb** and **ifnb**, but they accept two arguments rather than one. As with **ifb** and **ifnb**, the arguments to **ifdif** and **ifidn** must be surrounded by angle brackets.

A relatively simple example of using **ifidn** is to test a macro parameter to ensure that it is one of the four 16-bit general-purpose registers. A macro that performs this function, **IsWordReg**, is shown in Listing 1.2.

```
 1:   ; Listing 1.2--IsWordReg
 2:   ;
 3:   ; IsWordReg--Determine whether the passed parameter is one
 4:   ; of the 16-bit general-purpose registers.
 5:   ;
 6:   Macro IsWordReg Reg
 7:     Flag = 0
 8:     ifidn <Reg>,<ax>
 9:       Flag = 1
10:     endif
11:     ifidn <Reg>,<bx>
12:       Flag = 1
13:     endif
14:     ifidn <Reg>,<cx>
15:       Flag = 1
16:     endif
17:     ifidn <Reg>,<dx>
18:       Flag = 1
19:     endif
20:     if Flag eq 0
21:       err
22:       Display "Not a valid register"
23:     endif
24:   endm IsValidReg
```

IsWordReg will set the **Flag** variable to 1 if the single parameter is one of the four 16-bit general-purpose registers. If the **Reg** parameter is not a valid register, an error message is displayed and the **Flag** variable is set to 0.

The only problem with this version of **IsWordReg** is that it is case sensitive. For example, if we were to invoke the macro with this statement:

```
IsWordReg AX
```

the macro would generate an error message to tell us that AX is not a valid register, because the macro is testing for "ax," not "AX."

Fortunately, both **ifdif** and **ifidn** have case-insensitive counterparts that compare their arguments without regard to case. If we replace the **ifidn** directives in the previous example with **ifidni** directives, for example:

```
ifidni <Reg>,<ax>
```

the macro will work correctly, regardless of how we capitalize the parameter.

All of the **ifxxx** directives have corresponding **elseifxxx** directives that can be used to make very flexible conditional structures. For example, we can shorten the code in our **IsWordReg** macro by using the **elseifidni** directive, as shown in Listing 1.3.

```
 1:   ; Listing 1.3--New IsWordReg macro
 2:   ;
 3:   ; IsWordReg--Determine whether the Reg parameter is one
 4:   ; of the 16-bit general-purpose registers.
 5:   ;
 6:   Macro IsWordReg Reg
 7:     Flag = 0
 8:     ifidni <Reg>,<ax>
 9:       Flag = 1
10:     endifidni <Reg>,<bx>
11:       Flag = 1
12:     elseifidni <Reg>,<cx>
13:       Flag = 1
14:     elseifidni <Reg>,<dx>
15:       Flag = 1
16:     elseif Flag eq 0
17:       err
18:       Display "Not a valid register"
19:     endif
20:   endm IsValidReg
```

Multiple Parameters and Defaults

A macro that shifts AX left a given number of times is surely a much-appreciated enhancement of assembly language. But suppose that you have a program that makes extensive use of shifting BX. We could write a replica of **LShift** that uses BX rather than AX, but again that seems like a lot of extra work. Wouldn't it be better to add a parameter to the existing **LShift** directive that tells the macro which register to shift? A macro that does just that appears in Listing 1.4.

```
 1:   ; Listing 1.4--LShift
 2:   ;
 3:   ; LShift--Shift the specified register left
 4:   ; a given number of times.
 5:   ;
 6:   Macro LShift Reg,Count
 7:     ;;
 8:     ;; If no register given, produce an error message.
 9:     ;;
10:     ifb <Reg>
11:       Err
12:       Display "Register parameter to LShift required"
13:       exitm
14:     elseifb <Count>
15:     ;;
16:     ;; If no Count given, shift left once
17:     ;;
18:       shl Reg,1
```

```
19:      else
20:      ;;
21:      ;; Otherwise, shift left the specified number of times.
22:      ;;
23:        rept Count
24:          shl Reg,1
25:        endm
26:      endif
27:  Endm LShift
```

As well as the addition of the **Reg** parameter, the new version of **LShift** differs from the previous version in that it assumes a shift count of 1 if the second parameter is not given. The **Reg** parameter, however, is required, and the macro produces an error message if it is not passed.

Listing 1.4 uses the **ExitM** directive, which tells the assembler to halt macro expansion prematurely and to continue processing with the assembler statement following the current macro invocation. **ExitM** exits only the current macro, just as the **ret** assembler instruction exits only the current procedure. **ExitM** is commonly used to halt expansion when a macro determines that an error has occurred so that continued macro expansion doesn't produce more errors.

The new **LShift** macro requires us to pass one more parameter whenever we use the macro. To multiply AX by 16, for example, we must now write the following:

```
LShift ax,4
```

but we can perform a single left shift (multiply by 2) by specifying only the register parameter, as shown here:

```
LShift bx    ; shift BX left one time
```

which produces the same code as does this:

```
LShift bx,1    ; shift BX left one time
```

1.3 Text Macros and EQU

Unlike **=**, which defines constant values, the **equ** directive defines *text macros*, which share many of the same attributes as macro procedures. A short example here will illustrate how the **=** and **equ** directives differ. You'll no doubt recognize the following data definitions from the ubiquitous "Hello, world" program that many introductory programming texts present as a first stab at programming in a new language. In this case, we're interested in the **cr** and **lf** label definitions and how they're used in defining a text string.

```
cr equ 13   ; ASCII Carriage Return
lf equ 10   ; ASCII Line Feed

Hello  db "Hello, world",cr,lf,"$"
```

When the assembler encounters the last line, it actually goes through a two-step process to assemble the code and allocate storage for the string. It first expands **cr** and **lf** in the definition of **Hello** to **13** and **10**, respectively—in effect creating a line that reads:

```
Hello  db "Hello, world",13,10,"$"
```

The assembler then rescans the line and assembles it, generating storage for the string.

This two-step process is transparent to us and, because it generates the proper code, we really don't care to examine why or how it works. But at times using **equ** in this manner produces some strange results.

For example, suppose you were to write this:

```
cr equ 13 ; ASCII Carriage Return
lf equ 10 ; ASCII Line Feed

radix 16        ; Default base = hexadecimal

Hello db "Hello there",cr,lf,"$"
```

You might expect this to work exactly like the first example. After all, **cr** is 13 and **lf** is 10. But if you were to examine the assembly language listing for this program, you might be surprised to find that the assembler did not assemble an ASCII carriage return and line feed at the end of the string. Why not?

Remember that **equ** defines a text macro that is evaluated *when it is used* and that the assembler uses a two-step process to evaluate the macro. In this case, the assembler expands **cr** and **lf**, again creating a line that reads:

```
Hello db "Hello there",13,10,"$"
```

which is then assembled. But because the default radix is hexadecimal, the assembler interprets the two numbers as hexadecimal constants and generates code equivalent to this:

```
Hello db "Hello there",13h,10h,"$"
```

which is not at all what was intended! This, by the way, is not a contrived example. I actually did this once and spent hours trying to find the problem. Fortunately, I discovered **=** before embarrassing myself further by reporting a bug.

Had we defined **cr** and **lf** using the **=** operator, the assembler would have substituted the actual values (13 and 10, respectively) rather than substituting the text that the labels represent.

The other major difference between **equ** and **=** is that text macros defined with **equ** cannot be redefined, whereas constants defined with **=** can be.

You will see more uses of **equ** later in this book. For now, remember that in most cases you want to use **=**, rather than **equ**, to define constants such as **cr** or **lf**.

%, the Expression Evaluate Operator

There are times when you may wish to use a text macro as a parameter to a macro procedure, but you want to pass the *value* of the text macro, not the label, as a parameter. For example, consider the **Something** macro, which displays a message in response to the parameter passed to it:

```
Macro Something Arg1
  ifb <Arg1>
    Display "No argument given"
  elseifidni <Arg1>,<"Hello">
    Display "Hello yourself"
  elseifdifi <Arg1>,<"Goodbye">
    Display "I don't understand that"
  else
    Display "Au revoir"
Endm Something
```

If you were to define the following text macro:

```
Greeting equ "Hello"
```

and then invoke the **Something** macro with this statement:

```
Something Greeting
```

you might be surprised to see that the macro displays **I don't understand that** rather than **Hello yourself**. Let's take a look at why this happens.

When you invoke the **Something** macro, the value of the **Arg1** parameter is **Greeting**. Since the argument is not blank, the first test fails, and the assembler encounters this next test instruction:

```
elseifidni <Arg1>,<"Hello">
```

which is replaced with:

```
elseifidni <Greeting>,<"Hello">
```

and then evaluated. Because arguments to the **ifxxx** family of directives are interpreted as literal text strings (they're enclosed in literal text string brackets!), no text substitution takes place and the test fails.

In order to allow text macros to be passed as macro parameters, the assembler's designers provided us with an operator that instructs the assembler to expand the text macro before passing it as a parameter. This operator is **%**, the *expression evaluate operator.*

Evaluating an expression is very simple—simply precede the expression to be evaluated with the expression evaluate operator, as shown here:

```
Something %Greeting
```

When the assembler encounters this line, it replaces **%Greeting** with the value of the text macro, passing the string "'Hello'" as the macro parameter, in effect modifying the macro invocation to read:

```
Something "Hello"
```

which will produce the desired response, **Hello yourself**.

Suppose you want macro **Something** to evaluate the expression within the angle brackets so you won't have to remember the expression evaluate operator every time you invoke the macro. We can't code the test like this:

```
elseifidni <%Greeting>,<"Hello">
```

because the literal text string brackets cause **<%Greeting>** to be taken literally—no special meaning is attached to the **%** operator in this context.

In order to evaluate expressions and expand text macros within angle brackets, the assembler must know beforehand that we want the evaluation to take place. The evaluate operator must occur before the opening bracket, or the assembler won't attach any special meaning to it. However, the evaluate operator can't appear just anywhere on the line because it *does* have a special meaning as the evaluate operator outside of angle brackets.

The solution is to place **%** at the beginning of the line as the first nonspace character and then follow it with at least one space. The assembler interprets this placement of the expression evaluate operator to mean "examine and evaluate all expressions on the current line before generating any code." In our sample macro, then, we would write this:

```
% elseifidni <Greeting>,<"Hello">
```

The expression evaluate operator is also good for passing the result of a mathematical expression to a macro. For example, if we were to write this macro invocation:

```
Something 5+4
```

the value of the **Arg1** parameter in macro **Something** would be the string
"5+4". If, on the other hand, we were to use the expression evaluate operator,
as shown here:

```
Something %5+4
```

the assembler would evaluate the expression before invoking the macro, passing the string "9" as a parameter.

If you're a little confused about how the expression evaluate operator
works, you're not alone. The only way to become familiar with **%** and all of its
uses is to experiment with it. And because label names can begin with **%**, there
are ambiguities that can be very confusing. In order to minimize the confusion,
I strongly suggest that you avoid creating labels that begin with **%**.

1.4 Local Labels

A very common operation in assembly language is branching conditionally
depending on the value in a register. For example, the following code uses
comparisons and conditional branches in order to determine whether the value
in AL represents one of the uppercase alphabetic characters (letters):

```
; Set Z flag if character is uppercase alpha (A..Z)
  cmp al,'A'
  jbe Around
  cmp al,'Z'
  ja Around
  cmp al,al
Around:
```

This is such a common operation that most high-level languages and
assembly language libraries provide an **IsUpper** subroutine. We can just as
easily put this code in a macro and, while we're at it, add the ability to check
any register rather than just AL. Our new macro, **IsUpper**, appears in Listing
1.5.

```
1:   ; Listing 1.5--IsUpper
2:   ;
3:   ; IsUpper--Set the Z flag if specified register contains
4:   ; an uppercase alpha letter (A..Z).
5:   Macro IsUpper Reg
6:     cmp Reg,'A'
7:     jbe Around
8:     cmp Reg,'Z'
```

```
 9:     ja Around
10:     cmp Reg,Reg
11:   Around:
12:   Endm IsUpper
```

To use this macro in our code, we simply pass it the register name, as in

```
IsUpper al
```

and then check the Zero flag. If Z is set, the character is uppercase.

Unfortunately, there is a slight problem. If we use **IsUpper** more than one time in a program, the assembler will create two **Around** labels. For example, these two macro invocations:

```
IsUpper al
IsUpper dl
```

will expand to this assembly language code:

```
  cmp al,'A'
  jbe Around
  cmp al,'Z'
  ja Around
  cmp al,al
Around:
  cmp dl,'A'
  jbe Around
  cmp dl,'Z'
  ja Around
  cmp dl,dl
Around:
```

And the assembler will issue an error message about a redefined symbol. How do we get the macro to generate a unique label every time we use it?

If we define a *local label* within the macro, our problem is solved. Take a look at the slightly modified version of **IsUpper** in Listing 1.6.

```
 1:   ; Listing 1.6--New IsUpper macro, using local labels
 2:   ;
 3:   Macro IsUpper Reg
 4:     Local Around
 5:     cmp Reg,'A'
 6:     jbe Around
 7:     cmp Reg,'Z'
 8:     ja Around
 9:     cmp Reg,Reg
10:   Around:
11:   Endm IsUpper
```

Around is now a local label—accessible only to the macro—so we can use **IsUpper** as many times as we like and the assembler will not complain.

A Friendly Warning

There is one caution to using local labels. When the assembler encounters a local label within a macro, it creates a unique internal name for that label so that the label can be referenced. The names that the assembler creates all begin with two question marks, **??**, and are followed by four hexadecimal digits. The first time it encounters a local label, the assembler assigns the name **??0000**, the next time, **??0001** and so on throughout the program. In the hypothetical case just shown, the two **IsUpper** invocations will expand to the following code:

```
  cmp al,'A'
  jbe ??0000
  cmp al,'Z'
  ja ??0000
  cmp al,al
??0000:
  cmp dl,'A'
  jbe ??0001
  cmp dl,'Z'
  ja ??0001
  cmp dl,dl
??0001:
```

Because the assembler creates labels in this format, you should avoid creating labels yourself that start with **??**. If, for some reason, you *must* use **??** at the start of a label, be sure to use something other than four hexadecimal digits for the following characters, or you run the risk of creating name conflicts with the assembler-generated labels.

1.5 Indefinite Repeats and More Macro Operators

One of the more tedious aspects of writing assembly language subroutines is saving and restoring registers on entry to and exit from the subroutine. For example, a routine that interfaces with a C program is expected to save **SI**, **DI**, **BP**, and **DS**, as well as the current stack. **SS** and **SP** normally take care of themselves, but saving and restoring the other registers requires several lines of code, as shown here:

```
Proc Something
  push ds ; save registers
  push bp
  push di
```

```
push si
...       ; do whatever processing
...
pop si   ; restore registers
pop di
pop bp
pop ds
ret
Endp Something
```

If we always had to save these four registers, we would write two macros, **SaveCRegs** and **RestoreCRegs**, that exactly duplicate the code just shown. Most subroutines, however, save only those registers that are used and that the calling program expects to be intact on return from the subroutine. If, for example, procedure **Something** did not change **DS**, there would be no reason to save and restore it.

We could also write a macro that accepts four parameters (or more if we needed to save more registers) and generates code to save the registers on the stack. A macro of this type is shown in Listing 1.7.

```
 1:   ; Listing 1.7--PushRegs
 2:   ;
 3:   ; PushRegs--Push the specified registers.
 4:   Macro PushRegs R1,R2,R3,R4
 5:     ifnb <R1>
 6:       push R1
 7:       ifnb <R2>
 8:         push R2
 9:         ifnb <R3>
10:           push R3
11:           ifnb <R4>
12:             push R4
13:           endif
14:         endif
15:       endif
16:     endif
17:   Endm PushRegs
```

To use **PushRegs** in our **Something** procedure, we would write this macro invocation:

```
PushRegs ds,bp,di,si
```

The only drawback to this method is that, in order to be truly general, **PushRegs** would have to accept at least 10 parameters (one for each register) and possibly more if for some reason we wanted to save the contents of memory locations. Although we could make such a macro work, the **irp** directive provides an easier and more flexible way to do the same thing.

The **irp** (Indefinite Repeat) directive works in much the same manner as **rept** in that it repeats a block of instructions. But, where **rept** repeats a given number of times, **irp** repeats once for each item in a comma-separated list. In the **Something** procedure, we can rewrite the first four instructions using **irp** as shown here:

```
Proc Something
  irp Reg,<ds,di,si,bp>
    push Reg
  endm
  ...
  ...
Endp Something
```

In the preceding macro, the **irp** block repeats four times—once for each item in the comma-separated list. Each time through the loop, **Reg** is assigned the next value in the list; starting with **ds** and ending with **bp**. When **irp** reaches the end of the list, the assembler continues with the instruction following the **endm** directive.

Using **irp**, we can write a much-simplified **PushRegs** macro and a corresponding **PopRegs** macro that accept any number of parameters, as shown in Listing 1.8.

```
 1:    ; Listing 1.8--PushRegs and PopRegs
 2:    ;
 3:    ; PushRegs--Push a list of registers onto the stack.
 4:    Macro PushRegs RegList
 5:      irp Reg,<RegList>
 6:        push Reg
 7:      endm
 8:    Endm PushRegs
 9:
10:    ; PopRegs--Pop a list of registers from the stack
11:    Macro PopRegs RegList
12:      irp Reg,<RegList>
13:        pop Reg
14:      endm
15:    Endm PopRegs
```

Using these two macros, we can then rewrite procedure **Something** as shown:

```
Proc Something
  PushRegs <ds,di,si,bp> ; save required registers
```

```
      ...          ; do processing
   PopRegs <bp,si,di,ds>  ; restore saved registers
   ret
Endp Something
```

Angle Brackets Revisited

In order to pass a list of four items to a macro as a single parameter, you've got to enclose the list in angle brackets, or the macro gets confused and thinks you're passing four separate parameters. Indeed, if you remove the brackets from the **PushRegs** invocation in procedure **Something**, the assembler generates a single instruction, **push ds**, and continues on its way—ignoring the other three registers. With the angle brackets surrounding the register names, however, **PushRegs** treats the list as a single parameter.

Any time you wish to pass a list of values or a multiword expression as a single parameter, you must enclose it in angle brackets.

Each level of macro expansion removes a single level of angle brackets, which is why we enclosed the **RegList** parameter in angle brackets when we used it with the **irp** directive. If we didn't do so, the macro would have expanded to **irp Reg,ds,di,si,bp**, which, as you saw, would generate code to save only **ds**.

Counting Arguments with IRP

When I first started programming in assembly language, one of my most common errors was to **PUSH** items on the stack when I entered a subroutine and then forget to **POP** them before returning from the routine; or I'd **POP** too many parameters from the stack. Either way, my program wouldn't be in Kansas anymore and I'd spend the next several hours trying to track down the tornado that took it away.

For example, the following subroutine has one more **PUSH** than **POP**. If you execute a program that calls this subroutine, the program will undoubtedly end up somewhere over the rainbow chanting "There's no place like home."

```
;
; Sample subroutine that PUSHes more than it POPs
;
Proc Rainbow
   PushRegs <ax,bx,cx,dx>
   ;
   ; Follow the yellow brick road
   ;
   PopRegs <dx,cx,bx>
   Ret
Endp Rainbow
```

Even with source code debuggers that make tracking this type of error easier, this common mistake is frustrating to beginning and advanced programmers alike.

I encountered this problem again recently when I started writing some rather involved macros and finally came up with a method by which the assembler can tell me whether any **PUSH** and **POP** pairs are out of balance.

By adding a global variable that gets incremented each time **PushRegs** **PUSH**es a register and gets decremented each time **PopRegs POP**s a register, we can always use an **if** test to determine whether our **PUSH** and **POP** pairs are in balance. Modified versions of **PushRegs** and **PopRegs** are shown in Listing 1.9, along with **PopCheck**, a macro that performs the **if** test and issues an error message if the **PUSH** and **POP** pairs don't match.

```
1:   ; Listing 1.9--PushRegs, PopRegs, PopCheck, and SetPushCount
2:   ;
3:   PushCount = 0              ; global variable initialized to 0
4:
5:   ; PushRegs--Push a list of registers onto the stack.
6:   ;  Increment PushCount once for each PUSH.
7:   ;
8:   Macro PushRegs RegList
9:     irp Reg,<RegList>
10:      push Reg
11:      PushCount = PushCount + 1
12:    endm
13:   Endm PushRegs
14:
15:   ; PopRegs--Pop a list of registers from the stack.
16:   ;  Decrement PushCount once for each POP.
17:   ;
18:   Macro PopRegs RegList
19:     irp Reg,<RegList>
20:      pop Reg
21:      PushCount = PushCount - 1
22:    endm
23:   Endm PopRegs
24:
25:   ; PopCheck--Verify that PushCount is 0.
26:   Macro PopCheck
27:     if PushCount ne 0
28:       Err
29:       Display "PUSH/POP out of balance"
30:     endif
31:   Endm PopCheck
32:
33:   ; SetPushCount--Set push count to predetermined value.
34:   Macro SetPushCount Count
```

```
35:    % PushCount = Count
36:  Endm
```

If we include an invocation of **PopCheck** at the end of our **RainBow** procedure, the assembler will inform us that our **PUSH** and **POP** pairs don't match, preventing us from trying to execute a program that is doomed to fail.

PopCheck can be used at any point in your program—anywhere you need to make sure that you've included a **POP** for everything you used **PUSH** for and that you haven't gone too far. This is an excellent debugging tool that costs nothing in runtime performance or code size. Use it often; you'll be glad you did.

For those rare cases in which you *must* push more registers than you pop (or vice versa), the **SetPushCount** macro shown after **PopCheck** enables you to adjust the count.

Processing Character Strings with irpc

The assembler provides one other repeating structure, **irpc** (Indefinite Repeat, Character), that is similar to **irp** but takes a character string rather than a list of values as its second parameter. This directive enables us to process a string one character at a time.

For example, most programs I write allow options that change the program's default behavior to be specified on the command line. Usually, the options are preceded by a dash (-) or slash (/). The routine I use to identify options is similar to the following:

```
lodsb
cmp al,'-'
jz DoOption
cmp al,'/'
jz DoOption
   ...
   ...
DoOption:
```

We can save ourselves a little bit of typing by using an **irpc** loop to generate the code, as shown by this example:

```
lodsb
irpc Char,<-/>
  cmp al,'&Char&'
  jz DoOption
endm
   ...
   ...
DoOption:
```

Of course, with only two characters to test for, using **irpc** presents little benefit. The real benefit of **irpc** becomes apparent when you have to test for five or more characters.

1.6 &, the Macro Substitute Operator

The first time I wrote code similar to the previous looping example, the line that compares a value with the AL register was written like this:

```
cmp al,'Char'
```

which seemed perfectly natural to me at the time. I expected the assembler to replace the reference to **Char** with the current character, as in

```
cmp al,'-'
```

Much to my surprise, the assembler left the line exactly as I had written it and spit out an error message saying that it couldn't compare the AL register with a 4-byte character string. Hindsight being what it is, I guess I shouldn't have been too surprised—how was the assembler to know that I wanted it to substitute the parameter's value within the string?

After much head scratching, an intensive search of the documentation and some sample code revealed the *macro substitute operator*, **&**, which instructs the assembler to substitute the value of a parameter in a place that it wouldn't normally do so. One place in which the assembler doesn't normally substitute parameters is within quoted strings. Preceding a parameter with the macro-substitute operator causes the assembler to perform the substitution.

The substitute operator is also commonly used to piece together label names from parameters passed to a macro. Suppose, for example, that you have a macro called **LenString** that defines a string and its associated length. The text string, its length, and the string's label name are passed as parameters to the macro, which then generates code to allocate storage and define a label name for the length. The desired result is a data definition similar to this:

```
Hello db "Hello, world"
HelloLen = 11
```

The **LenString** macro that creates these definitions is shown in Listing 1.10. This macro uses the substitute operator to "glue" the label name together from the passed parameter and the **Len** suffix.

```
1:   ; Listing 1.10--LenString
2:   ;
3:   ; Define an ASCII string and its associated length.
```

```
4:  ;
5:  Macro LenString String,StrLen,LblName
6:     LblName db String
7:     &LblName&Len = StringLen
8:  Endm LenString
```

Using this macro, the following **LenString** invocation generates the desired definitions:

```
LenString <"Hello there">,11,Hello
```

1.7 Nesting Macros

Macros can include repeat blocks, as you saw in the previous sections. They can also make reference to other macros. This ability to *nest* macro invocations enables us to define one macro using other macros in much the same way that procedures in high-level languages are written using other procedures and functions.

A simple example of nested macros can be found in a macro that determines whether the character in a particular register is uppercase and, if so, converts the character to lowercase. This macro, **ToLower**, is shown in Listing 1.11.

```
 1:  ; Listing 1.11--ToLower
 2:  ;
 3:  ; ToLower--Convert register character to lowercase.
 4:  ;
 5:  Macro ToLower Reg
 6:     Local Around
 7:     IsUpper <Reg>
 8:     jnz Around
 9:     or Reg,20h
10:  Around:
11:  Endm ToLower
```

When **ToLower** is invoked with the following statement:

```
ToLower al
```

the macro is expanded to the following code:

```
; ToLower al
  IsUpper <al>     ; see whether character is uppercase
  jnz ??0000
  or al,20h
??0000:
```

The **IsUpper** invocation is further expanded, resulting in this final code:

```
; ToLower al
; IsUpper <al>
  cmp al,'A'
  jb ??0001
  cmp al,'Z'
  ja ??0001
  cmp al,al
??0001:
  jnz ??0000
  or al,20h
??0000:
```

Just as high-level language procedures enable us to break a large problem into smaller parts, nested macros enable us to write small, generalized "helper" macros that can be used as building blocks for larger and more task-specific macros.

Suppose now that we want a macro that will identify lowercase rather than uppercase letters. We could easily write a new macro called **IsLower**, as shown in Listing 1.12, which differs from **IsUpper** only in name and the characters tested.

```
1: ; Listing 1.12--IsLower
2: ;
3: ; IsLower--Determine whether the register contains a lowercase letter.
4: ;
5: Macro IsLower Reg
6:   Local Around
7:   cmp Reg,'a'
8:   jbe Around
9:   cmp Reg,'z'
10:   ja Around
11:   cmp Reg,Reg
12: Around:
13: Endm IsLower
```

Similarly, if we needed a macro to test for digits, we could write an **IsDigit** macro; copying **IsUpper** and changing **A** to **0** and **Z** to **9**. With a little thought, however, we can write a new macro called **IsRange** that enables us to test any register or memory location against *any* given range of values. This new macro is shown in Listing 1.13.

```
1: ; Listing 1.13--IsRange
2: ;
3: ; IsRange--Set the Z flag if the value in the specified
```

```
 4:   ; register falls within the lower and upper bounds.
 5:   ;
 6:   Macro IsRange Reg,Lower,Upper
 7:      Local Around
 8:      cmp <Reg>,<Lower>      ;; test lower bound
 9:      jbe Around            ;; if lower than lower bound, exit
10:      cmp <Reg>,<Upper>      ;; test upper bound
11:      ja Around             ;; if higher than upper bound, exit
12:      test <Reg>,0          ;; set Z flag to indicate success
13:   Around:
14:   Endm IsRange
```

The final instruction, **test Reg,0**, is similar to the **cmp Reg,Reg** instruction we used in **IsUpper**, but the **test** instruction enables us to test memory locations as well as registers.

We can then define **IsUpper** and similar macros using **IsRange**, thereby reducing the amount of duplication required for each macro. Sample uses of **IsRange** are shown in Listing 1.14.

```
 1:   ; Listing 1.14--IsUpper, IsLower and IsDigit
 2:   ;
 3:   ; IsUpper--Set the Z flag if the value in the specified
 4:   ; register or memory location is an uppercase letter.
 5:   Macro IsUpper Reg
 6:      IsRange <Reg>,'A','Z'
 7:   Endm IsUpper
 8:
 9:   ; IsLower--Set the Z flag if the value in the specified
10:   ; register or memory location is a lowercase letter.
11:   Macro IsLower Reg
12:      IsRange <Reg>,'a','z'
13:   Endm IsLower
14:
15:   ; IsDigit--Set the Z flag if the value in the specified
16:   ; register or memory location is a digit.
17:   Macro IsDigit Reg
18:      IsRange <Reg>,'0','9'
19:   Endm IsDigit
```

As an added benefit, we now have a general-purpose range-testing macro that we can use to test any register or memory location against any given range of values. For example, the data input screen for a payroll program may contain code similar to the following, which verifies a new employee's pay rate:

```
; Ensure that PayRate is in the proper range.
mov ax,[PayRate]
cmp ax,[MinimumWage]
```

```
  jbe Around
  cmp ax,[MaximumWage]
  ja Around
  test ax,0
Around:
; If the Z flag is set, the pay rate is within the required range.
; If the C flag is set, the pay rate is less than the minimum.
; If both Z and C are clear, the pay rate is greater than the maximum.
```

With our new **IsRange** macro, we can shorten the code to just three lines, making it more readable as well:

```
; Ensure that PayRate is in the proper range.
  mov ax,[PayRate]
  IsRange ax,[MinimumWage],[MaximumWage]
```

For all practical purposes, macros may be nested to any depth, subject to the amount of memory available to the assembler. The assembler itself places no limit on the depth of macro nesting, and I've never run into a situation where the use of nested macros has caused the assembler to run out of memory.

1.8 Macro Libraries, Listings, and Purging Macro Definitions

An extensive macro library wouldn't be of much use if we had to retype the macros for every program that we create. Fortunately, the assembler provides a directive, **include**, that allows us to place the macros in a separate file and then copy the contents of that file into the programs that need it.

For example, a complete listing of all the macros we've developed, as well as some companion macros, is included at the end of this chapter in Listing 1.15. Chapter 2 shows how to use the **include** directive to read this macro library from disk into the programs that need it.

Listing Controls

When you use the **include** directive to read a macro library during assembly, all of the text of the **include**d file is placed in the assembler-generated listing file. Although there's nothing *wrong* with this behavior, it does create some really bloated .LST files, which are full of unnecessary lines of code.

Fortunately, there is an assembler directive, **%NoIncl**, that tells the assembler not to list the contents of **include**d files. As we begin to write real programs using our macros, we'll use the **%NoIncl** directive to prevent the inclusion of all the macro definitions in the listing file. If you want to enable the listing of included text, the **%Incl** directive reverses the effect of **%NoIncl**.

One other listing control determines how much detail is provided in the listing file when a macro is expanded. Normally, only macro expansion lines that actually generate code are shown in the listing file. Most of the time this is just fine, but when you're trying to debug a new macro, you need more detail. The **%Macs** directive instructs the assembler to list *all* macro expansion lines, providing you with more information about how macros are expanded during assembly. You can reverse the effects of **%Macs** using the **%NoMacs** directive.

The example in Figure 1.2(a) shows an expansion of **ToLower** as it would appear in the listing using the default listing mode (**%NoMacs**). Figure 1.2(b) shows the same expansion as it would appear if **%Macs** were enabled.

Purging Macro Definitions

In order to expand a macro when it's used, the assembler must store the entire text of the macro definition in memory. As a result, macros take up valuable memory space during assembly. This is not normally a problem, but if you're

---

Figure 1.2(a). Listing expansion of ToLower with %NoMacs

```
      11                              ToLower al
3     12 0000   3C 41                 cmp al,'A'
3     13 0002   76 06                 jbe ??0001
3     14 0004   3C 5A                 cmp al,'Z'
3     15 0006   77 02                 ja ??0001
3     16 0008   A8 00                 test al,0
3     17 000A                       ??0001:
1     18 000A   75 02                 jnz ??0000
1     19 000C   0C 20                 or al,20h
1     20 000E                       ??0000:
```

Figure 1.2(b). Listing expansion of ToLower with %Macs

```
;
      10                              ToLower al
1     11                              IsUpper al
2     12                              IsRange <al>,'A','Z'
3     13 0000   3C 41                 cmp al,'A'
3     14 0002   76 06                 jbe ??0001
3     15 0004   3C 5A                 cmp al,'Z'
3     16 0006   77 02                 ja ??0001
3     17 0008   A8 00                 test al,0
3     18 000A                       ??0001:
1     19 000A   75 02                 jnz ??0000
1     20 000C   0C 20                 or al,20h
1     21 000E                       ??0000:
```

assembling a large program that makes use of extensive macro libraries, the assembler can very quickly run out of space. If this happens, you will receive an out-of-memory error, and the assembler will stop processing your program.

The **Purge** directive can be used to remove unnecessary macro definitions from the assembler's memory. Once a macro is removed using this directive, the assembler "forgets" it and you can no longer use the macro. For example, the assembler will display an error for the last line of the following code:

```
Macro MultiplyBy16
  rept 4
    shl ax,1
  endm
endm MultiplyBy16
MultiplyBy16
Purge MultiplyBy16
MultiplyBy16
```

The assembler displays an error when it encounters the last line, because the definition of **MultiplyBy16** has been removed from its memory. From then on, the assembler no longer knows that this macro exists.

1.9 Advantages and Disadvantages of Macros

Macros have several distinct advantages over traditional coding methods. First, placing repetitive or often-used code sequences in macros helps to reduce the chances of making a typing error and allows faster program development. In addition, using macros to perform commonly used functions enhances program readability by eliminating a level of detail that is not always necessary. The macro invocation, **IsUpper al**, for example, is much more informative and easier to read than the five lines of code that it replaces, even if the five lines are adequately documented.

Second, a macro to perform a given function will always execute faster than an equivalent subroutine, because of the subroutine's inherent **call** and **ret**urn overhead. The **IsUpper** macro, for example, executes three times as fast as an equivalent subroutine in small code models. The speed advantage would be even greater in large code models. *Three times*! In a program that uses **IsUpper** frequently, this speed advantage is well worth the added code space of seven bytes for each use of the macro.

Admittedly, if a program contains many calls to an **IsUpper** subroutine, replacing each **call** instruction with a macro invocation will produce some very bloated code. But because most programs use **IsUpper** and similar routines within loops, there will be few actual expansions of the code in a given program, resulting in a generous speed improvement at little or no cost in program size.

Including macros in your source files is going to slow assembly. And making multiple passes to resolve forward references (using the /m switch in Turbo Assembler) will slow the assembly process even more. But the knowledge you gain from this book will enable you to write macros that reduce your typing and debugging efforts to an extent that a few extra seconds assembly time will be a small price to pay.

A Note About the Listings

You may ask yourself why I provide 10 lines of documentation for a macro that's only 5 lines long and generates only 2 or 3 lines of code. In my opinion, it is not possible to overdocument any piece of code—especially assembly language code—*assuming the documentation is correct*. If the information provided is pertinent to the use of the tool, provide as much as you think is needed.

I have not added any information to the listings that is not in the macro files that I use in my everyday programming, although I have cast the documentation in a more presentable format. You can, of course, eliminate the comments entirely and rely on your memory.

A Final Note on Code Efficiency

The macros developed in this chapter generate code that is far from optimized. In fact, some of the generated code is downright *slow*. Chapter 5 discusses efficiency issues and revamps these macros to make them produce much better code. Remember, it is easier to make a working program efficient than to make an efficient program work. Right now we're interested in getting our programs working and getting you to understand how to use macros to make writing and maintaining those programs easier.

We've covered quite a bit of ground in this chapter and developed a number of macros that will recur throughout this book. The entire text of all our macros is shown in Listing 1.15, which makes up the include file MACROS.INC.

```
 1:   ; Listing 1.15--MACROS.INC
 2:   ;
 3:   ; MACROS.INC--General-purpose macros
 4:   ;
 5:   ; To use these macros in your programs, you must have the statement
 6:   ; include "macros.inc"
 7:   ; in your source file after the program header.
 8:
 9:   ; IsRange Reg,Lower,Upper
10:   ;  Determines whether the contents of the specified register or
11:   ; memory location is within the boundaries specified by Lower
```

```
12:  ; and Upper, inclusive.
13:  ;
14:  ; Parameters
15:  ;  Reg (Required) - Register or memory reference
16:  ;  Lower (Required) - Lower range boundary
17:  ;  Upper (Required) - Upper range boundary
18:  ;
19:  ; Returns
20:  ;  Z flag set if value is within range.
21:  ;  Z flag clear if value is not within range.
22:  ;
23:  ; Preserves the contents of all registers.
24:  ;
25:  Macro IsRange Reg,Lower,Upper
26:     Local Around
27:  ;;
28:  ;; Check for required parameters.
29:  ;;
30:     ifb <Reg>
31:       err
32:       Display "Register or memory reference must be specified"
33:       exitm
34:     elseifb <Lower>
35:       err
36:       Display "Lower boundary must be specified"
37:       exitm
38:     elseifb <Upper>
39:       err
40:       Display "Upper boundary must be specified"
41:       exitm
42:     endif
43:  ;;
44:  ;; All parameters exist. Generate code to perform the tests.
45:  ;;
46:     cmp Reg,Lower
47:     jbe Around
48:     cmp Reg,Upper
49:     ja Around
50:     test Reg,0
51:  Around:
52:  Endm IsRange
53:
54:  ;
55:  ; IsUpper Reg
56:  ;  Determine wehther the contents of the specified register or
57:  ; memory location is an uppercase alpha letter (A..Z).
58:  ;
59:  ; Parameters
```

```
60:   ;  Reg--Register or memory reference
61:   ;
62:   ; Returns
63:   ;  Z flag set if character is uppercase.
64:   ;  Z flag clear if value is not uppercase.
65:   ;
66:   ; Preserves the contents of all registers.
67:   ;
68:   Macro IsUpper Reg
69:     IsRange <Reg>,'A','Z'
70:   Endm IsUpper
71:
72:   ;
73:   ; IsLower Reg
74:   ;  Determine whether the contents of the specified register or
75:   ; memory location is a lowercase alpha letter (a..z).
76:   ;
77:   ; Parameters
78:   ;  Reg (Required)--Register or memory reference
79:   ;
80:   ; Returns
81:   ;  Z flag set if character is lowercase.
82:   ;  Z flag clear if value is not lowercase.
83:   ;
84:   ; Preserves the contents of all registers.
85:   ;
86:   Macro IsLower Reg
87:     IsRange <Reg>,'a','z'
88:   Endm IsLower
89:
90:   ;
91:   ; IsAlpha Reg
92:   ; Determine whether the contents of the specified register or
93:   ; memory location is an uppercase or lowercase alpha letter.
94:   ;
95:   ; Parameters
96:   ;  Reg (Required)--Register or memory reference
97:   ;
98:   ; Returns
99:   ;  Z flag set if character is alphabetic.
100:  ;  Z flag clear if value is not alphabetic.
101:  ;
102:  ; Preserves the contents of all registers.
103:  ;
104:  Macro IsAlpha Reg
105:    Local Around
106:    IsUpper <Reg>
107:    jbe Around
```

```
108:        IsLower <Reg>
109:    Around:
110:    Endm IsAlpha
111:
112:    ;
113:    ; IsDigit Reg
114:    ; Determine whether the contents of the specified register or
115:    ; memory location is a digit (0..9).
116:    ;
117:    ; Parameters
118:    ;   Reg (Required)--Register or memory reference
119:    ;
120:    ; Returns
121:    ;   Z flag set if character is a digit.
122:    ;   Z flag clear if value is not a digit.
123:    ;
124:    ; Preserves the contents of all registers.
125:    ;
126:    Macro IsDigit Reg
127:        IsRange <Reg>,'0','9'
128:    Endm IsDigit
129:
130:    ;
131:    ; ToUpper Reg
132:    ; Determine whether the contents of the specified register or
133:    ; memory location is a lowercase alpha character (a..z), and
134:    ; if so, convert it to uppercase.
135:    ;
136:    ; Parameters
137:    ;   Reg (Required)--Register or memory reference
138:    ;
139:    ; Returns
140:    ;   Reg converted to uppercase (if applicable).
141:    ;
142:    ; Preserves the contents of all registers except the one
143:    ; specified in the Reg parameter.
144:    ;
145:    Macro ToUpper Reg
146:        Local Around
147:        IsLower Reg          ;; see whether it's lowercase
148:        jnz Around           ;; if not, then ignore;
149:        and Reg,0DFh         ;; otherwise, convert to uppercase
150:    Around:
151:    Endm ToUpper
152:
153:    ;
154:    ; ToLower Reg
155:    ; Determine whether the contents of the specified register or
```

```
156:    ; memory location is an uppercase alpha character (A..Z) and
157:    ; if so, convert it to lowercase.
158:    ;
159:    ; Parameters
160:    ;   Reg (Required)--Register or memory reference
161:    ;
162:    ; Returns
163:    ;   Reg converted to uppercase (if applicable)
164:    ;
165:    ; Preserves the contents of all registers but the one
166:    ; specified in the Reg parameter.
167:    ;
168:    Macro ToLower Reg
169:      Local Around
170:      IsUpper Reg              ;; see whether it's uppercase
171:      jnz Around              ;; if not, then ignore;
172:      or Reg,20h              ;; otherwise, convert to lowercase
173:    Around:
174:    Endm ToLower
175:
176:    ;
177:    ; LShift Reg,<Num>
178:    ; Shift the specified register or memory location left the
179:    ; number of bit positions specified by the Num parameter.
180:    ; If Num is not specified, perform a one-bit shift.
181:    ;
182:    ; Parameters
183:    ;   Reg (Required)--Register or memory reference
184:    ;   Num (Optional)--Number of bits to shift
185:    ;
186:    ; Returns
187:    ;   Nothing
188:    ;
189:    ; Preserves the contents of all registers except the one
190:    ; specified in the Reg parameter.
191:    ;
192:    Macro LShift Reg,Num
193:    ;;
194:    ;; Check parameters
195:    ;;
196:      ifb <Reg>
197:        err
198:        Display "Register or memory reference must be specified"
199:        exitm
200:      elseifb <Num>
201:      ;;
202:      ;; If Num is blank then generate code
203:      ;; to do only a single shift.
```

```
204:     ;;
205:       shl Reg,1
206:     else
207:     ;;
208:     ;; Otherwise, generate code to do the specified number of shifts.
209:     ;;
210:       rept Num
211:         shl Reg,1
212:       endm
213:     endif
214:   Endm LShift
215:
216:   ;
217:   ; RShift Reg,<Num>
218:   ; Shift the specified register or memory location right the
219:   ; number of bit positions specified by the Num parameter.
220:   ; If Num is not specified, perform a one-bit shift.
221:   ;
222:   ; Parameters
223:   ;   Reg (Required)--Register or memory reference
224:   ;   Num (Optional)--Number of shifts to perform
225:   ;
226:   ; Returns
227:   ;   Nothing
228:   ;
229:   ; Preserves the contents of all registers except the one
230:   ; specified in the Reg parameter.
231:   ;
232:   Macro RShift Reg,Num
233:   ;;
234:   ;; Check parameters.
235:   ;;
236:     ifb <Reg>
237:       err
238:       Display "Register or memory reference must be specified"
239:       exitm
240:     elseifb <Num>
241:     ;;
242:     ;; If Num is blank then generate code
243:     ;; to do only a single shift.
244:     ;;
245:       shr Reg,1
246:     else
247:       ;;
248:       ;; Otherwise, generate code to do
249:       ;; the specified number of shifts.
250:       ;;
251:       rept Num
```

```
252:        shr Reg,1
253:      endm
254:    endif
255:  Endm RShift
256:
257:  ; PushCount is used by PushRegs and PopRegs to help keep
258:  ; the number of PUSHes and POPs in balance. PopCheck tests
259:  ; PushCount and issues an error message if it is not 0.
260:  PushCount = 0
261:
262:  ; PushRegs <RegList>
263:  ; Push a list of registers onto the stack.
264:  ; Increment PushCount once for each PUSH.
265:  ;
266:  Macro PushRegs RegList
267:    irp Reg,<RegList>
268:      push Reg
269:      PushCount = PushCount + 1
270:    endm
271:  Endm PushRegs
272:
273:  ; PopRegs <RegList>
274:  ; Pop a list of registers from the stack.
275:  ; Decrement PushCount once for each POP.
276:  ;
277:  Macro PopRegs RegList
278:    irp Reg,<RegList>
279:      pop Reg
280:      PushCount = PushCount - 1
281:    endm
282:  Endm PopRegs
283:
284:  ; PopCheck
285:  ; Verify that PushCount is 0.
286:  ;
287:  Macro PopCheck
288:    if PushCount ne 0
289:      Err
290:      Display "PUSH/POP out of balance"
291:    endif
292:  Endm PopCheck
```

The DOS Tamers

he last chapter looked at how macros are used and some of the ways they can save time and effort. We also wrote a small library of useful macros that can make program development a little easier. Up to now, however, we haven't had any real programs to test the macros on. This chapter introduces a test program skeleton that we'll use for further experiments, and we'll develop a small library of DOS-access macros to use in future chapters. In addition, we'll continue our exploration of the assembler's macro language and learn a few new techniques along the way.

Because I assume you're somewhat familiar with accessing DOS using assembly language, this chapter is not going to be a tutorial on how to use each of the DOS services. Rather, the chapter examines in detail several of the most commonly used functions and creates macros that make using these DOS functions much easier.

2.1 Hello Again

Darned near every introductory book on any programming language exhibits the "Hello, world" program as your first coding effort in the new language. You may mentally groan whenever you see a similar program, but face it: This one program teaches you many things about a new programming language and produces instant positive feedback. "I *can* program in APL!"

And so it is with our exploration of macros—the "Hello, world" program is small enough to be easily understood, but still contains enough features to allow us to learn from it. Listing 2.1 shows our version of HELLO.ASM, written in the format we will use for all code examples in this book.

```
 1:    ; Listing 2.1
 2:    ;
 3:    ; HELLO.ASM--Everybody's first program.
 4:    ; Simply displays a message,
 5:    ; "Hello, world," on the standard output device and returns
 6:    ; to DOS.
 7:    ;
 8:      Ideal              ; use TASM Ideal mode
 9:      Model Small        ; use small code & data model
10:      Stack 100h         ; 256 bytes of stack is plenty
11:
12:      DataSeg
13:
14:  Hello db 'Hello, world',13,10,'$'
15:
16:      CodeSeg
17:
18:  Proc Main
```

```
19:        mov ax,@Data
20:        mov ds,ax                ; set up data segment
21:
22:    ; Set up registers and display greeting.
23:        mov dx,offset Hello      ; message offset in DX
24:        mov ah,9                 ; DOS Display String function
25:        int 21h                  ; call DOS
26:
27:    ; Exit program
28:        mov al,0                 ; return code 0 - no error
29:        mov ah,4ch               ; exit with return code function
30:        int 21h                  ; exit program
31:    Endp Main
32:
33:    End Main                     ; end of program
```

In order to run this program, we must first assemble and link it to create an executable (.EXE) file. To assemble the program, enter this command at the DOS prompt:

```
tasm /l /m hello
```

The **/l** TASM command line switch instructs the assembler to create a listing file, HELLO.LST, and the **/m** switch causes the assembler to make multiple passes over the file in order to optimize jumps and resolve forward references. **/m** won't be necessary for HELLO.ASM, but we'll use it quite a bit as we dig deeper into macro programming.

/l is very useful in developing macros because it enables us to see what's being generated by the macros we create. Although this book won't show many examples of the listing (.LST) files, you'll want to examine them to familiarize yourself with the results of macro expansion.

To link the program, enter the following command at the DOS prompt.

```
tlink /m hello
```

The **/m** TLINK switch instructs the linker to create a .MAP file of the executable program. The .MAP file includes a list of all external symbols as well as their addresses and some other useful debugging information. We won't be using the .MAP file for the time being, but we will examine it in later chapters.

To execute the program, simply enter the command *hello* at the DOS prompt. The program should display **Hello, world** and return to the DOS prompt.

Granted, it's not a very exciting program, but now we've got a starting point for our experiments.

2.2 Improving HELLO.ASM

HELLO.ASM is a simple enough program that you'd think we couldn't improve on it. In terms of execution speed, you're right, although we could make it write directly to the screen rather than use the DOS output function. But execution speed is not our major concern right now. What we want to reduce is the amount of time it takes to write and maintain the program.

The program header starting with the **Ideal** directive and ending with the **Stack** directive will be used for all of the programs in this book. Rather than trying to remember to type those three lines in every program, I've created **ProgramHeader** (Listing 2.2), a macro that, given the memory model and stack size, generates the header. The default values for memory model and stack size are **Small** and **0100h**, respectively. This macro should be placed in your MACROS.INC file.

```
 1:   ;
 2:   ; Listing 2.2
 3:   ; ProgramHeader <ModelName>,<StackSize>
 4:   ; Generates program header directives.
 5:   ;
 6:   Macro ProgramHeader ModelName,StackSize
 7:     %PushLCtl              ; save listing controls
 8:     %Macs                 ; enable listing of all macro expansions
 9:     Jumps                 ; enable automatic jump sizing
10:     MASM51                ; enable special MASM 5.1 features
11:     ifnb <ModelName>
12:       Model ModelName
13:     else
14:       Model Small
15:     endif
16:     ifnb <StackSize>
17:       Stack StackSize
18:     else
19:       Stack 100h
20:     endif
21:     %PopLCtl              ; restore listing controls
22:   Endm ProgramHeader
```

ProgramHeader enables listing of all macro expansions so that the listing file shows exactly which directives are enabled at the start of the program. **%PushLCtl** and **%PopLCtl** are used to save and restore the listing controls at the start and end of the macro.

If we include MACROS.INC in all of our programs, our new program header looks like this:

```
Ideal
include "macros.inc"
  ProgramHeader Small,0100h
```

The **Ideal** directive is required because the assembler's default MASM compatible mode does not recognize quoted arguments to the **include** directive. We could simply leave the quotes off the first **include**, but I chose to include the **Ideal** directive so that all of our **include** directives use the same format.

With the program header out of the way, we'll continue our examination of HELLO.ASM with the definition of **Hello**.

Defining Strings

How many times have you forgotten to place the terminating dollar sign ($) at the end of a string? I've done it more times than I can remember and finally came up with a macro that ensures I'll never do it again. Take a look at the macro **$String**:

```
; Define a $-terminated string
Macro $String String
  db String,'$'
Endm $String
```

We can replace the definition of **Hello** in our program with an invocation of **$String**, like this:

```
Label Hello Byte
$String <"Hello, world",13,10>
```

and never worry again about that silly dollar-sign terminator. If you think that the macro invocation is more trouble than it's worth, you're right. We'll come back to **$String** shortly.

LABEL Versus :

We could also rewrite the definition of **Hello** to eliminate the first line by writing:

```
Hello: $String <"Hello, world",13,10>
```

The colon (:) after the label name is required in this case because of the way macros are expanded. Without the colon, TASM will report an "Illegal instruction" error, which is a bit confusing and caused me great concern until I figured out what was going on. However, defining data labels in this way forces

TASM to make assumptions about the label's type. In this case it would not be a problem, but there are cases in which type assumptions matter a great deal.

In order to provide the assembler with as much information as possible, I've opted to always use the **Label** directive in defining data but to reserve the right to use the colon notation when I define code labels.

It makes sense that any macro that creates more work than it saves shouldn't be used. **$String** in its current form is one such macro. I find that I forget the **Label** directive or what its purpose is at least as often as I forget the dollar-sign terminator. Because I choose not to use the colon notation (it causes the assembler to assume type information), I have no other choice but to go back to the traditional method of defining strings unless a better way can be found.

The better way, of course, is to have the macro create the **Label** directive as well as the terminating dollar sign. If we add another parameter, **LblName**, to the macro, we can make using the macro even easier. Listing 2.3 shows **$String** with this modification.

```
 1:    ; Listing 2.3
 2:    ;
 3:    ; $String <LblName>,String
 4:    ;    Defines a $-terminated string with optional label.
 5:    ;
 6:    ; Parameters
 7:    ;    LblName (Optional)--label name to assign to this string.
 8:    ;    String (Required)--a string of characters.
 9:    ;
10:    ; No registers or status flags are affected by this macro.
11:    ;
12:    Macro $String LblName,String
13:      ifnb <LblName>
14:        Label LblName Byte   ;; define label
15:      endif
16:      db String,'$'          ;; allocate storage for string
17:    Endm $String
```

With this macro, defining the **Hello** variable is very simple:

```
$String Hello,<"Hello, world",cr,lf>
```

Because the label name is optional, we can continue using either the colon notation or the manual **Label** directive if we want, the only catch being that we have to remember to pass a blank first parameter. For example, this code:

```
Label Hello Byte
$String ,<"Hello, world",cr,lf>
```

is equivalent to the previous line of code.

Setting Up the Segments

In HELLO.ASM, the first two lines of the **Main** procedure set up the DS register so that it references the default data segment. Almost every .EXE file that we create will need to do this. Although I've never forgotten to add this initialization, I've many times had to examine other programs to remember exactly what I was supposed to put here. Listing 2.4 presents **ExeStart**, a macro that performs the required initialization for an .EXE file in **Small** model.

```
 1:   ;
 2:   ; Listing 2.4
 3:   ; ExeStart
 4:   ;  Set up DS register to reference the default data segment.
 5:   ;
 6:   ; Parameters
 7:   ;    None
 8:   ;
 9:   ; Registers
10:   ; On completion, AX and DS will contain the address of the
11:   ; default data segment. All other registers are preserved.
12:   ; No flags are affected.
13:   ;
14:   Macro ExeStart
15:      mov ax,@Data
16:      mov ds,ax
17:   Endm ExeStart
```

This macro saves just a single line of code, true, but it saves me the time I used to spend looking up the proper code sequence. In addition, later chapters show that most programs do a great deal more initialization than simply setting up the segment registers. It is at that point that we will see the real value of an expanded **ExeStart** macro.

Taming INT 21h with DosCall

If you've done much assembly language programming at all, you'll appreciate the amount of coding it takes to access DOS functions via INT 21h. Even with adequate comments, loading registers in preparation for a call to INT 21h obscures the meaning of what is actually going on. Any macro that reduces the amount of effort we expend accessing DOS functions will free that much more time for other, more important, tasks.

As a first attempt at taming the INT 21h interface, I put forth **DosCall** (Listing 2.5), a macro that accepts a single optional parameter—the INT 21h function number—and generates code to load the AH register and access INT 21h.

```
 1:   ;
 2:   ; Listing 2.5
 3:   ; DosCall <Fcn>
 4:   ;   Load AH with optional function number and call INT 21h.
 5:   ;
 6:   ; Parameters
 7:   ;   Fcn (Optional) - INT 21h function number. If blank, the
 8:   ; current contents of the AH register is used.
 9:   ;
10:   ; Registers
11:   ; Registers and flags affected by this macro are as
12:   ; documented for the particular INT 21h function number.
13:   ;
14:   Macro DosCall Fcn
15:     ifnb <Fcn>
16:       mov ah,Fcn
17:     endif
18:     int 21h
19:   Endm DosCall
```

Using **DosCall** is a simple matter of providing the macro with a function number. For example, to display the greeting in HELLO.ASM, we would write this:

```
mov dx,offset Hello ; message address in DX
DosCall 9           ; display message
```

which expands to exactly the same code that appears in Listing 2.1, but is slightly easier to type and concentrates more on what is happening rather that how it is being accomplished.

Although **DosCall** is somewhat useful in and of itself, it relieves us of only a fraction of the tedium of using DOS calls in assembly language. Even with this macro, we're forced to remember function numbers—and with something over 100 documented (officially or unofficially) functions, you would be unwise to do much DOS programming without a function reference close at hand. One solution to this dilemma is to create an include file of equates that provides labels with descriptive names that can be used in place of the function numbers. For example, this code:

```
DisplayString = 9
   ...
   ...
mov dx,offset Hello
DosCall DisplayString
```

is much easier to write than trying to remember function numbers.

Displaying Strings with DosDisplayString

In all honesty, I have to tell you that I used the technique just described for quite a few years before I discovered a better way. I was working on my pet editor one evening when a thought entered my mind without warning: *Whenever I display a string, I load DE and then access CP/M.* (DE is a register pair on the 8080 that is roughly analogous to the 8088's DX register. CP/M was the dominant operating system for 8080- and Z80-based computers 10 years ago. "Calling CP/M" is how operating system functions were accessed—much like the MS-DOS INT 21h interface.) The specifics of each call changed, but the general form of the code remained constant. In the case of function 9, the only thing that changes is the value that gets loaded into the DX register.

This particular insight may seem obvious to you, but I had never considered it. The result of about five minutes reflection after that fortunate revelation is the **DosDisplayString** macro in Listing 2.6. This macro accepts a string address and produces the code required to display the string using DOS function 9.

```
 1:    ;
 2:    ; Listing 2.6
 3:    ; DosDisplayString <String>
 4:    ; Display $-terminated string on standard output device.
 5:    ;
 6:    ; Parameters
 7:    ; String (Optional) - offset of a $-terminated string within
 8:    ; the current data segment defined by DS.
 9:    ;
10:    ; Registers
11:    ; AH, DX, and Flags affected by the macro. On exit, AH = 9,
12:    ; DX = address of string displayed.
13:    ;
14:    Macro DosDisplayString String
15:       ifnb <String>
16:         mov dx,offset String
17:       endif
18:       DosCall 9
19:    Endm DosDisplayString
```

Using this macro is much easier and more understandable than the traditional method of accessing DOS. We can replace three lines of code in HELLO.ASM with a single invocation of **DosDisplayString**, like this:

```
DosDisplayString Hello
```

This line provides all the functionality at one-third the price—and it's more readable to boot!

The single parameter to **DosDisplayString** is optional, so we can use the macro to output a string whose address has previously been loaded into DX. For example, a subroutine may return the address of an information message in DX, expecting the calling program to display the message. Because DX already contains the address of the message string, it would be wasteful for the calling program to reload DX, even if the program knew which error message to use. The following code invokes **DosDisplayString** without a parameter:

```
call DoSomething  ; DoSomething returns message address
                  ; in the DX register
DosDisplayString
```

The preceding code will assemble to

```
call DoSomething
mov ah,9
int 21h
```

Armed with the knowledge I gained creating **DosDisplayString**, I went hunting through my programs searching for similarities. Sure enough, any particular CP/M function was called in exactly the same way. Form was constant—content was different. There followed several hours that evening (and several of the following weeks) writing, testing, and rewriting an extensive macro library for accessing CP/M functions. The macro library was one of the first pieces of code ported when I began programming in assembly language on the PC.

Exiting the Program

DOS function 4Ch, Exit with Return Code, has a calling sequence similar to that of function 9: Load a register, put the function number in AH, and issue an INT 21h. It follows that we should be able to create a macro similar to **DosDisplayString** that accepts a return code value and generates code to access function 4Ch. You're probably way ahead of me already, but Listing 2.7 shows **DosExitProgram**, a macro to do exactly that.

```
1:  ;
2:  ; Listing 2.7
3:  ; DosExitProgram <ReturnCode>
4:  ; Set return code and exit program
5:  ;
6:  ; Parameters
7:  ; ReturnCode (Optional) - Program exit status. Normally,
8:  ; a return code of 0 indicates successful program completion.
9:  ; Any other return code indicates failure. Return codes are
```

```
10:  ; user-defined and may depart from the normal usage.
11:  ;
12:  ; This function causes the program to terminate.
13:  ;
14:  Macro DosExitProgram ReturnCode
15:    ifnb <ReturnCode>
16:      mov al,ReturnCode
17:    endif
18:    DosCall 4Ch
19:  Endm DosExitProgram
```

A line of code that reads

```
DosExitProgram 1    ; exit with error status 1
```

makes more sense to me than does this:

```
mov ax,4c01h
int 21h   ; exit with error status 1
```

and it's easier to type as well. We can replace the final two lines of our **Main** procedure with

```
DosExitProgram 0  ; successful completion
```

Using the New Macros

With our three new macros safely hidden away in an include file called DOSMACS.INC, we can include them in our program without having to retype them. Listing 2.8 shows our new program, HELLO1.ASM, written using the new macros.

```
1:  ; Listing 2.8
2:  ;
3:  ; HELLO1.ASM
4:  ;   Everybody's first program rewritten using the new macros.
5:  ; Simply displays a message, "Hello, world," on the standard
6:  ; output device and returns to DOS.
7:  ;
8:    Ideal
9:  include "macros.inc"
10: include "dosmacs.inc"
11:
12:   ProgramHeader Small,0100h
13:
14:   DataSeg
15:
```

```
16:    $String Hello,<'Hello, world',13,10>
17:
18:    CodeSeg
19:
20:    Proc Main
21:       ExeStart
22:       DosDisplayString Hello
23:       DosExitProgram 0
24:    Endp Main
25:
26:    End Main
```

Not only is this version of HELLO.ASM easier to type and understand, it also produces *exactly* the same program as does the previous version shown at the beginning of this chapter. If you assemble and link this program and compare the resulting .EXE file with the original HELLO.EXE, you will find not one difference in the programs.

Our little program is not very complex, but it illustrates this point: Very simple macros can be created that significantly reduce the number of source lines in any program that uses DOS services. As an added benefit, the program becomes easier to develop, simpler to maintain, and more likely to be comprehensible to the person who returns later to add a feature. In the case of HELLO.ASM, we reduced the number of lines in our **Main** procedure from eight to three and made it more readable as well.

Not a bad bargain by my reckoning, especially considering that the final products (the executable programs) are identical.

But there are a lot of DOS services! Does this mean I have to write a macro to access each one? Not exactly, although you'll probably want to create a macro for each service that you use regularly. Even if you only *think* you'll use a DOS service more than once, why not put it in your macro library so you're sure to get it right every time? All it costs you is a little time during the assembly process. The time and effort spent developing my macro library was time well spent. The investment has been repaid many times over in reduced code development and debugging time.

2.3 A More Concrete Example: TRAL.ASM

For all the revisions we made to it, HELLO.ASM is not very useful other than as a demonstration of what we can do with the tools the assembler makes available. We can, however, write useful programs that take advantage of the time-saving features provided by macros.

Listing 2.9 shows TRAL.ASM; a simple filter program that copies one text file to another and in the process converts all uppercase characters in the file to lowercase.

TRAL is fairly representative of DOS filter programs, although I've omitted some features—most notably reading the names of the input and output files from the command line. The input and output file names are hard-coded in the program so that we don't have to deal with the command line just yet. The error reporting is not quite as sophisticated as would normally be included in a production program. Also, I used single-character input and output rather than block operations in order to keep from getting bogged down in details too soon. All of these features and more will be added to TRAL in later chapters.

```
 1:   ; Listing 2.9--TRAL.ASM
 2:   ;
 3:   ; TRAL.ASM--TRanslate All to Lowercase
 4:   ;   Convert uppercase characters to lowercase.
 5:   ;
 6:     Ideal
 7:     model small
 8:     stack 0100h
 9:
10:   cr = 0dh                  ; ASCII carriage return
11:   lf = 0ah                  ; ASCII line feed
12:   StdErr = 2                ; DOS standard error device
13:
14:     DataSeg
15:
16:   ; Filenames
17:   InputFile db "tral.asm",0      ; input filename
18:   OutputFile db "lowcase",0      ; output filename
19:
20:   ; Error messages
21:
22:   InFileErr db "Cannot open input file",cr,lf
23:   InFileErrLen = $ - InFileErr
24:
25:   OutFileErr db "Cannot open output file",cr,lf
26:   OutFileErrLen = $ - OutFileErr
27:
28:   ReadErr db "Read Error",cr,lf
29:   ReadErrLen = $ - ReadErr
30:
31:   WriteErr db "Write Error",cr,lf
32:   WriteErrLen = $ - WriteErr
33:
34:   DiskFull db "Disk Full",cr,lf
35:   DiskFullLen = $ - DiskFull
36:
37:   InHandle dw ?             ; input file handle
38:   OutHandle dw ?           ; output file handle
```

```
39:   InChar db ?               ; file I/O buffer
40:
41:     CodeSeg
42:
43:   Proc Main
44:     mov ax,@Data            ; set up data segment
45:     mov ds,ax
46:
47:   ; Open the files.
48:     call OpenInputFile      ; open the input file
49:     jc DoError              ; carry indicates error
50:     mov [InHandle],ax       ; save handle
51:
52:     call OpenOutputFile     ; create output file
53:     jc DoError              ; check for error
54:     mov [OutHandle],ax      ; if no error, save handle
55:
56:   ; Convert each character to lowercase
57:   ; and write to output file.
58:
59:   CharLoop:
60:     call ReadChar           ; read character into buffer
61:     jc DoError              ; check for error
62:     jz Done                 ; ZF means done
63:
64:     mov al,[InChar]         ; get character
65:     call ToLower            ;   convert to lowercase
66:     mov [InChar],al         ;   and save it
67:
68:     call WriteChar          ; write character from buffer
69:     jc DoError              ; check for error
70:     jnz CharLoop            ; or disk full
71:
72:   ; Display the error message on StdErr.
73:   DoError:
74:     mov bx,StdErr           ; error messages to StdErr
75:     mov ah,40h              ; DOS Write Device function
76:     int 21h
77:     stc                     ; set error flag
78:
79:   ; Processing complete.
80:   ; Close the files and exit program with return code
81:   ; indicating status.
82:   Done:
83:     pushf                   ; save error flag
84:     call CloseFiles         ; close the files
85:     popf                    ; restore error flag
86:
```

```
 87:     mov ax,4c00h
 88:     adc al,0                ; set up return code
 89:     int 21h                 ; and exit program
 90:  Endp Main
 91:
 92:  ; Open the input file defined by InputFile.
 93:  Proc OpenInputFile
 94:    mov dx,offset InputFile
 95:    mov al,0                ; open input
 96:    mov ah,3Dh              ; DOS Open File function
 97:    int 21h
 98:    jnc @@Done              ; check for error
 99:  ; An error occurred, set up registers for error routine.
100:    mov dx,offset InFileErr
101:    mov cx,InFileErrLen
102:  @@Done:
103:    ret
104:  Endp OpenInputFile
105:
106:  ; Open the output file defined by OutputFile.
107:  Proc OpenOutputFile
108:    mov cx,0               ; normal file attribute
109:    mov dx,offset OutputFile
110:    mov ah,3Ch             ; DOS Create File function
111:    int 21h
112:    jnc @@Done
113:  ; Error--set up registers for error routine.
114:    mov dx,offset OutFileErr
115:    mov cx,OutFileErrLen
116:  @@Done:
117:    ret
118:  Endp OpenOutputFile
119:
120:  ; Read one character from the input file into [InChar].
121:  Proc ReadChar
122:    mov bx,[InHandle]; file handle in BX
123:    mov cx,1               ; number of chars in CX
124:    mov dx,offset InChar   ; destination in DX
125:    mov ah,3Fh             ; DOS Read File function
126:    int 21h
127:    jnc CheckEof           ; check for error
128:  ; Error--set up registers for error routine
129:    mov dx,offset ReadErr
130:    mov cx,ReadErrLen
131:    jmp @@Done
132:  CheckEof:
133:    or ax,ax               ; check for EOF
134.    clc
```

```
135:    @@Done:
136:      ret
137:    Endp ReadChar
138:
139:    ; Write one character from [InChar] to the output file.
140:    Proc WriteChar
141:      mov bx,[OutHandle]    ; handle in BX
142:      mov cx,1             ; count in CX
143:      mov dx,offset InChar  ; buffer address in DX
144:      mov ah,40h           ; DOS Write File function
145:      int 21h
146:      jnc CheckFull        ; check for error
147:      mov dx,offset WriteErr
148:      mov cx,WriteErrLen
149:      jmp @@Done
150:    CheckFull:             ; check disk full
151:      or ax,ax
152:      jnz @@Done
153:      mov dx,offset DiskFull
154:      mov cx,DiskFullLen
155:    @@Done:
156:      ret
157:    Endp WriteChar
158:
159:    ; Convert the character in AL to lowercase.
160:    Proc ToLower
161:      cmp al,'A'            ; see whether it's uppercase
162:      jb @@Done
163:      cmp al,'Z'           ; if so...
164:      ja @@Done
165:      or al,20h            ; convert to lowercase
166:    @@Done:
167:      ret
168:    Endp ToLower
169:
170:    ; Close the input and output files.
171:    Proc CloseFiles
172:      mov bx,[InHandle]
173:      mov ah,3Eh           ; close input file
174:      int 21h
175:      mov bx,[OutHandle]
176:      mov ah,3Eh           ; close output file
177:      int 21h
178:      ret
179:    Endp CloseFiles
180:
181:    End Main
```

To assemble and link TRAL, you'll need to enter the following commands at the DOS command-line prompt:

```
tasm /l /m tral
tlink /m tral
```

To test the program, enter this command:

```
tral
```

When TRAL.EXE is done, you should have a new file on disk named LOWCASE that is the same size as TRAL.ASM, but that contains TRAL.ASM's source code converted entirely to lowercase.

An Aside: Snakes in the Refrigerator

When I was a boy, a friend and I were out exploring the vacant land near his house one day when we happened on a small snake of the harmless variety snuggled up next to a hot rock beneath a cactus. Having nothing better to do, we quickly decided to make the snake our pet and to find him a home. We returned to Scott's house and placed Boris (hey, I was a kid, okay?) in the refrigerator for safe keeping.

When Scott's mother returned from wherever it is that mothers run off to on Saturday afternoons, she found our newly acquired pet wrapped around a carton of milk. She *shrieked* and scooped poor Boris out of the refrigerator onto the floor. With a stream of language the like of which I'd never heard, she instructed us to remove our newfound friend from her refrigerator, return it to its home among the refuse, and refrain from inviting similar visitors to her home in the future. As an afterthought, she reminded us that we were more than welcome to take up residence with Boris if his was the kind of company we preferred.

If you can imagine Boris—frozen to the bone after an hour in cold storage—trying to crawl away from this shrieking madwoman, you'll understand what I mean when I tell you that TRAL is about as fast as a snake crawling out of a refrigerator.

So why is TRAL so slow? Because I used single-character file I/O rather than faster block operations in order to keep the program simple. Calling DOS for each character to be read or written is the bottleneck here, and no amount of code tweaking will make much of a difference in the speed of the program. You'll see in later chapters that modifying the program to work with larger blocks is a fairly straightforward enhancement that makes a dramatic improvement in performance but requires quite a bit more code—code that would only distract you from our current purpose of understanding how macros can save development time.

2.4 Improving TRAL

Even with its missing features and its slow single-character I/O, TRAL weighs in at over 150 lines and a substantial amount of development time. I'm embarrassed about how long it took me to write and debug this simple program. Looking in a DOS reference manual to verify the calling sequence and function number for a particular operation is time consuming.

Despite the fairly large number of comments and the liberal use of subroutines, TRAL's operation is not immediately obvious—we see the details of how it's accomplishing its task, but *what* it is doing is not readily apparent. At the moment, the program's performance is not relevant. It works; it's marginally useful in and of itself; and it's an excellent candidate for rewriting while we develop our DOS access macros.

More Data Types

Let's start again with data definitions, just as we did with HELLO.ASM. There aren't any dollar-sign terminated strings in this program, so **$String** won't do us any good. However, there are two ASCIIZ strings—strings delimited with a zero byte. DOS Open File, Create File, and other functions expect filename or pathname strings to be in ASCIIZ format. Listing 2.10 presents **zString**, which is an almost exact duplicate of **$String** that defines NUL-terminated strings.

```
 1:    ; Listing 2.10--zString
 2:    ;
 3:    ; zString <LblName>,String
 4:    ;    Defines a nul-terminated string with optional label
 5:    ;
 6:    ; Parameters
 7:    ;    LblName (Optional)--label name to assign to this string.
 8:    ;    String (Required)--a string of characters.
 9:    ;
10:    ; No registers or status flags are affected by this macro.
11:    ;
12:    Macro zString LblName,String
13:      ifnb <LblName>
14:        Label LblName Byte  ;; define label
15:      endif
16:      db String,0           ;; allocate storage for string
17:    Endm zString
```

Remember Chapter 1's two macros, **IsUpper** and **IsLower**, which were identical in form but differed slightly in detail? We developed **IsRange**, a "helper" macro to handle the common areas, leaving us free to concentrate only on the parts that differ. **$String** and **zString** differ only in name and the terminating character. Wouldn't it be easier to write a helper macro to define terminated strings? Such a macro, along with the new **$String** and **zString** macros that make use of it, appears in Listing 2.11.

```
 1:   ; Listing 2.11--TermString, $String, and zString
 2:   ;
 3:   ; TermString <LblName>,String,Terminator
 4:   ;   Defines a string with any given terminator
 5:   ;
 6:   ; Parameters
 7:   ;   LblName (Optional)--label name to assign to this string
 8:   ;   String (Required)--a string of characters
 9:   ;   Terminator (Required)--character to place at end of
10:   ; string.
11:   ;
12:   ; No registers or status flags are affected by this macro.
13:   ;
14:   Macro TermString LblName,String,Terminator
15:     ifnb <LblName>
16:       Label LblName Byte   ;; define label
17:     endif
18:     db String,Terminator   ;; allocate storage for string
19:   Endm TermString
20:
21:   ; $String <LblName>,String
22:   ; Define a $-terminated string.
23:   ;
24:   Macro $String Lblname,String
25:     TermString <LblName>,<String>,"$"
26:   Endm $String
27:
28:   ; zString <LblName>,String
29:   ; Define a nul-terminated string.
30:   ;
31:   Macro zString LblName,String
32:     TermString <LblName>,<String>,0
33:   Endm zString
```

In addition to saving us the trouble of typing all that code for each terminated string type, **TermString** enables us to define a string with any given terminator. For example, if we need to terminate strings with carriage return and line feed combinations, we can replace the code sequence

```
aString db "B string",cr,lf ; crlf-delimited string
```

with an invocation of **TermString**, like this:

```
TermString aString,<"B string">,<cr,lf>
```

although it would make more sense to define a **crlfString** macro similar to **zString** and **$String** if we were going to use CRLF-delimited strings often.

Other than two word-sized file handles and a byte-sized input-output buffer, the only data type in the program is a string with associated length, which is used by the program to display error messages on the DOS standard error device. The DOS Read File and Write File functions require a byte count to be passed in the CX register so that they know how many bytes to output. Fortunately, the assembler can be made to figure the string length for us—saving a lot of character counting—but these strings can still be particularly difficult to deal with. The macro in Listing 2.12, **LenString**, creates associated-length strings in much the same way that **TermString** creates terminated strings.

```
 1:   ;
 2:   ; Listing 2.12
 3:   ; LenString <LblName>,String
 4:   ;    Defines an ASCII string with associated length.
 5:   ;
 6:   ; Parameters
 7:   ;    LblName (Optional)--label name to assign to this string.
 8:   ;    String (Required)--a string of characters.
 9:   ;
10:   ; No registers or status flags are affected by this macro.
11:   ; If LblName is not given, no labels will be generated.
12:   ; If LblName is given, the label that contains the strings
13:   ; length will be named LblName&Len. For example, the
14:   ; call 'LenString Hello,<"Hello there">' will generate
15:   ;   Label Hello Byte
16:   ;   db "Hello there"
17:   ;   HelloLen = $ - Hello
18:   ;
19:   Macro LenString LblName,String
20:     ifnb <LblName>
21:       Label LblName Byte   ;; define label
22:     endif
23:     db String                ;; allocate storage for string
24:     ifnb <LblName>           ;; define string length
25:       &LblName&Len = $ - LblName
26:     endif
27:   Endm LenString
```

Using this macro, we can define error message strings with a single line of code, as shown here:

```
LenString DiskFull,<"Disk Full",cr,lf>
```

LenString uses the macro substitute operator, **&**, to create a label that defines the string's length. The ability to create labels by "gluing" pieces of the label's name together is a feature that we'll use often as we continue to explore the assembler's macro language.

2.5 TRAL's Code and More DOS Tamers

That's all of TRAL's data. Before we examine the code, let's take a look at what our new data definition macros can do. Listing 2.13 shows the first part of TRAL.ASM rewritten using the new macros.

```
1:    ;
2:    ; Listing 2.13
3:    ;   The first part of TRAL.ASM rewritten using our new data
4:    ; definition macros.
5:    ;
6:       Ideal
7:    include "macros.inc"
8:    include "dosmacs.inc"
9:       ProgramHeader Small,0100h
10:
11:      DataSeg
12:
13:   ; Input and output filenames
14:   zString InputFile,<"tral.asm">
15:   zString OutputFile,<"lowcase">
16:
17:   ; Error messages
18:   LenString InFileErr,<"Cannot open input file",cr,lf>
19:   LenString OutFileErr,<"Cannot open output file",cr,lf>
20:   LenString ReadErr,<"Read Error",cr,lf>
21:   LenString WriteErr,<"Write Error",cr,lf>
22:   LenString DiskFull,<"Disk Full",cr,lf>
23:
24:   InHandle dw ?           ; input file handle
25:   OutHandle dw ?          ; output file handle
26:   InChar db ?             ; file I/O buffer
27:
28:      CodeSeg
```

Listing 2.13 is quite an improvement over the original version. It's smaller, easier to read, and doesn't bother us with implementation details at the expense of clarity. The macros have all been encapsulated into DOSMACS.INC, as have the definitions of **cr**, **lf**, **StdIn**, and the other constants shown in Listing 2.21.

Macros Replacing Subroutines

The subroutines in TRAL.ASM are not what anybody would call reusable. For example, **OpenInputFile** accesses three global variables: **InputFile**, **InFileErr**, and **InFileErrLen**. To reuse this subroutine in another program, we would have to modify the labels for that particular program. The subroutines serve only to remove some of the complexity from the main program by breaking it into smaller, more manageable pieces. Even so, the program is difficult to comprehend at a glance because the subroutines cannot handle all of the error checking. The main program must examine the return status of each subroutine before continuing—a process that obscures the big picture. In fact, the big picture is sufficiently obscured that you could question the advantages of using subroutines at all in this case.

What we need, then, is a set of general-purpose macros similar to **DosDisplayString** that can take the place of the subroutines and also provide complete error checking so that we are free to concentrate our efforts at a higher level: *what* gets done rather than *how* it is performed. We will move the code from each subroutine into the main program so we can examine it in context. When we are finished, we will have an equivalent program (unlike HELLO.ASM in which we had an exact duplicate) that is easier to write, understand, and maintain. As an added bonus, we will add a number of useful macros to our growing collection of DOS-taming tools.

2.6 Opening Files

FCBs Versus Handles

Starting with DOS version 2, there are two methods of accessing files: handle functions and the older, CP/M-derived, FCB (File Control Block) functions. Although FCB functions have their uses, they suffer from a number of short-comings, most notably a lack of support for the hierarchical file structure. As a result, FCB functions are normally used only when there is no corresponding handle function to perform a specific task. In general, the handle functions are more versatile and easier to use, so we will concentrate our efforts on them.

Opening TRAL's Files

Listing 2.14 shows the **OpenInputFile** subroutine expanded inline in place of the **call OpenInputFile** statement in the **Main** procedure.

```
1:   ; Listing 2.14
2:   ; TRAL's OpenInputFile subroutine expanded to inline code
3:   ;
4:     mov al,0              ; open input
```

```
 5:        mov dx,offset InputFile
 6:        mov ah,3Dh              ; DOS Open File function
 7:        int 21h
 8:        jnc @@1                 ; check for error
 9:        mov dx,offset InFileErr
10:        mov cx,InFileErrLen
11:        jmp DoError             ; branch to error routine
12:     @@1:
13:        mov [InHandle],ax       ; save handle
```

Drawing freely from **DosDisplayString**, we can easily create a macro to duplicate the first four lines of code and access the macro with a single statement. Listing 2.15 shows our new **DosOpenInput** macro; Listing 2.16 shows how we would use it in the new version of TRAL.ASM.

```
 1:     ; Listing 2.15--DosOpenInput
 2:     ;
 3:     ; DosOpenInput <FileName>
 4:     ;    Open a file for input using DOS function 3Dh.
 5:     ;
 6:     Macro DosOpenInput FileName
 7:       mov al,0
 8:       ifnb <FileName>
 9:         mov dx,FileName
10:       endif
11:       DosCall 3dh
12:     Endm DosOpenFile
```

```
 1:     ; Listing 2.16--Opening the input file with DosOpenInput
 2:     ;
 3:        DosOpenInput <offset InputFile>
 4:        jnc @@1                 ; check for error
 5:        mov dx,offset InFileErr
 6:        mov cx,InFileErrLen
 7:        jmp DoError             ; branch to error routine
 8:     @@1:
 9:        mov [InHandle],ax       ; save handle
```

The Big Picture

Listing 2.16 is a slight improvement over Listing 2.14, in that we don't have to worry about loading the registers—**DosOpenInput** takes care of that for us. But there is still quite a bit of code required to check the return status, set up registers if an error occurs, and save the file handle if the call is successful.

Before we go on to opening the output file, let's look at the big picture. What exactly do we do when we open an input file?

I looked back recently at some of my old assembly language code. Nearly every time I opened a file for input, I wrote almost identical code. Sometimes I loaded AH before DX, or the error processing routine didn't require CX and DX to hold error message information. However, *every* "open input" routine I looked at had a structure roughly equivalent to the following pseudocode:

```
Load registers and access DOS
If no error occurred (Carry Clear) Then
  Save returned file handle
Else (Carry Set)
  Set registers for error routine
  Branch to error routine
Endif
```

The first part—loading the registers and accessing DOS—is already being handled by **DosOpenInput**, but we still have to handle the rest of it ourselves. This process causes us to lose sight of what we are doing in favor of how it's getting done. But if we step back and think about it for a moment, we can write a macro that, given the required information, can generate *all* of this code automatically.

Listing 2.17 shows an enhanced **DosOpenInput** macro that accepts the filename, a storage address for the returned handle, an error message, and a label to branch to if the file cannot be opened. Given these parameters the macro generates code identical to Listing 2.14.

```
 1:    ; Listing 2.17--DosOpenInput
 2:    ;
 3:    ; DosOpenInput <FileName>,Handle,ErrJmp,ErrMsg
 4:    ;   Open a file for input using DOS function 3Dh and branch
 5:    ; to error routine or save returned handle as appropriate.
 6:    ;
 7:    Macro DosOpenInput FileName,Handle,ErrJmp,ErrMsg
 8:       Local Around,Done
 9:       mov al,0               ;; open input, compatibility mode
10:       ifnb <FileName>
11:         mov dx,FileName       ;; DX points to file name
12:       endif
13:       DosCall 3dh
14:       jnc Around             ;; if no error, branch around
15:       mov dx,offset ErrMsg   ;; DX = error message address
16:       mov cx,ErrMsg&Len      ;; CX = error message length
17:       jmp ErrJmp             ;; branch to error routine
18:    Around:                   ;; success!
19:       mov Handle,ax          ;; save returned handle
20:    Done:
21:    Endm DosOpenInput
```

Likewise, the following single statement generates code that is identical to Listing 2.14:

```
DosOpenInput <offset InputFile>,[InHandle],DoError,InFileErr
```

DosOpenInput does, however, have its restrictions; the most important is that the statement depends on the error message being defined with **LenString** (or by hand, using the same naming conventions that **LenString** uses). We could change this behavior by adding an optional **ErrMsgLen** parameter, but I've never had occasion to. My error messages are typically known beforehand and therefore are generated using **LenString**.

Beyond the assumption about the error message parameter, **DosOpenInput** assumes that we always want all of the code to be generated—in effect acting like a high-level language in which we have no control over the generated code. Suppose we don't want the macro to handle the error checking?

Optional Parameters and DosOpenInput

The only way to change the default behavior of any macro is to make some or all of the macro parameters optional. In the case of **DosOpenInput**, there is no need to require that *any* of the parameters be given, so we'll make them all optional. Listing 2.18 shows **DosOpenInput** with optional parameters.

```
 1:   ; Listing 2.18--DosOpenInput with optional parameters
 2:   ;
 3:   ; DosOpenInput <FileName>,Handle,ErrJmp,ErrMsg
 4:   ;    Open a file for input using DOS function 3Dh.
 5:   ;
 6:   ; Expanded version of the macro in which all parameters are
 7:   ; optional.
 8:   ;
 9:   Macro DosOpenInput FileName,Handle,ErrJmp,ErrMsg
10:      Local Around
11:      mov al,0                ;; open mode = input only
12:      ifnb <FileName>
13:        mov dx,FileName       ;; filename pointer in DX
14:      endif
15:      DosCall 3dh             ;; access DOS--try to open file
16:   ; If error message address given, check error
17:      ifnb <ErrJmp>
18:        jnc Around            ;; branch around if no error
19:      endif
20:      ifnb <ErrMsg>
21:        mov dx,offset ErrMsg       ;; DX = error message address
22:        mov cx,ErrMsg&Len   ;; CX = error message length
23:      endif
```

```
24:      ifnb <ErrJmp>
25:        jmp ErrJmp
26:      endif
27:    Label Around Near
28:    ;; If handle given, generate code to save handle.
29:      ifnb <Handle>
30:        mov Handle,ax        ;; save returned handle
31:      endif
32:    Endm DosOpenInput
```

This version of **DosOpenInput** is by far the most involved macro we've
seen to this point, so let's take a few minutes to examine the code from some
sample uses.

If all parameters are given, the macro generates exactly the code we expect.
This statement:

```
DosOpenInput <offset InputFile>,[InHandle],DoError,InFileErr
```

generates the following assembly language code:

```
mov al,0                  ; set mode to input
mov dx,offset InputFile   ; DX is file name address
mov ah,3Dh
int 21h                   ; tell DOS to open the file
jnc ??0000                ; if okay, branch around error check;
mov dx,offset InFileErr   ; otherwise, set up error message
mov cx,InFileErrLen       ;   and length
jmp DoError               ;   and branch to error handler
Label ??0000 Near         ; come here if file opened okay
mov [InHandle],ax         ; save file handle
```

which is identical to what we used in TRAL. If we don't specify the **Handle**
parameter, then the last line, **mov [InHandle],ax** won't be generated, and if we
don't pass the **FileName** parameter, the second line, **mov dx,offset InputFile**,
won't be generated because the macro assumes that we've already got the
proper address in DX. Similarly (or minimally), if no parameters at all are
passed, **DosOpenInput** generates this code:

```
mov al,0
mov ah,3Dh
int 21h
```

and we can do our own error checking if we want to.

The last two parameters, **ErrJmp** and **ErrMsg**, however, are more difficult
to deal with. If one of them is not specified, the macro generates incorrect or
nonoptimum code for the other. For example, if we drop the **ErrMsg** parameter, as in

```
DosOpenInput <offset InputFile>,[Handle],DoError
```

the macro generates the following code after the **int 21h** instruction:

```
  jnc ??0000        ; branch around if okay;
  jmp DoError       ; otherwise, branch to error handler
Label ??0000 Near   ; come here if okay
  mov [InHandle],ax ; save returned file handle
```

This is clearly nonoptimum, in that **jc DoError** should have been generated rather than the "jump around a jump" code that is shown. Similarly, giving the **ErrMsg** parameter but dropping the **ErrJmp** parameter, as in

```
DosOpenInput <offset InputFile>,[InHandle],,InFileErr
```

produces the following code (after **int 21h**)

```
  mov dx,offset InFileErr  ; load error message address
  mov cx,InFileErrLen      ; and length
Label ??0000 Near
  mov [InHandle],ax
```

which is clearly *not* what we want. The file handle is saved whether or not there was an error, and the CX and DX registers are changed even if no error occurred. Are we stuck with macros that generate *almost* optimum (or worse, almost correct) code?

Optimization, Macro Style

Optimizing a macro or (more correctly) modifying it to generate optimum code, invariably requires a number of **if** tests to ensure that only the required code is generated for any given calling sequence. As a result, macros tend to grow by leaps and bounds and become very complex—we move the problem from our source to the macro code. Unfortunately, there's not much we can do about this except be very careful to document our macros extensively.

On the other hand, we can easily test the macro with all possible input permutations to verify its correctness. We can then use the macro in our programs without worry, safe in the knowledge that it works. This is preferable to hand-coding every DOS call.

The final version of **DosOpenInput**, which generates the correct code for all possible combinations of parameters, is shown in Listing 2.19. Study this macro carefully until you understand *exactly* how it works.

```
1:   ; Listing 2.19--DosOpenInput with optimizations
2:   ;
3:   ; DosOpenInput <FileName>,<Handle>,<ErrJmp>,<ErMsg>
```

```
 4:    ;    Open a file for input using INT 21h function 3Dh.
 5:    ;
 6:    Macro DosOpenInput FileName,Handle,ErrJmp,ErMsg
 7:      Local Around,Done
 8:      mov al,0               ;; open mode = input only
 9:      ifnb <FileName>
10:        mov dx,FileName       ;; filename pointer in DX
11:      endif
12:      DosCall 3dh            ;; access DOS--try to open file
13:    ;; If Error Message address given, check for error.
14:      ifnb <ErMsg>
15:        jnc Around           ;; branch around if no error
16:        mov dx,offset ErMsg ;; DX = error message address
17:        mov cx,ErMsg&Len    ;; CX = error message length
18:        ifnb <ErrJmp>
19:          jmp ErrJmp         ;; branch to failure routine
20:        elseifnb <Handle>
21:          jmp Done
22:        endif
23:        Label Around Near
24:    ;; If no error message, but error routine defined, generate
25:    ;; conditional branch there. Otherwise, generate conditional
26:    ;; branch to end of macro.
27:      elseifnb <ErrJmp>
28:        jc ErrJmp
29:      else ifnb <Handle>
30:        jc Done
31:      endif
32:    ;; If handle is given, write code to save returned handle.
33:      ifnb <Handle>
34:        mov Handle,ax        ;; save returned handle
35:        Label Done Near
36:      endif
37:    Endm DosOpenInput
```

We'll study optimization more closely in Chapter 5. For now, rest assured that it *is* possible to create macros that generate optimized, correct, code.

Opening the Output File

With the input file open, let's take a look at opening the output file. Expanding the **OpenOutputFile** subroutine inline produces the code shown in Listing 2.20.

```
 1:   ; Listing 2.20
 2:   ; TRAL's OpenOutputFile subroutine expanded to inline code
 3:   ;
 4:     mov cx,0                       ; normal file attribute
```

```
 5:      mov dx,offset OutputFile
 6:      mov ah,3Ch                     ; DOS Create File function
 7:      int 21h                        ; tell DOS to create the file
 8:      jnc @@1                        ; skip around; if no error
 9:      mov dx,offset OutFileErr        ; set up error message
10:      mov cx,OutFileErrLen           ; and length and
11:      jmp DoError                    ; branch to error handler
12:   @@1:
13:      mov [OutHandle],ax             ; save file handle
```

If you compare Listing 2.20 with the **OpenInputFile** code in Listing 2.14, you'll notice more than a passing similarity. In fact, they're identical in terms of form; differing only in label names and the function number that's called. We could easily duplicate our final version of **DosOpenInput** and produce a **DosOpenOutput** macro that provides similar flexibility. But if we expand our thinking and apply what we've learned up to this point, we can create a generalized **DosOpenFile** macro that takes care of all contingencies for us and provides additional capabilities as well.

DosOpenFile is going to be quite a bit more complex than Chapter 1's **IsRange** macro, so let's take a close look at what we want it to do before we jump into creating a macro to handle all cases.

2.7 A Closer Look at Opening Files

DOS enables users to open files in four distinctly different ways:

- Input only (as handled by **DosOpenInput**)
- Input/output
- Append
- New file opened for input/output (as shown in Listing 2.20)

In addition, DOS versions 3.0 and later add new file-sharing modes. Finally, the DOS Create or Truncate File function enables us to specify attributes for the newly created file. Figure 2.1 summarizes the Create and Open File functions.

Let's concentrate first on opening existing files, assuming that once we get that working, the modifications for creating files using function 3Ch will be fairly straightforward.

Our new macro, **DosOpenFile**, will have an interface similar to the **DosOpenInput** macro shown in Listing 2.19. We will add two parameters— **OpenMode** to indicate read, write, read/write, or create; and **ShareMode** to indicate file-sharing mode (for opening existing files) or file attributes (for new files). The macro header, then, will look like this:

```
Macro DosOpenFile FileName,OpenMode,ShareMode,Handle,ErrJmp,ErrMsg
```

Figure 2.1. Summary of INT 21h functions 3Ch (Create or Truncate File) and 3Dh (Open File)

Function 3Ch—Create or Truncate File
Creates designated file if it doesn't exist or truncates the existing file to zero length. The file is opened with read/write access. The function fails if no handles are available, if the path is invalid or if a read-only file or a subdirectory with the same name already exists.

Calling Registers: AH = 3Ch
  CX = File Attribute
  00h Normal
  02h Hidden
  04h System
  06h Hidden and System
  DS:DX = pointer to ASCIIZ file specification

Return Registers: Carry flag clear if successful
  AX = returned file handle
  Carry flag set if error
  AX = Error code
  03h = path not found
  04h = too many files open
  05h = access denied

Function 3Dh—Open Existing File
Opens the designated file and returns a file handle in AX. Under DOS version 2, bits 7-3 are not used and should be set to 0. This function fails if the file doesn't exist, if the path is invalid, if there are no available file handles or if an invalid access code is specified.

Calling Registers: AH = 3Ch
  AL = Access and file-sharing mode
  Bit 7
  0 = inherited by child process
  1 = private to current process
  Bits 6-4 - File-Sharing Mode
  000 = compatibility mode
  001 = read/write access denied
  010 = write access denied
  011 = read access denied
  100 = full access permitted
  Bit 3 = Reserved
  Bits 2-0 - Access Mode
  000 = Read Access
  001 = Write Access
  010 = Read/Write access
  DS:DX = pointer to ASCIIZ file specification

Return Registers: Carry flag clear if successful
  AX = returned file handle
  Carry flag set if error
  AX = Error code
  01h = invalid function
  02h = file not found
  03h = path not found
  04h = too many files open
  05h = access denied
  06h = invalid access code

It seems pointless to provide time-saving macros that create all this wonderful code if we're still forced to remember numeric codes for things like **OpenMode** and **ShareMode**. It's simple enough to remember that an **OpenMode** of 0 means "open for read" and that a **ShareMode** of 0 means "compatibility mode," but trying to remember all the possible values for these two parameters is difficult and unnecessary. In order to save time, effort, and possibly some hair, Listing 2.21 defines named constants for these parameters as well as some other commonly used constants. This should be placed at the beginning of your DOSMACS.INC file.

```
 1:    ; Listing 2.21--Constant definitions for DOSMACS.INC
 2:    ;
 3:    bs = 08h                      ; ASCII backspace
 4:    tab = 09h                     ; ASCII vertical tab
 5:    lf = 0ah                      ; ASCII line feed
 6:    ff = 0ch                      ; ASCII form feed
 7:    cr = 0dh                      ; ASCII carriage return
 8:    eof = 1ah                     ; DOS end-of-file character
 9:    Escape = 1bh                  ; ASCII ESCape character
10:
11:    ; Standard file handles
12:    StdIn = 0                     ; standard input device
13:    StdOut = 1                    ; standard output device
14:    StdErr = 2                    ; standard error device
15:    StdAux = 3                    ; standard auxiliary device
16:    StdPrn = 4                    ; standard list device
17:
18:    ; File open modes
19:    omRead = 0                    ; read only
20:    omWrite = 1                   ; write only
21:    omRW = 2                      ; read/write
22:    omCreate = 3                  ; create new file
23:
24:    ; File-sharing modes
25:    smCompat = 0                  ; compatibility mode
26:    smDenyRW = 10h                ; read/write access denied
27:    smDenyWrite = 20h             ; write access denied
28:    smDenyRead = 30h              ; read access denied
29:    smAllowAll = 40h              ; full access permitted
30:    smPrivate = 80h               ; private to current process
31:
32:    ; File Attributes
33:    faNormal = 00h                ; normal file
34:    faReadOnly = 01h              ; read only
35:    faHidden = 02h                ; hidden file
36:    faSystem = 04h                ; system file
37:    faVolume = 08h                ; volume label
```

```
38:    faDirec = 10h          ; directory
39:    faArchive = 20h        ; archive
```

Using the constants in Listing 2.21, we can open a file for input with exclusive access using the following statement:

```
DosOpenFile <offset InputFile>,omRead,smDenyRW+smPrivate,\
          [InHandle],DoError,InFileErr
```

which is much easier to remember than specifying **0** for **OpenMode** and **1001000b** for **ShareMode**.

This is the first time we've had to use the \ continuation character in order to keep the program statements within the confines of the margins. While it's perfectly acceptable to allow program text to extend beyond the margins, I prefer to have it all fit on the screen so I don't overlook whatever is hidden off-screen.

Our interim version of **DosOpenFile** is an exact copy of **DosOpenInput**, with the addition of logic to process the **OpenMode** and **ShareMode** parameters. As with the other parameters, both of the new parameters are optional. The code to process the open and file-sharing modes replaces the line in **DosOpenInput** that reads:

```
mov al,0     ;; open mode = input/compatibility mode
```

The new code is shown here:

```
ifnb <OpenMode>
  ifnb <ShareMode>
    mov al,OpenMode+ShareMode
  else
    or al,OpenMode
else
  or al,ShareMode
endif
```

Beware Defaults

If you look closely at the code just listed, you may wonder why we **or** the values of **OpenMode** and **ShareMode** into AL if only one of the parameters is specified. The macro assumes that you know what you're doing and leaves the other bits alone if you don't tell it to modify them. All of this book's macros work this way. *If you don't specifically tell the macro to change something, it's left alone with the assumption that you know what you're doing.*

If you're not careful, the default behavior can get you into trouble. For example, if you were to invoke **DosOpenFile** with the statement

```
DosOpenFile <offset InputFile>,,smDenyRW+smPrivate,\
           [InHandle],DoError,InFileErr
```

with the intention of opening a file for input, you might end up with an error message or a file opened for *output*. To see why this happens, examine the generated code:

```
  or al,ShareMode          ; set sharing mode
  mov dx,offset InputFile   ; DX is file name address
  mov ah,3Dh
  int 21h                   ; tell DOS to open the file
  jnc ??0000                ; if okay, branch around error check
  mov dx,offset InFileErr   ; otherwise, set up error message
  mov cx,InFileErrLen       ;  and length
  jmp DoError               ;  and branch to error handler
Label ??0000 Near          ; come here if file opened okay
  mov [InHandle],ax         ; save file handle
```

Notice that the first line sets only the sharing-mode bits—*the open-mode bits are left untouched.* As a result, the open mode passed to function 3Dh is whatever happens to be in the first four bits of AL when the function is called. If you're lucky, you'll get the right mode. More likely, Murphy's Law being what it is, function 3Dh will return with an error status indicating an illegal function request.

Remember: Unless you're absolutely certain that a register contains the proper value, always specify the parameter.

Opening Output Files . . . Continued

Finally we return to creating a new file. With **DosOpenFile** modified to open an existing file in any mode, the modifications for creating a new file are minor and very straightforward. The only complication is that the macro must examine **OpenMode** to determine whether it is equal to **omCreate** and, if so, to generate code to access function 3Ch (Create or Truncate File) rather than function 3Dh (Open File). Because the macro depends on the **OpenMode** parameter to determine which function to call, we must either require that the parameter be given in the macro invocation or define a default behavior for the macro if the parameter is omitted. I choose to have the macro default to function 3Dh (Open File) if the open mode is not specified. This decision allows for some flexibility and also prevents us from inadvertently destroying a file's contents—something that could very well happen if the macro defaulted to function 3Ch (Create or Truncate File).

The final version of **DosOpenFile**, which will be included in DOSMACS.INC, is shown Listing 2.22. This is indeed a monster macro—not the largest we'll develop in this book, but certainly nontrivial. When you deal with macros as involved as **DosOpenFile**, it is imperative to comment them heavily and correctly so that people who will use them know beyond a doubt what will be generated in any given case. *Be verbose in documenting your macros.* You may have to go back and modify them sometime in the future.

```
 1:   ; Listing 2.22
 2:   ; DosOpenFile <FileName>,<OpenMode>,<ShareMode>,<Handle>,
 3:   ;                <ErrJmp>,<ErrMsg>
 4:   ;
 5:   ; Open or create a file in the given mode and store the
 6:   ; returned handle at the address given in the Handle
 7:   ; parameter. On error, branch to the error handler,
 8:   ; ErrJmp, with registers set to display ErrMsg.
 9:   ;
10:   ; Parameters
11:   ;   FileName (Optional) - Offset address of ASCIIZ file spec.
12:   ;   OpenMode (Optional) - File open mode (omRead, omWrite,
13:   ;     omRW or omCreate)
14:   ;   ShareMode (Optional) - If OpenMode is omCreate, ShareMode
15:   ;     specifies the attributes for the new file. Otherwise
16:   ;     ShareMode is the DOS V3 file sharing mode.
17:   ;   Handle (Optional) - Address to store returned file handle.
18:   ;   ErrJmp (Optional) - Address to branch to on error
19:   ;   ErrMsg (Optional) - Address of error message to pass to
20:   ;     error handler.
21:   ;
22:   ; Returns
23:   ;   If successful, the carry flag is clear, DX holds the address
24:   ; of the ASCIIZ file spec and AX contains the returned file
25:   ; handle.
26:   ;   If unsuccessful, carry will be set. If ErrMsg was given, DX
27:   ; holds the offset of the error message and CX contains the error
28:   ; message length. If ErrJmp is given, the routine will branch to
29:   ; that address. The contents of the AX register is undefined.
30:   ;
31:   Macro DosOpenFile FileName,OpenMode,ShareMode,Handle,ErrJmp,ErrMsg
32:     Local Around,Done
33:   ;;
34:   ;; Load registers with optional parameters
35:   ;;
36:     ifnb <FileName>
37:       mov dx,FileName              ;; DX = ASCIIZ file spec
38:     endif
39:   ;;
40:   ;; If the Create File function was requested, load CX with
41:   ;; the third parameter--the file attribute (assuming it was
```

```
42:    ;; passed). Then generate code to make a "Create file"
43:    ;; call (Function 3Ch).
44:    ;;
45:      if OpenMode eq omCreate
46:        ifnb <ShareMode>
47:          mov cx,ShareMode          ;; CX is file attribute
48:        endif
49:        DosCall 3Ch
50:      else
51:       ;;
52:       ;; Open an existing file. If both OpenMode and ShareMode were
53:       ;; given, load AL. Otherwise, simply mask in the bits for
54:       ;; the parameter that was specified.
55:       ;;
56:        ifnb <OpenMode>              ;; if both Open and Share modes,
57:          ifnb <ShareMode>
58:            mov al,OpenMode+ShareMode ;; set AL;
59:          else
60:            or al,OpenMode           ;; otherwise, just mask in
61:          endif
62:        else
63:          or al,ShareMode            ;; the required bits
64:        endif
65:        DosCall 3Dh
66:      endif
67:    ;;
68:    ;; The following is the same for both functions.
69:    ;; If an error message address is given, generate code to
70:    ;; test error flag and branch or load registers accordingly.
71:    ;;
72:      ifnb <ErrMsg>
73:        jnc Around                   ;; branch around if no error
74:        mov dx,offset ErrMsg         ;; DX = error message address
75:        mov cx,ErrMsg&Len            ;; CX = error message length
76:        ;;
77:        ;; If ErrJmp is passed, generate branch to that address.
78:        ;; Otherwise, generate branch to end of macro.
79:        ;;
80:        ifnb <ErrJmp>
81:          jmp ErrJmp
82:        elseifnb <Handle>
83:          jmp Done
84:        endif
85:        Label Around Near
86:    ;;
87:    ;; If no ErrMsg is given, generate conditional branch to error
88:    ;; routine (if given) or end of macro (if handle given). If
89:    ;; neither ErrJmp nor handle is given, generate nothing.
```

```
 90:     ;;
 91:     elseifnb <ErrJmp>
 92:       jc ErrJmp
 93:     elseifnb <Handle>
 94:       jc Done
 95:     endif
 96:   ;;
 97:   ;; If handle given, generate code to save returned handle.
 98:   ;;
 99:     ifnb <Handle>
100:       mov Handle,ax
101:       Label Done Near
102:     endif
103:   Endm DosOpenFile
```

Before we continue improving TRAL, take a look at the following code:

```
ExeStart
DosOpenFile <Offset InputFile>,omRead,smCompat,[InHandle],\
    DoError,InFileErr
DosOpenFile <Offset OutputFile>,omCreate,smDenyRW,[OutHandle],\
    DoError,OutFileErr
```

These three statements take the place of all the **Main** procedure code that initializes the program and opens the files. In addition, they eliminate the **OpenInputFile** and **OpenOutputFile** subroutines entirely.

2.8 Accessing Disk Files and Devices

We're done opening files, at least for the time being, so let's take a close look at the processing loop. However obscured it appears in the code, the logic for the main loop is simple, as shown by the following pseudocode:

```
Read a character
While there is input available and no errors occur
  Convert character to lowercase
  Output the character
  Read the next character
End While
```

As you can readily see from Listing 2.9, most of the code that makes up this loop is involved with checking the completion status of the **ReadChar** and **WriteChar** subroutines. The logic of the loop itself is obscured by details that really have no bearing on the overall picture. By now you can probably ask the question: Why not let a macro worry about how things get done?

Indeed. Why should we have to worry about the details? Using the techniques we've learned up to this point, we can easily create macros that handle all of that stuff for us.

Listing 2.23 shows the **ReadChar** subroutine expanded inline in the **Main** procedure.

```
 1:   ; Listing 2.23
 2:   ; In-line expansion of ReadChar subroutine
 3:   ;
 4:       mov bx,[InHandle]      ; handle in BX
 5:       mov cx,1               ; number of chars in CX
 6:       mov dx,offset InChar   ; destination in DX
 7:       mov ah,3Fh             ; DOS Read File function
 8:       int 21h
 9:       jnc CheckEof           ; no error, go check for EOF
10:       mov dx,offset ReadErr  ; setup registers for
11:       mov cx,ReadErrLen
12:       jc DoError             ; branch to error routine
13:   CheckEof:
14:       or ax,ax               ; check for EOF
15:       jz Done
```

The code is very similar to what we've already written for opening the files. It's so similar, in fact, that you could probably write a fully functional **DosReadFile** macro on your own without my help. The only difference in form is that **DosReadFile** must define two branch addresses—one to be taken when function 3Fh returns an error, and another if an end-of-file character is encountered. The header for our new macro will read

```
Macro DosReadFile Handle,NumChar,Buffer,EofJmp,ErrJmp,ErrMsg
```

where **EofJmp** and **ErrJmp** are the addresses to branch to when an end-of-file character and error, respectively, are encountered. The entire macro is shown in Listing 2.24.

```
 1:   ; Listing 2.24--DosReadFile
 2:   ;
 3:   ; DosReadFile <Handle>,<NumChar>,<Buffer>,<EofJmp>,<ErrJmp>,
 4:   ;             <ErrMsg>
 5:   ;
 6:   ; Use the DOS Read Device function (3Fh) to read NumChar bytes
 7:   ; from the specified file into buffer. On end-of-file,
 8:   ; branch to EofJmp. On error, branch to ErrJmp with the address
 9:   ; and length of an error message in DX and CX, respectively.
10:   ;
11:   ; Parameters
```

```
12:   ;    Handle (Optional) - File handle of file to read from. If
13:   ;      not specified, uses the contents of the BX register.
14:   ;    NumChar (Optional) - Number of characters to read. If not
15:   ;      specified, uses the contents of the CX register.
16:   ;    Buffer (Optional) - Offset address (in the currently active
17:   ;      data segment) of a buffer to hold the retrieved data. If
18:   ;      not specified, DX is used.
19:   ;    EofJmp (Optional) - Address to branch on end-of-file
20:   ;    ErrJmp (Optional) - Address to branch to on error
21:   ;    ErrMsg (Optional) - Address of error message to pass to
22:   ;      error handler.
23:   ;
24:   ; Returns
25:   ;    If successful, the carry flag is clear and AX holds the
26:   ; number of bytes read. CX will hold number of bytes requested
27:   ; and DX will contain the address of the input buffer.
28:   ;    On end-of-file, AX is 0, the Z flag is set,  and the macro
29:   ; branches to the optional ErrJmp address or to the end of the
30:   ; routine.
31:   ;    If carry is clear and AX < CX, a partial block was read.
32:   ;    If unsuccessful, carry will be set. If ErrMsg was given, DX
33:   ; holds the offset of the error message and CX contains the error
34:   ; message length. If ErrJmp is given, the routine will branch to
35:   ; that address. The contents of the AX register is undefined.
36:   ;
37:   Macro DosReadFile Handle,NumChar,Buffer,EofJmp,ErrJmp,ErrMsg
38:     Local CkEof,Done
39:   ;;
40:   ;; Load registers with optional parameters
41:   ;;
42:     ifnb <Handle>
43:       mov bx,Handle               ;; BX = handle
44:     endif
45:     ifnb <NumChar>
46:       mov cx,NumChar              ;; CX = number of bytes to read
47:     endif
48:     ifnb <Buffer>
49:       mov dx,Buffer               ;; DX = buffer address
50:     endif
51:     DosCall 3Fh                   ;; tell DOS to read the file
52:   ;;
53:   ;; If an error message address is given, generate code to
54:   ;; test error flag and branch or load registers accordingly.
55:   ;;
56:     ifnb <ErrMsg>
57:       jnc CkEof                   ;; branch around if no error
58:       mov dx,offset ErrMsg        ;; set error message address
59:       mov cx,ErrMsg&Len           ;; and length
60:         ;;
```

```
61:        ;; Generate branch to error routine (if given) or to
62:        ;; end of macro.
63:        ;;
64:        ifnb <ErrJmp>
65:          jmp ErrJmp
66:        else
67:          jmp Done
68:        endif
69:        Label CkEof Near
70:      ;;
71:      ;; If no error message given, generate conditional branch
72:      ;; to error routine (if given) or end of macro.
73:      ;;
74:      elseifnb <ErrJmp>
75:        jc ErrJmp
76:      else
77:        jc Done
78:      endif
79:      or ax,ax                    ;; check for end of file
80:    ;;
81:    ;; Generate conditional branch to EOF processing
82:    ;; routine (if defined).
83:    ;;
84:      ifnb <EofJmp>
85:        jz EofJmp                 ;; and branch if required
86:      endif
87:    ;;
88:    ;; If no error routine defined, define target label for
89:    ;; end of macro.
90:    ;;
91:      ifb <ErrJmp>
92:        Label Done Near
93:      endif
94:    Endm DosReadFile
```

As with our other DOS access macros, all of the parameters are optional, and **DosReadFile** will correctly generate only that code required by the parameters we supply it with.

This statement:

```
DosReadFile [InHandle],1,<offset InChar>,Done,DoError,ReadErr
```

generates code that is functionally equivalent to Listing 2.23.

DosReadFile doesn't contain any new concepts— every feature we put in this macro has been used in the other macros we've developed. We simply examined (albeit quickly) the *context* of the DOS call and wrote a macro that duplicates the most common uses.

Short Blocks and DosReadFile

We did leave one test out of this macro—the test for a short block. It's not added here because I find it of limited use, but it warrants some quick discussion.

Function 3Fh attempts to read a block of a given size from a file or device. Under certain circumstances, the number of bytes requested is not available. Most often, this happens when end of file is reached on a block device (such as a disk file) or when a carriage return is received from a character device (like the keyboard). Because no error occurred (there simply weren't enough characters to fill the buffer), function 3Fh reports successful completion and AX contains the number of characters that were actually read. Unless AX is 0, however, we can't be sure that end-of-file has been reached. The *only* time we're sure that no more input is available is when function 3Fh returns with the carry flag cleared and 0 in AX.

Because character devices may return short blocks as a normal course of action, our programs must be made flexible enough to handle that inevitable situation. Rather than deal with the short block as a special case, we can easily design our code to work properly with any size block. With TRAL, which expects only one character, the problem of short blocks does not concern us. In Chapter 6, however, we will develop some input routines that anticipate and correctly handle short blocks returned from function 3Fh.

Writing the Characters with DosWriteFile

DosWriteFile, as I'm sure you expect, is very similar to **DosReadFile**. You might think we could combine these two into a single **DosFileIO** macro, and we could. But we won't, because input and output are two fundamentally different operations and there are some subtle differences in how return values are handled. These differences make writing a generalized **DosFileIO** macro difficult.

Recall that the DOS Read File function returns two values—the carry flag indicates completion status and the AX register reports how many characters were read.

The DOS Write File function uses the same two registers for return values—the carry flag indicates completion status, and AX tells how many bytes were written—but there is a subtle difference in how the value returned in AX is interpreted. If the carry flag is clear (indicating successful completion), AX indicates how many bytes were written. However, if the value in AX is not equal to the value in CX (that is, the number of bytes actually written does not match the number of bytes that we requested to be written), then an error occurred. As a result, **DosWriteFile** must handle the returned values slightly differently than **DosReadFile**.

As with **DosReadFile**, the **DosWriteFile** macro shown in Listing 2.25 presents no new concepts. Using this new macro is similar to using the other DOS macros in this chapter.

```
 1:   ; Listing 2.25--DosWriteFile
 2:   ;
 3:   ; DosWriteFile <Handle>,<NumChar>,<Buffer>,<EofJmp>,<ErrJmp>,
 4:   ;              <ErrMsg>,<FullMsg>
 5:   ;
 6:   ; Use the DOS Write Device function (40h) to write NumChar
 7:   ; bytes from Buffer to the specified file. On disk full or
 8:   ; other error, branch to ErrJmp with the address and length of
 9:   ; the appropriate error message in DX and CX, respectively.
10:   ;
11:   ; Parameters
12:   ;   Handle (Optional) - File handle of file to write to. If
13:   ;      not specified, uses the contents of the BX register.
14:   ;   NumChar (Optional) - Number of characters to write. If not
15:   ;      specified, uses the contents of the CX register.
16:   ;   Buffer (Optional) - Offset address (in the currently active
17:   ;      data segment) of the buffer that is to be written. If not
18:   ;      specified, DX is used.
19:   ;   ErrJmp (Optional) - Address to branch to on error
20:   ;   ErrMsg (Optional) - Address of error message to pass to
21:   ;      error handler in case of error.
22:   ;   FullMsg (Optional) - Address of error message to pass to
23:   ;      error handler in case of disk full.
24:   ;
25:   ; Returns
26:   ;    If successful, the carry flag is clear and AX holds the
27:   ; number of bytes written. CX holds number of bytes requested
28:   ; and DX will contain the address of the output buffer.
29:   ;    If unsuccessful, carry will be set. If ErrMsg was given, DX
30:   ; holds the offset of the error message and CX contains the error
31:   ; message length. If ErrJmp is given, the routine will branch to
32:   ; that address. The contents of the AX register is undefined.
33:   ;    If carry is clear and AX <> CX, then either the disk is
34:   ; full or some other error occurred. In this case, DX holds the
35:   ; address of FullMsg and CX holds the FullMsg error length and
36:   ; the routine branches to ErrJmp.
37:   ;
38:   Macro DosWriteFile Handle,NumChar,Buffer,ErrJmp,ErrMsg,FullMsg
39:     Local CkFull,Done
40:   ;;
41:   ;; Load registers with optional parameters.
42:   ;;
43:     ifnb <Handle>
44:       mov bx,Handle                  ;; BX = handle
```

```
45:     endif
46:     ifnb <NumChar>
47:       mov cx,NumChar                ;; CX = number of bytes to write
48:     endif
49:     ifnb <Buffer>
50:       mov dx,Buffer                 ;; DX = address of buffer
51:     endif
52:     DosCall 40h                     ;; tell DOS to write the data
53:   ;;
54:   ;; If an error message address is given, generate code to
55:   ;; test error flag and branch or load registers accordingly.
56:   ;;
57:     ifnb <ErrMsg>
58:       jnc CkFull                    ;; branch around if no error
59:       mov dx,offset ErrMsg          ;; set error message address
60:       mov cx,ErrMsg&Len             ;; and length
61:       ;;
62:       ;; Generate branch to error routine (if given) or to
63:       ;; end of macro.
64:       ;;
65:       ifnb <ErrJmp>
66:         jmp ErrJmp
67:       else
68:         jmp Done
69:       endif
70:       Label CkFull Near
71:     ;;
72:     ;; If no error message given, generate conditional branch
73:     ;; to error routine (if given) or end of macro.
74:     ;;
75:     elseifnb <ErrJmp>
76:       jc ErrJmp
77:     else
78:       jc Done
79:     endif
80:     cmp ax,cx                       ;; check for full block write
81:   ;;
82:   ;; If "disk full" message address is given, generate code to
83:   ;; test condition and branch or load registers accordingly.
84:   ;;
85:     ifnb <FullMsg>
86:       jz Done                       ;; if AX = CX then everything's okay;
87:       mov dx,offset FullMsg         ;; otherwise, set up registers
88:       mov cx,FullMsg&Len            ;; for branch to error handler
89:       ;;
90:       ;; Generate branch to error routine (if given) or code to
91:       ;; set the error flag.
92:       ;;
```

```
 93:         ifnb <ErrJmp>
 94:           jmp ErrJmp              ;; branch to error routine
 95:         else
 96:           stc                     ;; set carry to indicate error
 97:         endif
 98:       ;;
 99:       ;; If "disk full" not defined, generate conditional branch
100:       ;; to error routine (if given) or to end of macro.
101:       ;;
102:       elseifnb <ErrJmp>
103:         jnz ErrJmp                ;; branch on error
104:       else
105:         jz Done                   ;; branch if okay
106:         stc                       ;; set carry to indicate error
107:       endif
108:     Label Done Near               ;; target for conditional jumps
109:     Endm DosWriteFile
```

Using **DosWriteFile** in TRAL, we can replace the **call WriteChar** statement, the **WriteChar** subroutine, and the associated error checking with this one statement:

```
DosWriteFile [OutHandle],1,<offset InChar>,DoError,\
    WriteErr,DiskFull
```

Closing the Files

The last DOS macro we'll create for TRAL is **DosCloseFile**. Compared to the other file-handling macros we've developed, this one is very simple—the only twist being that the DOS Close File function *can* return an error code, so we must make our macro generate code to check it. TRAL doesn't make use of this error code, but other programs we write might want to know whether the file closed successfully. **DosCloseFile** is shown in Listing 2.26.

```
 1:   ;
 2:   ; Listing 2.26
 3:   ; DosCloseFile <Handle>,<ErrJmp>,<ErrMsg>
 4:   ;
 5:   ; Uses INT 21h function 3Eh to close a previously opened file and
 6:   ; branches to error routine with registers set to display an error
 7:   ; message if an error occurs.
 8:   ;
 9:   ; Parameters
10:   ;   Handle (Optional) - The handle to close. If not specified,
11:   ;      the current contents of BX are used.
12:   ;   ErrJmp (Optional) - Address to branch if an error occurs.
```

```
13:   ;    ErrMsg (Optional) - On error, DX will hold the offset of the
14:   ;      error message and CX will hold the length.
15:   ;
16:   ; Returns
17:   ;   On success, carry will be clear.
18:   ;   If an error occurs, carry is set, DX holds error message
19:   ; address, and CX contains error message length. AX will hold
20:   ; the DOS error code.
21:   ;
22:   Macro DosCloseFile Handle,ErrJmp,ErrMsg
23:     Local Around
24:   ;;
25:   ;; Load register with optional handle
26:   ;;
27:     ifnb <Handle>
28:       mov bx,Handle               ;; BX = file handle
29:     endif
30:     DosCall 3Eh                   ;; tell DOS to close the file
31:   ;;
32:   ;; If error message passed, generate code to test error flag
33:   ;; and branch or load registers accordingly.
34:   ;;
35:     ifnb <ErrMsg>
36:       jnc Around                  ;; branch around if no error
37:       mov dx,offset ErrMsg        ;; DX = error message address
38:       mov cx,ErrMsg&Len           ;; CX = error message length
39:       ;;
40:       ;; Generate branch to error routine (if given)
41:       ;;
42:       ifnb <ErrJmp>
43:         jmp ErrJmp
44:       endif
45:       Label Around Near
46:     ;;
47:     ;; If no error message is defined but error routine is defined,
48:     ;; generate conditional branch to error routine.
49:     ;;
50:     elseifnb <ErrJmp>
51:       jc ErrJmp
52:     endif
53:     Endm DosCloseFile
```

Using the macro in Listing 2.26 to close TRAL's files is a simple matter of replacing the call to **CloseFiles** in the **Main** procedure with these two lines of code:

```
DosCloseFile [InHandle]
DosCloseFile [OutHandle]
```

2.9 The Final TRAL

Two other sections of TRAL's code can be simplified using macros. The **ToLower** subroutine and the statement that calls it can be replaced by the **ToLower** macro that we developed in Chapter 1. And the **DoError** routine, shown here:

```
DoError:
  mov bx,StdErr        ; error messages to StdErr
  mov ah,40h           ; DOS Write Device function
  int 21h
  stc                  ; set error flag
```

is replaced with an invocation of our **DosWriteFile** macro, like this:

```
DoError:
  DosWriteFile StdErr    ; output error message
  stc                    ; set error flag
```

Notice that the preceding code specified only the file handle. The error message address and message length are already in DX and CX. In addition, we don't do any error checking on output to the standard error device (where could we report the error?), so no **ErrJmp** or **ErrMsg** parameter is given.

The resulting program, shown in Listing 2.27, generates an executable file that is equivalent in function to the original TRAL.ASM program shown in Listing 2.9. At 73 lines, Listing 2.27 is 60 percent smaller and much easier to work with than the original version. The generated code, although functionally equivalent, is 15 bytes shorter and a little bit faster, although you probably won't notice the speed difference because the program spends so much time getting characters from DOS.

```
 1:  ; Listing 2.27--TRALM.ASM
 2:  ;
 3:  ; TRALM.ASM--TRanslate All to Lowercase
 4:  ;   Convert uppercase characters to lowercase
 5:  ;
 6:      Ideal
 7:      %NoIncl
 8:  include "macros.inc"
 9:  include "dosmacs.inc"
10:      ProgramHeader Small,0100h
11:
12:      DataSeg
13:
14:  ; Input and output filenames
15:  zString InputFile,<"tral.asm">
16:  zString OutputFile,<"lowcase">
```

```
17:
18:     ; Error messages.
19:     LenString InFileErr,<"Cannot open input file",cr,lf>
20:     LenString OutFileErr,<"Cannot open output file",cr,lf>
21:     LenString ReadErr,<"Read Error",cr,lf>
22:     LenString WriteErr,<"Write Error",cr,lf>
23:     LenString DiskFull,<"Disk Full",cr,lf>
24:
25:     InHandle dw ?                       ; input file handle
26:     OutHandle dw ?                      ; output file handle
27:     InChar db ?                         ; file I/O buffer
28:
29:       CodeSeg
30:
31:     Proc Main
32:       ExeStart
33:       DosOpenFile <offset InputFile>,omRead,smCompat,[InHandle],\
34:                   DoError,InFileErr
35:       DosOpenFile <offset OutputFile>,omCreate,faNormal,[OutHandle],\
36:                   DoError,OutFileErr
37:     ;
38:     ; Loop until end-of-file or error.
39:     ;   Read character.
40:     ;   Convert character to uppercase.
41:     ;   Write character.
42:     ; EndLoop
43:     ;
44:     CharLoop:
45:       DosReadFile [InHandle],1,<offset InChar>,Done,DoError,ReadErr
46:       mov al,[InChar]
47:       ToLower al
48:       mov [InChar],al
49:       DosWriteFile [OutHandle],1,<offset InChar>,DoError,WriteErr,\
50:                   DiskFull
51:       jmp CharLoop
52:
53:     ; Display the error message on StdErr
54:     DoError:
55:       DosWriteFile StdErr
56:       stc                               ; set error flag
57:
58:     ; Processing complete.
59:     ; Close the files and exit program with return code
60:     ; indicating status.
61:     Done:
62:       pushf                             ; save error flag
63:       DosCloseFile [InHandle]
64:       DosCloseFile [OutHandle]
```

```
65:     popf                           ; restore error flag
66:   ;
67:   ; Carry flag will be set if an error occurred.
68:     mov al,0
69:     adc al,0                       ; set up return code
70:     DosExitProgram                 ; and exit program
71:   Endp Main
72:
73:   End Main
```

2.10 DOS Tamers and You

Although TRAL is but minimally useful—especially as it is currently written—it illustrates my point. Well thought-out macros can entirely eliminate the tedious "load registers, call INT 21h, check error flags" process that we must endure to access DOS functions from assembly language. The macros also provide us with a common interface to similar DOS functions and standardized error checking without sacrificing flexibility or code efficiency. Finally, our macros free us from the drudgery of accessing DOS functions so we can concentrate our efforts on the problem we're trying to solve rather than on interfacing with DOS.

In our experiments with HELLO and TRAL, we explored only a small number of the many DOS functions that are commonly used by application programs, but we laid the groundwork for developing macros that make use of many more. As you continue to develop and modify your own programs, look for opportunities to turn those long sequences of DOS access instructions into macros that remove the drudgery of operating system interfacing.

As you develop your new macros, concentrate on making them both simple to use and flexible enough to handle the most common uses. There may be times when you simply cannot use the macros, but those will be few and far between. If you use a DOS function more than once, be it several times in a single program or once in each of several programs, you're better off creating a macro to generate the code for you. Once the macro is created, using it will be easier, shorter, faster, and more reliable than writing all of that code by yourself.

Current Macro Libraries

You've now got two macro libraries that contain macros that we'll be using in the following chapters. The original library, MACROS.INC, has not changed much in this chapter. We only added one macro—the **ProgramHeader** macro of Listing 2.2.

DOSMACS.INC, though, has quite a few new macros. Rather than listing the entire contents of this new file, I've listed the macros and corresponding listing numbers that make up our working version of DOSMACS.INC:

3

Data Definition

I guess I was browsing "Dear Abby" or one of the other newspaper "advice" columns one day (Yeah? Well *you* try eating alone at Burger King with nothing else to read) when I ran across a story about a woman who was teaching her young daughter to cook dinner.

Having prepared the roast, heated the oven, and completed all the other preliminary steps, the girl was eager to pop the main course into the oven and get on with preparing the rest of the meal. Her mother, however, stopped her before she could get the pan in the oven and, pulling out a knife, proceeded to chop about four inches off one end of the roast.

"Why did you do that?" asked the little girl.

"Because," mother replied, "that's the way my mom taught me to do it."

Being at the age when *everything* must have a reason, this particular response did not satisfy the little girl and she was determined to get a better answer. After several minutes of hearing her daughter ask "why, why, why," Mom finally gave in and called *her* mother.

"Mom," she asked, "why do you cut four inches off the end of a roast before putting it in the oven?"

"Well, I don't know, dear," replied the older woman. "My mom taught me that and I never thought to ask why. Why don't you call her?"

Determined to get to the bottom of this in order to get her daughter's mind off the subject, the woman looked up her grandmother's number and dialed the phone.

"Grandma," she asked after some small talk, "why is it that you always cut four inches off the end of a roast before cooking it?"

Grandmother, after thinking a moment, said, "Oh, I don't do that any more since I got my new roast pan. You see, the old pan was so small I couldn't get a whole roast in it."

"That's the way we've always done it"

I've always been frustrated by programming languages that force me to define my data in one place and the code in another. In most cases the data is defined at the top of the source program and the code that operates on it is placed further down in the file. Most modern block-structured languages reduce this headache somewhat by allowing global data definitions outside of any block and local definitions within a block. Even so, most programmers define their data at the top of the program because that's the way it's always been done. They simply don't know any better.

If the current rage about object-oriented programming has taught us anything, it's to *attach your code to the data it operates on.* I know you're thinking "Sure, that's fine in high-level languages, but this is *assembly* language!" Yes, it is assembly language, and that's precisely why we want to keep the code and data together. Assembly language is complex enough without having to flip through thousand-page listings looking for a variable name or error message that's used only once.

Except for languages that require no data definition at all (such as BASIC or AWK, in which variables are defined at first use), Turbo Assembler provides perhaps the most flexible means of data definition. Unlike block-structured languages in which data definitions can occur only outside of a block or at the beginning of a local block, Turbo Assembler allows data to be defined at any point within the program. Properly used, this capability can be turned very much to our advantage.

3.1 HELLO Once More

Let's return to our first program, HELLO.ASM, to illustrate a point. In Listing 3.1, the definition of the "Hello, world" message has been moved so that the message is defined near the code that accesses it. Examine closely how this works.

```
 1:    ; Listing 3.1--HELLO.ASM
 2:    ;
 3:    ; HELLO.ASM
 4:    ; Everybody's first program rewritten using the new macros.
 5:    ; Simply displays a message, "Hello, world," on the standard
 6:    ; output device and returns to DOS.
 7:    Ideal
 8:    include "macros.inc"
 9:    include "dosmacs.inc"
10:      ProgramHeader Small,0100h
11:
12:      CodeSeg
13:
14:    Proc Main
15:      ExeStart
16:
17:      DataSeg
18:    $String Hello,<'Hello, world',cr,lf>
19:      CodeSeg
20:
21:      DosDisplayString Hello
22:      DosExitProgram 0
23:    Endp Main
24:
25:    End Main       ; End of program
```

ExeStart is expanded in the code segment as we expect. Then, the **DataSeg** directive instructs the assembler to switch segments and place anything that follows into the data segment. After **$String** is used to define the welcome message, the **CodeSeg** directive switches back to the code segment, where the rest of the program is assembled. As easily as that, we can define the data where it's used.

Listing 3.1 produces the same code as Listing 2.8. The advantage of Listing 3.1 is not apparent in such a small program, but consider a 2,000-line assembly language program. Wouldn't you rather have the data defined where it is used rather than in a single data section at the top or bottom of the program listing?

The only real disadvantage to this method of defining data is that it's awkward to work with, because we're again forced to remember details best left up to the assembler. If we forget one of the segment directives, we will end up with data in the code segment or, even worse, code in the data segment. Either way, even if the assembler doesn't report an error, our program will probably crash.

We can easily rewrite **TermString** as shown in Listing 3.2 so that it generates the **DataSeg** and **CodeSeg** directives automatically.

```
 1:    ; Listing 3.2--Segment switching TermString macro
 2:    ;
 3:    Macro TermString LblName,String,Terminator
 4:      DataSeg
 5:      ifnb <LblName>
 6:        Label LblName Byte
 7:      endif
 8:      db String,Terminator
 9:      CodeSeg
10:    Endm TermString
```

We can then use the new **TermString** macro as shown in Listing 3.3, but this creates another problem.

```
 1:    ; Listing 3.3--Using the new TermString macro
 2:    ;
 3:    ; HELLO.ASM code segment rewritten using the new TermString macro
 4:    ;
 5:      CodeSeg
 6:    Proc Main
 7:      ExeStart
 8:      ; Define welcome message in data segment.
 9:      $String Hello,<'Hello, world',cr,lf>
10:      DosDisplayString Hello
11:      DosExitProgram 0
12:    Endp Main
```

Although Listing 3.3 does indeed work as expected, we've broken the **TermString** macro! How? Imagine defining a string and a word variable in the data segment using the following code:

```
; Program header above
  DataSeg
$String Hello,<"Hello, world",cr,lf>
AWord dw ?
```

This seems perfectly normal and should do just what we expect. But the assembler expands the above code to this:

```
  DataSeg
  DataSeg
Label Hello Byte
  db "Hello, world",cr,lf,"$"
  CodeSeg
AWord dw ?
```

which is incorrect and will undoubtedly cause some strange results, because the variable **AWord** is defined in the code segment.

The problem here is that **TermString** assumes that it was invoked from within the code segment. In order to define the data, it must switch to the data segment, generate the definition, and then return to the code segment. **TermString** works fine when it's invoked from within the code segment, but when it's invoked from within the data segment, the segment switching causes erroneous code to be generated. In order to generate correct code for either case, **TermString** must be smart enough to determine which segment is currently active.

Where Am I?

As well as providing directives that change the currently active segment, Turbo Assembler also provides a text equate, **@curseg**, that can be used to determine the current segment name. Although this equate is normally used for **Assume** statements and segment overrides, it can also be used by a macro in conjunction with the **@code** equate to determine what code to generate in a given situation.

Three text equates are used to determine the code and data segment names, and the currently active segment.

The **@code** equate holds the name of the default code segment. This is the segment name that becomes active when the **CodeSeg** directive is used. Similarly, **@data** holds the name of the default data segment, which becomes active when **DataSeg** is used.

Finally, **@curseg** holds the name of the currently active segment. The value of this equate changes during assembly to reflect the current segment name.

Macro **CheckSeg**, shown in Listing 3.4, compares two segment names for equality and, if the segment names match, issues the specified directive and sets a flag to indicate that segment switching took place. If no match is found, no segment-switching directive is issued and the flag is cleared.

The new **TermString** macro in this listing uses **CheckSeg** to switch segments so that code and data are always assembled into their proper segments.

```
1:   ; Listing 3.4--CheckSeg and corrected TermString
2:   ;
3:   ; CheckSeg <Cur>,<Target>,<Directive>,<YesNo>
4:   ; Compare segment names, if equal, issue directive and set flag
5:   ; indicating that the segment was changed.
6:   ;
7:   ; Parameters
8:   ;   Cur (Optional) - Current segment name
9:   ;   Target (Optional) - Segment name to compare against
10:  ;   Directive (Optional) - Directive to issue if
11:  ; segment names match
12:  ;   YesNo (Optional) - Flag that indicates whether
13:  ; the segment names match. 1 = yes, 0 = no.
14:  ;
15:  ; Returns
16:  ;   The label specified by YesNo is set to indicate whether
17:  ; the segment names match.
18:  ;
19:  Macro CheckSeg Cur,Target,Directive,YesNo
20:    ifidni <Cur>,<Target>
21:      Directive
22:      ifnb <YesNo>
23:        YesNo = 1
24:      endif
25:    elseifnb <YesNo>
26:      YesNo = 0
27:    endif
28:  Endm CheckSeg
29:
30:  ;
31:  ; TermString--define a terminated string
32:  ;
33:  Macro TermString LblName,String,Terminator
34:    Local YesNo
35:  ;;
36:  ;; If currently in the code segment, switch to data segment.
37:  ;;
38:    CheckSeg %@curseg,%@code,DataSeg,YesNo
39:    ifnb <LblName>
40:      Label LblName Byte
41:    endif
42:    db String,Terminator
43:  ;;
```

```
44:   ;; Go back to code segment if that's where we came from.
45:   ;;
46:     if YesNo eq 1
47:       CodeSeg
48:     endif
49:   Endm TermString
```

This is the first time we've used the expression evaluate operator, **%**, in a nontrivial macro. Let's take a moment for a quick review of what this operator does and how it works.

Recall from Chapter 1 that the expression evaluate operator causes an expression to be evaluated immediately, so that the assembler uses the result of the evaluation, rather than the expression itself. **TermString** uses this operator to pass the segment names rather than the equate names to **CheckSeg**. Let's take a look at how this is done.

If we assume that **TermString** is the first macro used by a program and that it is invoked from the code segment, line 38, which reads

```
CheckSeg %@curseg,%@code,DataSeg,YesNo
```

is converted internally by the assembler to this:

```
CheckSeg _TEXT,_TEXT,DataSeg,??0000
```

and **CheckSeg** receives the proper parameters.

If we were to omit the expression evaluate operators in line 38 and write the line like this:

```
CheckSeg @curseg,@code,DataSeg,YesNo
```

then **CheckSeg** would receive the strings **@curseg** and **@code** for parameters, which would cause the **ifidni** test to fail, regardless of the values that these equates represent.

Recall that, if the expression evaluate operator is the first nonspace character on a line and is followed by at least one space, *all* expressions on that line will be evaluated before the line is assembled. We could use this feature in macro **CheckSeg** to evaluate the expressions in the **ifidni** test and avoid having to include the expression evaluate operator on each parameter to **CheckSeg**. To do this, simply replace line 20 in Listing 3.4 with a line that reads

```
% ifidni <Cur>,<Target>
```

and then change the macro invocation in **TermString** (line 38) to read

```
CheckSeg @curseg,@code,DataSeg,YesNo
```

With the addition of **CheckSeg**, and the enhanced **TermString** macro, we can now define a string from either segment and rest assured that it will be assembled in the data segment and that control will return to the segment that was active prior to the data definition. This flexibility does come at a small price. It is no longer possible to use **TermString** or its derivatives to define strings that reside in the code segment. Fortunately, data that resides within the code segment is not very common, so our new macros should work in most situations.

3.2 Data and Code . . . Together

Even with the new **TermString** macro, displaying strings in assembly language requires too much work. Granted, using the macros we've developed so far reduces the required code from a half dozen lines to two, but that's still one more than what's required in higher-level languages.

It would be nice to have **DosDisplayString** work in much the same way as the BASIC **PRINT** statement, which displays either a string or the contents of a variable. For example, to display a string in BASIC, you simply write

```
PRINT "Hello, world"
```

and if you want to define a string variable and then display the variable's contents, you can write this:

```
HELLO$ = "Hello, world"
PRINT HELLO$
```

The BASIC interpreter (or compiler) can identify the different argument types and generate the appropriate code. We can do the same thing with an assembly language macro and even go one better by defining and displaying the string with a single statement. All we need is for the assembler to tell us what kind of symbol is passed as a parameter to our macro.

Who Are You?

The Turbo Assembler **SymType** operator returns a byte that provides information about a symbol. The information returned is coded as shown in Table 3.1. Table 3.2 shows the **SymType** values that are returned for some of the symbols in HELLO.ASM.

Unfortunately, **SymType** produces an error if it is passed an undefined symbol, if the argument evaluates to a constant that exceeds 16 bits (32 bits if assembling in 80386 mode), or if the argument contains commas. For example, both of the following statements will produce an error:

Table 3.1. SymType information bits

Usage: **SymType** expression

Bit	Description
0	Program relative symbol
1	Data relative symbol
2	Constant
3	Direct addressing mode
4	Register
5	Symbol is defined
6	Unused bit
7	Symbol is external

If bits 2 and 3 are both zero, the expression is a register indirect reference (i.e. [DI]).

SymType will report an error if the expression contains an undefined symbol.

```
SymType <10,13>         ; Error!
SymType <"Hello, world"> ; Error!
```

Clearly, if we want to write a macro that will work with any type of argument, we must find some way of filtering quoted strings and value lists so that **SymType** does not encounter something that it can't process. We don't have to look far.

Examining Strings with InStr

Turbo Assembler provides three operators that greatly enhance the assembler's ability to deal with string data during assembly. **InStr** reports on the existence of a substring within a string; **CatStr** concatenates two strings to form a single string; and **SubStr** extracts substrings from a given string. All three operators are useful, but right now we're interested only in **InStr**.

Table 3.2. Typical SymType values

	Returned Value	**Meaning**
SymType 1	0024	Defined, Constant
SymType Hello	002A	Defined, Direct addressing, Data relative
SymType Main	0021	Defined, Program relative
SymType ax	0030	Register

InStr works in much the same way as the Turbo Pascal **Pos** function or the C **strchr()** and **strstr()** functions. Given a string and a substring, **InStr** returns an integer indicating the position that the substring occupies within the string. If **InStr** returns 0, the substring is not contained within the string. For example, this statement:

```
Apos = InStr <Hello, world>,<world>
```

sets **Apos** to 8, and a statement that reads:

```
Apos = InStr <Hello, world>,<z>
```

sets **Apos** to 0 because there is no *z* in "Hello, world."

The **WhatType** macro in Listing 3.5 uses **irpc** and **InStr** to test an argument for occurrences of quote, apostrophe, or comma. If none of these characters is found in the argument, **WhatType** assumes that the argument is a defined symbol and uses **SymType** to return the symbol's type. If one of the searched-for characters *does* occur in the argument, **WhatType** returns 0, indicating that the argument is either a string or a comma-separated list of values.

```
 1:   ; Listing 3.5--WhatType
 2:   ;
 3:   ; WhatType Arg1,Arg2
 4:   ;   Set Arg2 to indicate type of Arg1. Returns 0 if Arg1 is
 5:   ; a quoted string or a list of values. Otherwise, Arg2 is set
 6:   ; as described in the documentation for SymType.
 7:   ;
 8:   Macro WhatType Arg1,Arg2
 9:     Local YesNo
10:   ;;
11:   ;; If the argument contains quote ("), apostrophe ('), or
12:   ;; comma (,), treat it as a string.
13:   ;;
14:     irpc TestChar,<"',>
15:       YesNo InStr <Arg1>,<TestChar>
16:       if YesNo ne 0
17:         exitm
18:       endif
19:     endm
20:   ;;
21:   ;; If YesNo is equal to 0, the argument does not contain
22:   ;; any of the three characters.
23:   ;;
24:     if YesNo eq 0
25:       Arg2 = SymType Arg1
26:     else
27:       Arg2 = 0
```

```
28:     endif
29:  Endm WhatType
```

Armed with a working **WhatType** macro, we can proceed to modify **DosDisplayString** as shown in Listing 3.6. Then the macro will be able to determine what kind of argument is being passed and thereby produce the correct code for any given situation.

```
1:   ; Listing 3.6--New DosDisplayString macro
2:   ;
3:   ; DosDisplayString <String>
4:   ;
5:   Macro DosDisplayString String
6:     Local ArgType,Temp
7:   ;;
8:   ;; If the parameter is not blank, check the type to determine
9:   ;; what kind of code to generate. The local variable ArgType
10:  ;; is set to indicate the type of argument.
11:  ;;
12:    ifnb <String>
13:      WhatType <String>,ArgType
14:       ;;
15:       ;; If it's a string (ArgType = 0) or a constant
16:       ;; (ArgType = 24), define the data and generate code
17:       ;; to display it.
18:       ;;
19:      if (ArgType eq 0) or (ArgType eq 24h)
20:        $String Temp,<String>
21:        mov dx,offset Temp
22:      else
23:        ;;
24:        ;; Otherwise, just generate code to display it.
25:        ;;
26:        mov dx,offset String
27:      endif
28:    endif
29:    DosCall 9
30:  Endm DosDisplayString
```

With the new **DosDisplayString** macro, HELLO.ASM becomes a very simple program indeed, as shown in Listing 3.7. This program assembles to *exactly* the same code as the original version of HELLO.ASM shown at the beginning of Chapter 2 (Listing 2.1).

```
1:   ; Listing 3.7--HELLO.ASM
2:   ;
3:   ; HELLO.ASM written using the new "type aware"
4:   ; DosDisplayString macro.
```

```
 5:    ;
 6:       Ideal
 7:
 8:    include "macros.inc"
 9:    include "dosmacs.inc"
10:
11:       ProgramHeader Small,0100h
12:
13:       CodeSeg
14:    Proc Main
15:       ExeStart
16:       DosDisplayString <"Hello, world">
17:       DosExitProgram 0
18:    Endp Main
19:
20:       End Main
```

3.3 Variable Arguments

Many times a program uses the same string in different parts of the code. The traditional way of handling this situation would be to use **$String** to define the string and then **DosDisplayString** to access it each time it's used. For example, if you wanted to display the "Hello, world" message twice, you would write this:

```
$String Hello,<"Hello, world",cr,lf>
DosDisplayString Hello
DosDisplayString Hello
```

Of course, we could have written this:

```
DosDisplayString <"Hello, world",cr,lf>
DosDisplayString <"Hello, world",cr,lf>
```

but that would have defined the string twice, which is a waste of memory. Many high-level language compilers perform *constant folding*—an optimization that merges duplicate string constants—in effect converting the second example above into code equivalent to the first example. The assembler has no such capability. We could write a set of macros that performs constant folding, but the result would be far from foolproof and the added functionality would hardly be worth the trouble.

We can, however, modify **DosDisplayString** as shown in Listing 3.8 so that it defines and displays a string with a single statement. Subsequent references to the string can then be made using the defined name.

```
 1:    ; Listing 3.8--DosDisplayString
 2:    ;
 3:    ; DosDisplayString <String>,Arg2
 4:    ;
 5:   Macro DosDisplayString String,Arg2
 6:     Local ArgType,Temp
 7:   ;;
 8:   ;; If the first parameter is not blank, check the second
 9:   ;; parameter and the first parameter's type to determine
10:   ;; what code to generate.
11:   ;;
12:     ifnb <String>
13:       ;;
14:       ;; If the second parameter is not blank, assume the first
15:       ;; parameter is a label name and define a string
16:       ;; with that name. Then display it.
17:       ;;
18:     ifnb <Arg2>
19:       $String String,<Arg2>
20:       mov dx,offset String
21:     else
22:       ;;
23:       ;; The second parameter is blank. Check the type of
24:       ;; first parameter.
25:       WhatType <String>,ArgType
26:       ;;
27:       ;; If it's a string (ArgType = 0) or a constant
28:       ;; (ArgType = 24) then define the data and generate
29:       ;; code to display it.
30:       ;;
31:       if (ArgType eq 0) or (ArgType eq 24h)
32:         $String Temp,<String>
33:         mov dx,offset Temp
34:       else
35:         ;;
36:         ;; Otherwise, just generate code to display it.
37:         ;;
38:         mov dx,offset String
39:       endif
40:     endif
41:   endif
42:   DosCall 9
43:   Endm DosDisplayString
```

Using the new **DosDisplayString** macro from Listing 3.8, the code to display the same string twice then becomes:

```
DosDisplayString Hello,<"Hello, world",cr,lf>
DosDisplayString Hello
```

The first use of **DosDisplayString** defines the label **Hello**, allocates storage for the string, and generates code to display it. The second statement works exactly as before—generating only the code necessary to display the string. The code generated from these statements is shown here:

```
; DosDisplayString Hello,<"Hello, world",cr,lf>
  DataSeg
Label Hello Byte
  db "Hello, world",cr,lf,"$"
  CodeSeg
  mov dx,offset Hello
  mov ah,9
  int 21h
; DosDisplayString Hello
  mov dx,offset Hello
  mov ah,9
  int 21h
```

More Uses of Variable Arguments

When I finally finished **DosDisplayString**, I started looking for other applications of this technique. One possibility that immediately came to mind was modifying **DosReadFile** and **DosWriteFile** so that the error message strings could be defined on the same line as their first use.

DosReadFile presents no problem at all, and we could very easily change the macro definition to allow for defining the error message string and its label, much as we do with **DosDisplayString**. If we were to make these modifications, the code in TRAL.ASM that reads a character from the file would be changed to:

```
DosReadFile [InHandle],1,<offset InChar>,Done,DoError,\
            ReadErr,<"Read Error",cr,lf>
```

I haven't presented these modifications here because they're relatively straightforward copies of what we've already done to **DosDisplayString** and because this technique won't work in all situations.

The modifications to make **DosWriteFile** accept either text strings or label names for the last two parameters are much like the first modifications we made to **DosDisplayString**. If we were to make these changes, this code fragment from TRAL.ASM that writes a character to the file

```
  DataSeg
LenString WriteErr,<"Write Error",cr,lf>
LenString DiskFull,<"Disk Full",cr,lf>
  CodeSeg
DosWriteFile [OutHandle],1,<offset InChar>,DoError,WriteErr,DiskFull
```

would be rewritten as

```
DosWriteFile [OutHandle],1,<offset InChar>,DoError, \
          <"Write Error",cr,lf>,<"Disk Full",cr,lf>
```

which will produce the same result as what TRAL uses, except that the **WriteError** and **DiskFull** labels are not defined. This is not a problem unless we want to use the same error messages in more than one **DosWriteFile** invocation.

But the modifications that allow **DosWriteFile** to optionally define labels for the error message strings present a bit of a problem. Why? Because the macro will accept two error message parameters. As an example, imagine if we changed the macro definition to this:

```
Macro DosWriteFile Handle,NumChar,Buffer,ErrJmp,ErrMsgL,ErrMsg,FullMsgL,FullMsg
```

where the two new parameters, **ErrMsgL** and **FullMsgL**, are the label names for the respective messages. We could then change TRAL's **DosWriteFile** invocation to read:

```
DosWriteFile [OutHandle],1,<offset InChar>,DoError,\
      WriteErr,<"Write Error",cr,lf>,DiskFull,<"Disk Full",cr,lf>
```

and the macro would generate the following data definitions:

```
Label WriteErr Byte
db "Write Error",cr,lf
WriteErrLen = $ - WriteErr
Label DiskFull Byte
db "Disk full",cr,lf
DiskFullLen = $ - DiskFull
```

But, if we then wanted to reuse the same error messages, we'd have to pass the label names and substitute a blank parameter for the **ErrMsg** parameter, like this:

```
DosWriteFile [OutHandle],1,<offset InChar>,DoError,\
          WriteErr,,DiskFull
```

(Notice the two commas after **WriteErr** that indicate a blank **ErrMsg** parameter.) Although this works, remembering to insert those blank parameters will quickly bring on the men in the white coats. There is a better way to handle this situation, but it requires another trip down memory lane and one last modification to **DosDisplayString** for an example.

Counting Arguments Revisited

Recall **PushRegs**, **PopRegs**, and **PopCheck**, the macros that help you ensure that you're managing the stack correctly. If these macros don't ring a bell, hop back to Chapter 1 and take a quick look at them. **PushRegs** increments a counter every time it **PUSH**es a register and **PopRegs** decrements the same counter every time a register is **POP**ped. The result is that we can always use **PopCheck** to see whether the numbers of **PUSH**es and **POP**s match.

We can use the same technique—a counter variable within an **irp** loop—to allow *any* macro parameter, not just the last one, to accept variable arguments. The result is a cleaner syntax and a more flexible macro.

Consider the **CountArgs** macro in Listing 3.9. All it does is count the number of items in the list passed as its only parameter. The result is stored in the global variable **ArgCount**.

```
 1:    ; Listing 3.9--CountArgs
 2:    ;
 3:    ; Return a count of the arguments in a list
 4:    ;
 5:    Macro CountArgs ArgList
 6:      ArgCount = 0              ;; ArgCount is a global variable
 7:      irp x,<ArgList>
 8:        ArgCount = ArgCount + 1
 9:      endm
10:    Endm CountArgs
```

To use this macro, we simply pass it a comma-separated list of items and then inspect the **ArgCount** variable once the macro is finished. For example, the following code will display a message indicating that three items were in the list passed to **CountArgs**:

```
CountArgs <1,2,3>
if ArgCount eq 3
  Display "Three items"
endif
```

Following are more sample uses of **CountArgs**. The comments to the right show what the value of **ArgCount** will be after each statement is assembled.

```
CountArgs 1                             ; ArgCount = 1
CountArgs 1,2,3                         ; ArgCount = 1
CountArgs <"Hello, world",cr,lf>        ; ArgCount = 3
CountArgs <Hello, <"Hello, world",cr,lf>> ; ArgCount = 2 (!)
```

The last example illustrates how we can use angle brackets to enclose any list of items so that the assembler treats the list as a single parameter. Because each level of macro expansion removes only a single level of brackets, the outer pair of brackets is removed by the **CountArgs** invocation, and the two arguments that **CountArgs** identifies are the label **Hello** and the bracketed list **<"Hello, world",cr,lf>**.

The ability of **CountArgs** to treat a list of items as a single argument enables us to pass variable arguments in any macro parameter.

The **DosDisplayString** macro in Listing 3.10 accepts a single parameter and uses **CountArgs** to determine how the parameter should be passed. The resulting macro is then used in much the same way as the macro in Listing 3.8. The advantage of this new method is that we can now use the same technique with **DosWriteFile** or any other macro that accepts text strings.

```
 1:    ; Listing 3.10--DosDisplayString
 2:    ;
 3:    ; DosDisplayString <StringDef>
 4:    ;
 5:    Macro DosDisplayString StringDef
 6:      Local ArgType,Temp
 7:    ;;
 8:    ;; If the parameter is not blank, count the arguments in the
 9:    ;; parameter list to determine how to proceed.
10:    ;;
11:      ifnb <StringDef>
12:        CountArgs <StringDef>
13:        if ArgCount gt 2
14:          ;;
15:          ;; If more than 2 arguments, display error and exit.
16:          ;;
17:          Err
18:          Display "Too many parameters to DosDisplayString"
19:          exitm
20:        elseif ArgCount eq 2
21:          ;;
22:          ;; If two arguments, assume the first is a label name
23:          ;; and the second is a string. Define a string and
24:          ;; then display it.
25:          ;;
26:          $String StringDef
27:          irp x,<StringDef>
28:            mov dx,offset x
29:            exitm
30:          endm
31:        else
32:          ;;
33:          ;; Only one argument was passed. Check its type.
34:          ;;
35:          WhatType StringDef,ArgType
```

```
36:          ::
37:          :: If it's a string (ArgType = 0) or a constant
38:          :: (ArgType = 24), define the data and generate
39:          :: code to display it.
40:          ::
41:          if (ArgType eq 0) or (ArgType eq 24h)
42:            $String Temp,StringDef
43:            mov dx,offset Temp
44:          else
45:            ::
46:            :: Otherwise, assume it's a label, so simply
47:            :: generate code to display it.
48:            ::
49:            mov dx,offset StringDef
50:          endif
51:        endif
52:      endif
53:      DosCall 9
54:    Endm DosDisplayString
```

The four different calling sequences for the new **DosDisplayString** macro are

```
DosDisplayString                    ; display a string from DX
DosDisplayString <<"Hello, world",cr,lf>> ; display a string
DosDisplayString Hello              ; display a string that's already defined
DosDisplayString <Hello,<"Hello, world",cr,lf>> ; define and display a string
```

Ambiguities and Assembler Quirks

If you were to write a program that included the last line above, the assembler would issue an error message similar to this:

```
**Error** X.ASM (8) DOSDISPLAYSTRING(1) Extra characters on line
```

where the number in parentheses is the line number of the **DosDisplayString** invocation. We can get around this problem using a quirk of the assembler, but let's take a look at what causes the problem.

Line 11 in Listing 3.10 is the one that the assembler doesn't like. This line reads

```
ifnb <StringDef>
```

In our example, the assembler substitutes the value of **StringDef** and ends up with a line that reads

```
ifnb <Hello,<"Hello, world",cr,lf>>
```

and then proceeds to evaluate the line.

Unfortunately, the assembler's expression evaluator doesn't know about nesting angle brackets. As a result, it interprets the first right angle bracket (immediately after the **lf**) as the closing bracket for the **ifnb** test. The final angle bracket, then, is not interpreted as part of the expression and the assembler doesn't know what to do with it, so an error message is issued.

Without getting into the details of how the assembler works, it's difficult to explain exactly *why* the assembler interprets the first right angle bracket as it does. An ambiguity in the language definition causes the assembler to get confused by this construct.

We can, however, get around this problem using the assembler's **QUIRKS** mode. The **QUIRKS** directive instructs Turbo Assembler to emulate some of the more arcane Microsoft MASM features—the "extra characters on line" problem being one of them.

The only problem with using **QUIRKS** mode is that it disables **Ideal** mode. So, we've got to reenable **Ideal** after making the test. Normally, this wouldn't be a problem, but consider the following code fragment:

```
quirks
ifnb <ErrMsg>
  ideal
  ;; Do one thing.
elseifnb <ErrJmp>
  ideal
  ;; Do another.
else
  ideal
  ;; Do something else.
endif
```

We've got to reenable **Ideal** mode inside each conditional block. Because **QUIRKS** mode has a slightly different syntax than **Ideal** mode, forgetting to reenable **Ideal** mode will undoubtedly lead to some very strange and difficult-to-find assembly errors.

Again, I have no idea why the assembler treats arguments to **ifnb** in this manner or why the assembler's designers decided that allowing what appears to be a valid construct is considered a quirk. The **QUIRKS** directive, however, enables us to get around the problem, and we'll need to use it in several of our macros.

Variable Arguments and DosWriteFile

Now that we know how to use **CountArgs** to determine how many arguments are included in a single parameter, modifying **DosReadFile** and **DosWriteFile** is a fairly simple matter of using the modifications we made to **DosDisplayString** in the new macros. Rather than duplicate all of that code inside each of the new macros (once in **DosReadFile** and twice in **DosWriteFile**), another "helper" macro, **MakeString**, accepts a string definition and generates the correct code for each of the three possible uses. Listing 3.11 contains **MakeString**, the two modified DOS macros, and a new **LenString** macro that understands segments just like the **TermString** macro of Listing 3.4.

```
 1:   ; Listing 3.11--New DosReadFile, DosWriteFile, LenString, and
 2:   ; MakeString macros.
 3:   Macro DosReadFile Handle,NumChar,Buffer,EofJmp,ErrJmp,ErrMsg
 4:     Local CkEof,Done
 5:     ;;
 6:     ;; Load registers with optional parameters.
 7:     ;;
 8:     ifnb <Handle>
 9:       mov bx,Handle              ;; BX = handle
10:     endif
11:     ifnb <NumChar>
12:       mov cx,NumChar             ;; CX = number of bytes to read
13:     endif
14:     ifnb <Buffer>
15:       mov dx,Buffer              ;; DX = buffer address
16:     endif
17:     DosCall 3Fh                  ;; tell DOS to read the file
18:     ;;
19:     ;; If an error message address is given, generate code to
20:     ;; test error flag and branch or load registers accordingly.
21:     ;;
22:     quirks
23:     ifnb <ErrMsg>
24:       ideal
25:       jnc CkEof                  ;; branch around if no error
26:       MakeString <ErrMsg>
27:       ;;
28:       ;; Generate branch to error routine (if given) or to
29:       ;; end of macro.
30:       ;;
31:       ifnb <ErrJmp>
32:         jmp ErrJmp
33:       else
34:         jmp Done
35:       endif
36:       Label CkEof Near
37:     ;;
38:     ;; If no error message given, generate conditional branch
39:     ;; to error routine (if given) or end of macro.
40:     ;;
41:     elseifnb <ErrJmp>
```

```
42:        ideal
43:        jc ErrJmp
44:      else
45:        ideal
46:        jc Done
47:      endif
48:      or ax,ax                    ;; check for end of file
49:   ;;
50:   ;; Generate conditional branch to EOF processing
51:   ;; routine (if defined).
52:   ;;
53:      ifnb <EofJmp>
54:        jz EofJmp                  ;; and branch if required
55:      endif
56:   ;;
57:   ;; If no error routine defined, define target label for
58:   ;; end of macro.
59:   ;;
60:      ifb <ErrJmp>
61:        Label Done Near
62:      endif
63:   Endm DosReadFile
64:
65:
66:   Macro DosWriteFile Handle,NumChar,Buffer,ErrJmp,ErrMsg,FullMsg
67:      Local CkFull,Done
68:   ;;
69:   ;; Load registers with optional parameters.
70:   ;;
71:      ifnb <Handle>
72:        mov bx,Handle              ;; BX = handle
73:      endif
74:      ifnb <NumChar>
75:        mov cx,NumChar             ;; CX = number of bytes to write
76:      endif
77:      ifnb <Buffer>
78:        mov dx,Buffer              ;; DX = address of buffer
79:      endif
80:      DosCall 40h                  ;; tell DOS to write the data
81:   ;;
82:   ;; If an error message address is given, generate code to
83:   ;; test error flag and branch or load registers accordingly.
84:   ;;
85:      quirks
86:      ifnb <ErrMsg>
87:        ideal
88:        jnc CkFull                 ;; branch around if no error
89:        MakeString <ErrMsg>
```

```
 90:        ;;
 91:        ;; Generate branch to error routine (if given) or to
 92:        ;; end of macro.
 93:        ;;
 94:        ifnb <ErrJmp>
 95:          jmp ErrJmp
 96:        else
 97:          jmp Done
 98:        endif
 99:        Label CkFull Near
100:      ;;
101:      ;; If no error message given, generate conditional branch
102:      ;; to error routine (if given) or end of macro.
103:      ;;
104:      elseifnb <ErrJmp>
105:        ideal
106:        jc ErrJmp
107:      else
108:        ideal
109:        jc Done
110:      endif
111:      cmp ax,cx                        ;; check for full block write
112:    ;;
113:    ;; If "disk full" message address is given, generate code to
114:    ;; test condition and branch or load registers accordingly.
115:    ;;
116:      quirks
117:      ifnb <FullMsg>
118:        ideal
119:        jz Done                        ;; if AX = CX, everything's OK
120:        MakeString <FullMsg>
121:        ;;
122:        ;; Generate branch to error routine (if given) or code to
123:        ;; set the error flag.
124:        ;;
125:        ifnb <ErrJmp>
126:          jmp ErrJmp                   ;; branch to error routine
127:        else
128:          stc                          ;; set carry to indicate error
129:        endif
130:      ;;
131:      ;; If "disk full" not defined, generate conditional branch
132:      ;; to error routine (if given) or to end of macro.
133:      ;;
134:      elseifnb <ErrJmp>
135:        ideal
136:        jnz ErrJmp                     ;; branch on error
137:      else
```

```
138:        ideal
139:        jz Done                        ;; branch if OK
140:        stc                            ;; set carry to indicate error
141:      endif
142: Label Done Near                       ;; target for conditional jumps
143: Endm DosWriteFile
144:
145: Macro MakeString StringDef
146:    Local Temp
147:    CountArgs <StringDef>
148:    if ArgCount gt 2
149:       ;;
150:       ;; If more than two arguments, display error and exit.
151:       ;;
152:       Err
153:       Display "Too many arguments"
154:       exitm
155:    elseif ArgCount eq 2
156:       ;;
157:       ;; If two arguments, assume the first is a label name
158:       ;; and the second is a string. Define a string and
159:       ;; then display it.
160:       ;;
161:       LenString StringDef
162:       irp x,<StringDef>
163:         mov dx,offset x              ;; set error message address
164:         mov cx,x&&Len                ;; and length
165:         exitm
166:       endm
167:    else
168:       ;;
169:       ;; Only one argument was passed. Check its type.
170:       ;;
171:       WhatType StringDef,ArgType
172:       ;;
173:       ;; If it's a string (ArgType = 0) or a constant
174:       ;; (ArgType = 24), define the data and generate
175:       ;; code to output it.
176:       ;;
177:       if (ArgType eq 0) or (ArgType eq 24h)
178:         LenString Temp,StringDef
179:         mov dx,offset Temp
180:         mov cx,Temp&Len
101:       clsc
182:         ;;
183:         ;; Otherwise, assume it's a label and simply
184:         ;; generate code to output it.
185:         ;;
```

```
186:         mov dx,offset StringDef
187:         mov cx,StringDef&Len
188:       endif
189:     endif
190:   Endm MakeString
191:
192:   ;
193:   ; LenString--Define an ASCII string with associated length
194:   ;
195:   Macro LenString Name,String
196:     Local IsCode
197:   ;;
198:   ;; If currently in code segment, switch to data segment.
199:   ;;
200:     CheckSeg %@curseg,%@code,DataSeg,IsCode
201:     ifnb <Name>
202:       Label Name Byte
203:     endif
204:     db String
205:     ifnb <Name>
206:       Name&Len = $ - Name
207:     endif
208:   ;;
209:   ;; Switch back to code segment if required.
210:   ;;
211:     if IsCode eq 1
212:       CodeSeg
213:     endif
214:   Endm LenString
```

Sample uses of the new **DosReadFile** and **DosWriteFile** macros are

```
DosWriteFile [OutHandle],1,<offset InChar>,DoError,\
  <WriteErr,<"Write Error",cr,lf>>,<DiskFull,<"Disk Full",cr,lf>>
DosWriteFile [OutHandle],1,<offset InChar>,DoError,\
  <<"Write Error",cr,lf>>,<<"Disk Full",cr,lf>>
DosWriteFile [OutHandle],1,<offset InChar>,DoError,WriteErr,DiskFull
DosReadFile [InHandle],1,<offset InChar>,DoError,<<"Read Error",cr,lf>>
DosReadFile [InHandle],1,<offset InChar>,DoError,<ReadErr,<"Read Error",cr,lf>>
DosReadFile [InHandle],1,<offset InChar>,DoError,ReadErr
```

3.4 Conversion Tables
ToLower Revisited

Chapter 1 mentioned that the macros we developed there did not create the fastest possible code and that we'd return to them in later chapters to make them generate better code. We won't spend a lot of time on optimization here—that's the subject of Chapter 5—but one optimization technique should be mentioned here because it involves defining data and code together.

One particularly inefficient macro from Chapter 1 is **ToLower**, the macro that converts a character in a given register from uppercase to lowercase. In my experience, the most common use of this macro is to convert a character in AL. Rarely do I have a character in some other register or memory location that needs to be converted.

As it turns out, the 8086 has a special instruction that makes quick work of converting characters in AL, and we can modify **ToLower** to take advantage of this instruction.

Conversions with XLAT

If you're not familiar with the 8086 **XLAT** instruction, you've missed out on one of the 8086's more unique instructions. **XLAT** performs a table lookup by adding the contents of the AL register to BX and then using the resulting address as an offset into the segment referenced by DS (the default) or any other segment register if a segment override is given. Figure 3.1 illustrates how **XLAT** works.

Figure 3.1. The operation of XLAT

Step 1: **XLAT** accesses memory by adding BX and AL to form an offset address into the DS segment.

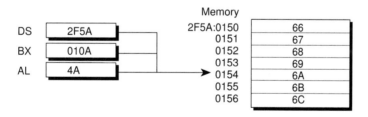

Step 2: The addressed byte is placed in AL. Only bytes can be accessed with **XLAT**, and the result is always placed in AL.

If we were to define a table that maps uppercase characters to lowercase and leaves all other characters alone, we could perform an uppercase to lowercase conversion with a single **XLAT** instruction. The code fragment in Listing 3.12 shows how this is accomplished.

```
 1:  ; Listing 3.12--Case conversions with XLAT
 2:  ;
 3:    DataSeg
 4:
 5:  ; Upper- to lowercase conversion table
 6:  radix 16
 7:  Label LCTable Byte
 8:    db 00,01,02,03,04,05,06,07,08,09,0a,0b,0c,0d,0e,0f
 9:    db 10,11,12,13,14,15,16,17,18,19,1a,1b,1c,1d,1e,1f
10:    db 20,21,22,23,24,25,26,27,28,29,2a,2b,2c,2d,2e,2f
11:    db 30,31,32,33,34,35,36,37,38,39,3a,3b,3c,3d,3e,3f
12:  ;
13:  ; Uppercase characters are ASCII codes 41h through 5Ah.
14:  ; Lowercase codes are 61h through 7Ah.
15:  ; Place the lowercase codes here to map upper to lower.
16:  ;
17:    db 40,61,62,63,64,65,66,67,68,69,6a,6b,6c,6d,6e,6f
18:    db 70,71,72,73,74,75,76,77,78,79,7a,5b,5c,5d,5e,5f
19:  ; Now continue from 60h through 0ffh
20:    db 60,61,62,63,64,65,66,67,68,69,6a,6b,6c,6d,6e,6f
21:    db 70,71,72,73,74,75,76,77,78,79,7a,7b,7c,7d,7e,7f
22:    db 80,81,82,83,84,85,86,87,88,89,8a,8b,8c,8d,8e,8f
23:    db 90,91,92,93,94,95,96,97,98,99,9a,9b,9c,9d,9e,9f
24:    db 0a0,0a1,0a2,0a3,0a4,0a5,0a6,0a7,0a8,0a9,0aa,0ab,0ac,0ad,0ae,0af
25:    db 0b0,0b1,0b2,0b3,0b4,0b5,0b6,0b7,0b8,0b9,0ba,0bb,0bc,0bd,0be,0bf
26:    db 0c0,0c1,0c2,0c3,0c4,0c5,0c6,0c7,0c8,0c9,0ca,0cb,0cc,0cd,0ce,0cf
27:    db 0d0,0d1,0d2,0d3,0d4,0d5,0d6,0d7,0d8,0d9,0da,0db,0dc,0dd,0de,0df
28:    db 0e0,0e1,0e2,0e3,0e4,0e5,0e6,0e7,0e8,0e9,0ea,0eb,0ec,0ed,0ee,0ef
29:    db 0f0,0f1,0f2,0f3,0f4,0f5,0f6,0f7,0f8,0f9,0fa,0fb,0fc,0fd,0fe,0ff
30:  radix 10
31:
32:    CodeSeg
33:  Proc Main
34:    ; Initialization code here. Open files, and so on.
35:    mov bx,offset LCTable ; BX points to conversion table
36:  MainLoop:
37:    ; Read character from file into AL.
38:    xlat                  ; convert AL to lowercase
39:    ; Write character to file.
40:    ; Loop until no more characters.
```

How much faster is **XLAT**? On my 10-MHz AT compatible, 1,000 iterations of **ToLower** execute in anywhere from 1,886 µs (when the character in AL is less than 65, the ASCII code for *A*) to 3,175 µs (when the character in AL is greater than or equal 65). **ToLower**, then, takes roughly 19 or 32 cycles, depending on the value in AL.

One thousand **XLAT** instructions, on the other hand, executed in an amazingly fast 628 µs, regardless of the value in AL. At something less than 7 cycles per occurrence, **XLAT** is almost three times as fast as **ToLower**'s *best* time and 4½ times as fast as **ToLower** when it actually has to convert a character.

XLAT won't always provide such dramatic performance increases; this test was run completely out of context without regard for actually *doing* anything. On the other hand, it could provide an even greater performance increase if a large amount of processing is required in order to do a particular character conversion.

Of course, using **XLAT** takes up memory—256 bytes for the conversion table—and typing that conversion table is a big pain in the fingers as well as an excellent opportunity to make an error. Memory, however, is cheap; and we can construct a macro that will generate the conversion table for us.

As shown in Listing 3.13, **rept** in conjunction with a counting variable can easily generate the table with considerably less work on our part. The **Char** variable is set to 0 and incremented each time through the loop. When **Char** represents one of the uppercase alpha characters, a lowercase character is generated in its place. Otherwise, the byte generated is equal to **Char**. This generates a table that is equivalent in content to the conversion table in Listing 3.12.

```
1:    ; Listing 3.13--Generating the lowercase conversion table
2:    ;
3:    Label LCTable Byte
4:      Char = 0                ; initialize count
5:      rept 256
6:        ;;
7:        ;; If Char is in the range of uppercase characters
8:        ;; then generate the lowercase equivalent. Otherwise,
9:        ;; generate a byte with value of Char.
10:       ;;
11:       if (Char ge 'A') and (Char le 'Z')
12:         db Char or 20h
13:       else
14:         db Char
15:       endif
16:       Char = Char + 1    ; go to next character
17:     endm
```

The only step left is to modify **ToLower** so that it will generate the table if required and also generate code to use **XLAT** when requested. It will be necessary to maintain the existing functionality so that other registers—or even AL—can be tested using the original "compare and jump" method. The new **ToLower** macro that includes these enhancements is shown in Listing 3.14.

```
 1:   ; Listing 3.14--ToLower with XLAT capability
 2:   ;
 3:   ; ToLower Reg,<UseXlat>,<LoadBX>
 4:   ; Determine whether the contents of the specified register or
 5:   ; memory location is an uppercase alpha character (A..Z), and
 6:   ; if so, convert it to lowercase.
 7:   ;
 8:   ; Parameters
 9:   ;   Reg (Required)--Register or memory reference
10:   ;   UseXlat (Optional)--meaningful only when Reg = AL
11:   ;   LoadBX (Optional)--meaningful only when Reg = AL and
12:   ; UseXlat is not blank.
13:   ;
14:   ;   This macro will automatically generate the conversion
15:   ;   table if required.
16:   ;
17:   ; Returns
18:   ;   Reg converted to uppercase (if applicable)
19:   ;
20:   ; Preserves the contents of all registers but the one
21:   ; specified in the Reg parameter and BX if the third parameter
22:   ; is given.
23:   ;
24:   Macro ToLower Reg,UseXlat,LoadBX
25:       Local Around
26:       ifidni <Reg>,<al>
27:           ;;
28:           ;; If the requested register is AL and the second parameter
29:           ;; is nonblank, generate code to use XLAT for the
30:           ;; conversion.
31:           ;;
32:           ifnb <UseXlat>
33:             ;;
34:             ;; If ??LcFlag = 0, the conversion table has not been
35:             ;; constructed. Construct it, set the flag, and purge
36:             ;; the construction macro.
37:             ;;
38:             if ??LcFlag eq 0
39:               MakeLcTable
40:               Purge MakeLcTable
41:             endif
42:             ;;
43:             ;; If the third parameter is not blank, load BX with the
44:             ;; address of the conversion table.
45:             ;;
46:             ifnb <LoadBX>
47:               mov bx,offset ??LcTable
48:             endif
```

```
49:         xlat                ;; do the conversion
50:         exitm
51:       endif
52:     endif
53:   ;;
54:   ;; If the macro executes to this point, generate code to
55:   ;; perform "compare and jump" translation.
56:   ;;
57:     IsUpper Reg             ;; see whether it's uppercase
58:     jnz Around              ;; if not, then ignore;
59:     or Reg,20h              ;; otherwise, convert to lowercase
60:   Around:
61:   Endm ToLower
62:
63:   ;
64:   ; The global variable ??LcFlag is used to determine whether the
65:   ; upper- to lowercase conversion table has been generated.
66:   ; It is set to 1 after the table is created.
67:   ;
68:   ??LcFlag = 0
69:
70:   ;
71:   ; MakeLcTable--generate the upper- to lowercase conversion
72:   ; table. This macro is used only by ToLower and is purged
73:   ; after it is used.
74:   ;
75:   Macro MakeLcTable
76:     Local Char,IsCode
77:
78:     ;; Switch to data segment if not already there.
79:     CheckSeg %@curseg,%@Code,DataSeg,IsCode
80:     Label ??LcTable Byte
81:     Char = 0                ;; initialize count
82:     rept 256
83:       ;;
84:       ;; If Char is in the range of uppercase characters,
85:       ;; generate the lowercase equivalent. Otherwise,
86:       ;; generate a byte with value of Char.
87:       ;;
88:       if (Char ge 'A') and (Char le 'Z')
89:         db Char or 20h
90:       else
91:         db Char
92:       endif
93:       Char = Char + 1        ;; go to next character
94:     endm
95:     ??LcFlag = 1            ;; set flag indicating that the table
96:                             ;; has been created
```

```
 97:     ;; Go back to code segment if required.
 98:     if IsCode eq 1
 99:        CodeSeg
100:     endif
101:  Endm MakeLcTable
```

In order to determine whether to generate the table, two additional parameters were added to **ToLower**, and a global flag, **??LcFlag**, was added. The first new parameter is used to instruct the macro to use **XLAT** rather than "compare and jump." Any nonblank value passed in this parameter will cause **ToLower** to generate **XLAT** code.

If you can't dedicate the BX register for this task and need to load it with the address of the conversion table each time through the loop, pass a nonblank third parameter to **ToLower**. Note that the second and third parameters are meaningful only when **Reg** is AL, and that the third parameter is meaningful only when the second is nonblank.

Don't be afraid to use the third parameter if you need to. Even if you load BX with a constant value each time through a conversion loop, using **XLAT** is still twice as fast as the fastest "compare and jump" algorithm.

The global variable **??LcFlag** is set to 0 when the file containing the macro (normally an included file) is read. If the **XLAT** version of **ToLower** is selected, the macro examines the flag to see whether the table has been defined. If **??LcFlag** is zero, **MakeLcTable** is invoked to generate the conversion table, **??LcFlag** is set to 1 to prevent the table from being generated again, and the **MakeLcTable** macro is purged from memory.

If we wanted to replace the old **ToLower** macro with the new, faster version in TRAL.ASM, we would make just one change. The line that reads

```
ToLower al
```

would be replaced with a line that reads

```
ToLower al,xlat,LoadBX
```

ToLower would define the conversion table and generate the following code:

```
mov bx,offset LcTable
xlat
```

Any nonblank value can be used for the second and third parameters to **ToLower**. The macro checks only to see if the parameters are nonblank. I could have used "ToLower al,1,1", but I find the use of descriptive names such as **XLAT** and **LoadBX** more informative when I have to go back and work on a program.

3.5 String Arrays

Defining and using arrays of strings in assembly language is very simple—if you're not concerned about how much memory you use. You simply make each string in the array as long as all of the others by padding the shorter strings with spaces. The only problem is that this technique wastes *lots* of memory.

Consider, for example, the error codes returned by DOS functions. In version 4.01, DOS functions can return error codes from 0 (success) to 90. Only 70 of these error codes are currently defined, and a large number of the error codes are specific to networks, but that still leaves quite a few error messages. The text of the error messages ranges from 9 to 39 bytes in length. Listing 3.15 shows an array of the first 13 DOS error messages. Error codes 0, 1, 2, 3, 4, 5, 6, and 12 are commonly returned by the handle I/O functions.

```
 1:   ; Listing 3.15--Commonly seen DOS I/O error messages
 2:   ;
 3:   ; 31 bytes per message
 4:   ;
 5:   Label FileErrTable Byte
 6:      db "Unknown error                 "  ; 0
 7:      db "Invalid function number       "  ; 1
 8:      db "File not found                "  ; 2
 9:      db "Path not found                "  ; 3
10:      db "No handles available          "  ; 4
11:      db "Access denied                 "  ; 5
12:      db "Invalid handle                "  ; 6
13:      db "Memory control blocks destroyed"  ; 7
14:      db "Insufficient memory           "  ; 8
15:      db "Invalid memory block address  "  ; 9
16:      db "Invalid environment           "  ; 10
17:      db "Invalid format                "  ; 11
18:      db "Invalid access code           "  ; 12
```

This table can be easily accessed by a program after executing a DOS function call, as shown in Listing 3.16. If the DOS function returns with the carry flag set, AX and DX are used to find the address of the proper error message, and then **DosWriteFile** is invoked to write the error message on the standard error device.

```
 1:   ; Listing 3.16--Accessing the error message array
 2:   ;
 3:      ; Registers were set above.
 4:      mov ah,3Dh
 5:      int 21h                    ; open file
 6:      jnc AllOk
 7:      mov dx,offset FileErrTable  ; DX points to error message table
 8:      cmp ax,12                   ; if error code > 12
```

```
 9:       jbe Around
10:       xor ax,ax                 ; ...then it's an unknown error
11:    Around:
12:       shl ax,1                  ; error code * 2 for indexing
13:       add dx,ax                 ; add to table base
14:       mov cx,31                 ; all messages are 31 bytes long
15:       mov bx,StdErr
16:       DosCall 40h               ; write message to StdErr
17:    AllOk:
```

FileErrTable in Listing 3.15 occupies 403 bytes, 40 percent of which (162 bytes) is padding. The full table of all 91 error messages occupies 3,549 bytes, almost 60 percent of which is blank space taken either by padding or the reserved error codes. Memory may indeed be cheap, but it's not free and should not be wasted. Clearly, we must find a more efficient way to store these strings while retaining ease of use.

Pointer Arrays

The solution can be found by examining how string arrays are stored in the C language. In C, our error message array is defined as shown in Listing 3.17.

```
 1:    ; Listing 3.17--Defining the error message array in C
 2:    ;
 3:    char *FileErrTable[] = {
 4:       "Unknown error",
 5:       "Invalid function number",
 6:       "File not found",
 7:       "Path not found",
 8:       "No handles available",
 9:       "Access denied",
10:       "Invalid handle",
11:       "Memory control blocks destroyed",
12:       "Insufficient memory",
13:       "Invalid memory block address",
14:       "Invalid environment",
15:       "Invalid format",
16:       "Invalid access code"
17:       }
```

The C compiler actually forms two data structures from this definition. The first structure contains the text for each error message stored as an ASCIIZ string, and the second is an array of 13 pointers to the start of each string. The resulting data structures are similar to those shown in Listing 3.18.

```
 1:    ; Listing 3.18--C-generated data structures
 2:    ;
```

```
 3:    ; Data structures created for the C code in Listing 3.17
 4:    ;
 5:
 6:    ; Error message text follows.
 7:    ; Each message is stored as an ASCIIZ string.
 8:    ;
 9:    Err00 db "Unknown error",0
10:    Err01 db "Invalid function number",0
11:    Err02 db "File not found",0
12:    Err03 db "Path not found",0
13:    Err04 db "No handles available",0
14:    Err05 db "Access denied",0
15:    Err06 db "Invalid handle",0
16:    Err07 db "Memory control blocks destroyed",0
17:    Err08 db "Insufficient memory",0
18:    Err09 db "Invalid memory block address",0
19:    Err10 db "Invalid environment",0
20:    Err11 db "Invalid format",0
21:    Err12 db "Invalid access code",0
22:
23:    ; Pointers to each of the error messages
24:    Label FileErrTable Word
25:        dw offset Err00
26:        dw offset Err01
27:        dw offset Err02
28:        dw offset Err03
29:        dw offset Err04
30:        dw offset Err05
31:        dw offset Err06
32:        dw offset Err07
33:        dw offset Err08
34:        dw offset Err09
35:        dw offset Err10
36:        dw offset Err11
37:        dw offset Err12
```

Accessing the strings is a simple matter of indexing the pointer array to find the address of the particular string in question. This method is slightly slower than directly accessing the string array, but it uses less memory and the small cost in performance will hardly be noticed, especially in a non–time-critical function, such as an error handler.

With a single change, we can use this technique to define our error message table. The single change involves storing the string's length rather than a 0 byte within the text. Using this method, our string array occupies 267 bytes, and another 26 bytes is taken up by the pointer table, making a total of 293 bytes—a 26 percent savings over Listing 3.15. The full table of 91 DOS error messages, complete with the pointer table, occupies only 1,763 bytes—a little less than half of the space required if we were to use a direct-access array of error messages.

Generating the Tables Automatically

Defining a table of this size by hand is not something I look forward to. At first glance, however, it doesn't appear that we can automate its generation. Although we can easily define the array of strings using successive **LenString** invocations, we can't define the pointer array at the same time. And once the array of strings has been defined, we lose the address information that the pointer array needs. How do we save the address of each message for later use in the pointer array?

You'll recall that, unlike **EQU**, the = operator enables us to create labels that can later be redefined. We used this capability in the previous section to determine whether the uppercase to lowercase conversation table had been defined. Once the table was defined, the **??LcFlag** variable was set to 1 so that the **ToLower** macro didn't attempt to create it more than once. The macros in Listing 3.19 use this technique to generate the pointer table.

```
 1:    ; Listing 3.19--Building the error table
 2:    ;
 3:    ; BuildErrTable
 4:    ; Generate the error message table and the pointer array.
 5:    ;
 6:    Macro BuildErrTable
 7:      Local IsCode
 8:      CheckSeg %@curseg,%@code,DataSeg,IsCode
 9:    ;;
10:    ;; Initialize the error message pointers so that all point
11:    ;; to error message 0 (Unknown error).
12:    ;;
13:      ??ErrNo = 0
14:      rept 13
15:        MakeErrLbl %??ErrNo
16:        ??ErrNo = ??ErrNo + 1
17:      endm
18:    ;;
19:    ;; Now define the error messages.
20:    ;;
21:      Label FileErrTable Byte
22:      ErrDef  0,<"Unknown error">
23:      ErrDef  1,<"Invalid function number">
24:      ErrDef  2,<"File not found">
25:      ErrDef  3,<"Path not found">
26:      ErrDef  4,<"No handles available">
27:      ErrDef  5,<"Access denied">
```

```
28:      ErrDef  6,<"Invalid handle">
29:      ErrDef  7,<"Memory control blocks destroyed">
30:      ErrDef  8,<"Insufficient memory">
31:      ErrDef  9,<"Invalid memory block address">
32:      ErrDef 10,<"Invalid environment">
33:      ErrDef 11,<"Invalid format">
34:      ErrDef 12,<"Invalid access code">
35:    ;;
36:    ;; Define the pointer table from the redefined message pointers.
37:    ;;
38:      ??ErrNo = 0
39:      Label ErrPtrs Word
40:      rept 13
41:        MakeErrPtr %??ErrNo
42:        ??ErrNo = ??ErrNo + 1
43:      endm
44:    ;;
45:    ;; Go back to code segment if required.
46:    ;;
47:      if IsCode eq 1
48:        CodeSeg
49:      endif
50:    Endm BuildErrTable
51:
52:    ;
53:    ; MakeErrLbl
54:    ; Define a single error label that points to the
55:    ; "Unknown Error" message.
56:    ;
57:    Macro MakeErrLbl ErrNo
58:      ??Err&ErrNo = offset FileErrTable
59:    Endm MakeErrLbl
60:
61:    ;
62:    ; ErrDef ErrNo,String
63:    ; Define a preceding length string error message and set
64:    ; the corresponding error message pointer to point to
65:    ; the first byte of the string.
66:    ;
67:    Macro ErrDef ErrNo,String
68:      Local Temp
69:      dw Temp&Len
70:      ??Err&ErrNo = $
71:      LenString Temp,<String>
72:    Endm ErrDef
73:
74:    ;
75:    ; MakeErrPtr
```

```
76:    ; Define a word that contains a pointer
77:    ; to the specified error message.
78:    ;
79:    Macro MakeErrPtr ErrNo
80:        dw ??Err&ErrNo
81:    Endm MakeErrPtr
```

BuildErrTable defines 13 labels (**??Err00** through **??Err12**) that initially point to the first error message. As the messages are defined with **ErrDef**, the labels are reassigned so that they point to their corresponding error message. After all error messages have been defined, **BuildErrTable** defines the pointer array using the values of the **??Errxx** labels. This technique has the added benefit of allowing for undefined error messages: the reserved error numbers are not reassigned, so their pointers point to the "Unknown error" message.

Using the Error Messages

Obviously, accessing the error messages through a pointer table requires a little more code than does accessing a simple array of fixed-length strings. The modifications are slight, and the resulting code is not much larger than that shown in Listing 3.16. The new routine is shown here in Listing 3.20.

```
1:    ; Listing 3.20--Accessing the error messages
2:    ;
3:        ; Registers were set above.
4:        mov ah,3Dh
5:        int 21h                ; open file
6:        jnc AllOk
7:        mov bx,offset ErrPtrs  ; DX points to error message table
8:        cmp ax,12              ; if error code > 12...
9:        jbe Around
10:       xor ax,ax              ; ...then it's an unknown error
11:   Around:
12:       shl ax,1               ; error code * 2 for indexing
13:       add bx,ax              ; add to table base
14:       mov bx,[bx]            ; BX holds address of error message
15:       mov dx,bx              ; put in DX for write device function
16:       mov cx,[bx-2]          ; load message length in CX
17:       mov bx,StdErr
18:       DosCall 40h            ; write message to StdErr
19:   AllOk:
```

The only change made to the code prior to the **Around** label changes the line that reads:

```
mov dx,offset FileErrTable
```

to

```
mov bx,offset ErrPtrs
```

because BX is used to index into the pointer array. The code after **Around** accesses the pointer array to find the address of the proper error message and then loads the message address into DX and the message length into CX.

I'm sure you can guess what the next step is: Write a macro that will automatically generate both the error message array and the code that accesses it. This macro will behave in much the same way as the version of **ToLower** developed in Listing 3.14. The first time the macro is invoked it defines the error table and generates the code to access the error messages. Subsequent uses only generate the code to access the error message array.

In addition to displaying the message corresponding to the error code in AX, **DosErrMsg** (Listing 3.21) also displays a user-defined error message that is passed to the macro in the same manner used by **DosDisplayString**. If the first parameter is a string or the first parameter is a label name and the second parameter is a string, storage is allocated and the string is then displayed. If the first parameter is a label name, no storage is allocated. In any case, if the first parameter is nonblank, the requested information message is written to the standard error device before the DOS error message is written.

```
 1:   ; Listing 3.21--DosErrMsg
 2:
 3:   ;
 4:   ; ??ErrTbl is initialized to 0 and then set to 1
 5:   ;  after the error message table is defined.
 6:   ;
 7:   ??ErrTbl = 0
 8:
 9:   ;
10:   ; DosErrMsg <String>,<Arg2>
11:   ; Write a user-defined error message and the standard DOS error
12:   ; message corresponding to the value in AX to the standard
13:   ; error device.
14:   ;
15:   ; Parameters
16:   ;    String (Optional) - Either a text string or the label name
17:   ; of a string to display. If it's a text string, the string is
18:   ; defined in the data segment before displaying.
19:   ;    Arg2 (Optional) - If this parameter is given, the first
20:   ; parameter is assumed to be a label name and Arg2 is assumed
21:   ; to be the string to define and display.
22:   ;
23:   ; If either or both of the above parameters is given, CX and DX
24:   ; are loaded with the appropriate values. If DosErrMsg is
```

```
25:     ; invoked without parameters, only the DOS error message
26:     ; corresponding to the value in AX is written to StdErr.
27:     ;
28:     ; Before this macro is invoked, AX must hold an error value
29:     ; returned by a DOS function.
30:     ;
31:     ; AX, BX, CX, DX and the flags are affected by the code created
32:     ; by this macro. All other registers are unaltered.
33:     ;
34:     ; The first time through this macro, the error message table
35:     ; and corresponding pointer array are defined.
36:     ;
37:     Macro DosErrMsg String,Arg2
38:       Local ArgType,Temp,Around,IsCode
39:       ;;
40:       ;; If the error message table has not been defined, create it
41:       ;; and the pointer array. Then remove the BuildErrTable macro
42:       ;; and set the ??ErrTbl flag to indicate that the tables have
43:       ;; been defined.
44:       ;;
45:       if ??ErrTbl eq 0
46:         CheckSeg %@curseg,%@code,DataSeg,IsCode
47:         BuildErrTable
48:         Purge BuildErrTable
49:         ??ErrTbl = 1
50:         ;;
51:         ;; Define the message separator and newline.
52:         ;;
53:         LenString SpaceDashSpace,<" - ">
54:         LenString CRLF,<cr,lf>
55:         if IsCode eq 1
56:           CodeSeg
57:         endif
58:       endif
59:       ;;
60:       ;; If the first parameter is not blank, check the second
61:       ;; parameter and the first parameter's type to determine
62:       ;; what code to generate.
63:       ;;
64:       ifnb <String>
65:         ;;
66:         ;; If the second parameter is not blank, assume the first
67:         ;; parameter is a label name and define a string
68:         ;; with that name.
69:         ;;
70:         ifnb <Arg2>
71:           LenString String,<Arg2>
72:           mov cx,String&Len
```

```
 73:            mov dx,offset String
 74:        else
 75:          ;;
 76:          ;; The second parameter is blank. Check the type of
 77:          ;; first parameter.
 78:          WhatType <String>,ArgType
 79:          ;;
 80:          ;; If it's a string (ArgType = 0) or a constant
 81:          ;; (ArgType = 24), define the data and generate
 82:          ;; code to display it.
 83:          ;;
 84:          if (ArgType eq 0) or (ArgType eq 24h)
 85:            LenString Temp,<String>
 86:            mov cx,Temp&Len
 87:            mov dx,offset Temp
 88:          else
 89:            ;;
 90:            ;; Otherwise, just generate code to display it.
 91:            ;;
 92:            mov cx,String&Len
 93:            mov dx,offset String
 94:          endif
 95:        endif
 96:        push ax              ;; save error code
 97:        mov bx,StdErr
 98:        DosCall 40h          ;; write the message to StdErr
 99:  ;;
100:  ;; Write the message separator (" - ").
101:  ;;
102:        mov cx,SpaceDashSpaceLen
103:        mov dx,offset SpaceDashSpace
104:        DosCall 40h
105:        pop ax              ;; restore error code
106:      endif
107:  ;;
108:  ;; Now generate code to lookup error code in table and
109:  ;; display the error on the stderr device.
110:  ;;
111:    mov bx,offset ErrPtrs;; BX points to error message pointer table
112:    cmp ax,12              ;; if error code > 12...
113:    jbe Around
114:    xor ax,ax              ;; ...then it's an unknown error
115:  Around:
116:    shl ax,1               ;; error code * 2 for indexing
117:    add bx,ax              ;; add to table base
118:    mov bx,[bx]            ;; BX holds address of error message
119:    mov dx,bx              ;; put in DX for write device function
120:    mov cx,[bx-2]          ;; load message length in CX
```

```
121:     mov bx,StdErr
122:     DosCall 40h              ;; write error message to StdErr
123:     ;;
124:     ;; Write a newline.
125:     ;;
126:     mov cx,CRLFLen
127:     mov dx,offset CRLF
128:     DosCall 40h
129:   Endm DosErrMsg
```

A sample use of the new **DosErrMsg** macro is shown in Listing 3.22.

```
1:    ; Listing 3.22--Sample use of DosErrMsg
2:    ;
3:    ; Registers were set above.
4:    mov ah,3Dh
5:    int 21h                ; open file
6:    jnc AllOk
7:    DosErrMsg "Error opening input file"
8:  AllOk:
```

This code fragment uses DOS function 3Dh to open a file. If DOS is unable to open the file, the program displays the following message on the standard error device:

```
Error opening input file - File not found
```

If no error occurs when opening the file, no message is output.

Although **DosErrMsg** is a useful macro, each use of it comes at a fairly high price in code: 38 bytes when no preliminary message is displayed and 63 bytes if a message is requested when the macro is invoked.

As I pointed out at the end of Chapter 1, large blocks of code that are not excessively time critical, and that are used more than once, should be placed in a subroutine in order to conserve code space. **DosErrMsg** is an excellent candidate for rewriting using a subroutine, and we will do just that in the next chapter when we discuss macros that work in conjunction with subroutines.

3.6 Out of Data

The data definition macros presented in this chapter are by no means an exhaustive library that can be used in all circumstances. On the contrary, the few macros presented here represent only a very small fraction of all the possible data types and operations that can be performed. Data by its very nature is problem specific; requiring different definition and manipulation procedures for each particular task. The macros we developed in this chapter, although useful, were presented primarily to make you aware of what is possible so that you can apply these techniques to your particular data definition problems.

Preparations

In the course of the last three chapters, we've developed quite a few macros and made many changes to several of them. In preparation for the following chapters, let's review the contents of our two macro libraries. These macro libraries will be required in order to assemble the programs that we'll be developing in the following chapters.

MACROS.INC includes all of Listing 1.15 and the **ProgramHeader** macro of Listing 2.2. Don't replace the original version of **ToLower** with Listing 3.14, though. In Chapter 4 we'll take another look at **ToLower** and we'll replace the version in MACROS.INC at that time.

Our other macro library, DOSMACS.INC, contains quite a few more macros than does MACROS.INC. Some of the macros in this file—**DosDisplayString** in particular—have been through a number of changes, so we'd better be sure to include the proper version in the library file that is used in the next few chapters. The macros that make up the most current DOSMACS.INC file are

Listing 2.21 Constant definitions
Listing 2.4 Macro **ExeStart**
Listing 2.5 Macro **DosCall**
Listing 2.7 Macro **DosExitProgram**
Listing 2.11 Macros **$String** and **zString**
Listing 2.22 Macro **DosOpenFile**
Listing 2.26 Macro **DosCloseFile**
Listing 3.4 Macros **CheckSeg** and **TermString**
Listing 3.5 Macro **WhatType**
Listing 3.9 Macro **CountArgs**
Listing 3.10 Macro **DosDisplayString**
Listing 3.11 Macros **DosReadFile**, **DosWriteFile**, **LenString**, and **MakeString**
Listing 3.19 Macros **BuildErrTable**, **MakeErrLbl**, **ErrDef**, and **MakeErrPtr**
Listing 3.21 Macro **DosErrMsg**

4

Macros and Subroutines

When all you have is a hammer, everything looks like a nail.

I've never been able to figure that one out. Most of the time, when I've got a hammer handy, everything looks like a screw. And whenever there are nails lying about, screwdrivers are plentiful, but the hammer's nowhere to be found.

The point here is this: If you have only one tool at your disposal, you'll have to shape whatever problem you're trying to solve into a form suitable for solving with that tool.

The idea, then, is to make more tools available.

The first three chapters explored assembly language macros and how to put them to use in many ways. We've developed some very useful tools in the process—tools that we will put to good use in the following chapters.

But some problems do not lend themselves well to macros. If we insist on using macros exclusively, we're going to end up in the hammer trap. We've got to enlarge our toolset.

This chapter discusses macros that define and use subroutines. In addition, we'll take a close look at how we can best incorporate commonly called subroutines into our programs. Although the macros we develop in this chapter will be much smaller than those we built in the previous two chapters, they will be just as useful. More importantly, the simple sample macros enable us to concentrate on the new concepts without being distracted by the specifics of a particular implementation.

4.1 Macros That Call Subroutines

The primary goal in developing our macros has been to simplify program development. To a lesser extent, we've been interested in generating efficient code. In Chapter 2, you discovered that macros can many times be used to replace subroutines. Why then would we want to have a macro *call* a subroutine?

Take another look at the **DosErrMsg** macro that we developed at the end of Chapter 3 (Listing 3.21). As useful as it is, this macro generates at least 38, and as many as 63, bytes of code each time it is invoked. Although the code it generates is plenty fast, it doesn't have to be fast at all. **DosErrMsg** uses a DOS function to output a message to the standard error device. No matter how much we tweak the macro's code, the bottleneck will always lie within DOS—something we can do nothing about. If we rewrote **DosErrMsg** so that it sets up the registers and calls a subroutine, we wouldn't notice a difference in execution speed and we'd save one heck of a lot of code space.

Before we tackle a macro as large and complex as **DosErrMsg**, let's take a closer look at how macros are used to define and call subroutines.

Do You Really Want to Do This?

It seems that I'm forever writing code that asks a question and then prompts the user for a "Yes" or "No" answer. For example, a file deletion program that I once wrote always prompts before deleting a directory. Getting a "Yes" or "No" answer from the user is something that many of my programs do. To keep myself from having to code this particular sequence over and over again, I developed the **YesNo** macro shown in Listing 4.1.

```
 1:    ; Listing 4.1--Macro YesNo
 2:    ;
 3:    ; YesNo
 4:    ; Wait for a 'Y' or 'N' response (upper- or lowercase).
 5:    ;
 6:    ; Sets Z flag if NO. Z flag is cleared if YES.
 7:    ;
 8:    Macro YesNo
 9:       Local GetKey,Done
10:    GetKey:
11:       DosCall 8              ;; get character, no echo
12:       ToUpper al             ;; convert to uppercase
13:       sub al,'N'             ;; if smaller than 'N'
14:       jc GetKey              ;; try again
15:       jz Done                ;; if it was 'N', done
16:       sub al,'Y'-'N'         ;; check for 'Y'
17:       jnz GetKey
18:       inc al                 ;; clear Z flag
19:    Done:
20:    Endm YesNo
```

To test the **YesNo** macro, I've written a simple program called DIDYOU, which asks a simple question, "Did you win? (Y/N)," and responds accordingly. This program is shown in Listing 4.2.

```
 1:    ; Listing 4.2--DIDYOU.ASM
 2:    ;
 3:    ; Ask a question and get a "Yes" or "No" answer.
 4:    ;
 5:       ideal
 6:    include "macros.inc"
 7:    include "dosmacs.inc"
 8:       ProgramHeader Small,0100h
 9:       CodeSeg
10:    Proc Main
11:       FxeStart
12:       DosDisplayString <<"Did you win? (Y/N) ">>
```

```
13:    YesNo
14:    jz DidntWin
15:    DosDisplayString <<cr,lf,"Congratulations!",cr,lf>>
16:    jmp Done
17:  DidntWin:
18:    DosDisplayString <<cr,lf,"Better luck next time",cr,lf>>
19:  Done:
20:    DosExitProgram 0
21:  Endp Main
22:
23:  End Main
```

Add macro **YesNo** to your DOSMACS.INC file and then type Listing 4.2 into a file called DIDYOU.ASM. To assemble and test the program, enter the following commands at the DOS prompt:

```
tasm /m didyou
tlink didyou
didyou
```

The only problem with macro **YesNo** is that it generates 30 bytes of code each time it's invoked. If those 30 bytes represented a significant performance improvement, there would be no problem at all leaving **YesNo** exactly as it is, but that's not the case. No matter how fast I make the code for **YesNo**, the routine's speed is determined entirely by the user's response time. Clearly, in a program that requires more than one Yes or No answer, we can save a lot of code space by turning **YesNo** into a subroutine.

But that doesn't mean we have to abandon the macro! If we take the proper precautions, we can easily make the **YesNo** macro *define and use* a subroutine. Listing 4.3 shows how this is done.

```
1:   ; Listing 4.3--Macro YesNo
2:   ;
3:   ; YesNo
4:   ; Wait for a 'Y' or 'N' response (upper- or lowercase).
5:   ;
6:   ; Sets Z flag if NO. Z flag is cleared if YES.
7:   ;
8:   YesNoFlag = 0
9:   Macro YesNo
10:    Local Around
11:    ;;
12:    ;; If this is the first time the macro is used,
13:    ;; define the GetYesNo procedure.
14:    ;;
15:    if YesNoFlag eq 0
16:      jmp Around          ;; jump around procedure
17:      Proc GetYesNo
```

```
18:        @@GetKey:
19:           DosCall 8          ;; get character, no echo
20:           ToUpper al         ;; convert to uppercase
21:           sub al,'N'         ;; if smaller than 'N'
22:           jc @@GetKey        ;; try again
23:           jz @@Done          ;; if it was 'N', done
24:           sub al,'Y'-'N'     ;; check for 'Y'
25:           jnz @@GetKey
26:           inc al             ;; clear Z flag
27:        @@Done:
28:           ret
29:        Endp GetYesNo
30:        Around:               ;; destination of jump around procedure
31:           call GetYesNo      ;; call the procedure
32:           YesNoFlag = 1
33:      else
34:           ;;
35:           ;; This part is used on second and subsequent macro invocations.
36:           ;;
37:           call GetYesNo
38:        endif
39:     Endm YesNo
```

We used the same technique in this version of **YesNo** that we used in our fast **ToUpper** macro of Chapter 3. The first time through the macro, the **YesNoFlag** variable is 0, causing the macro to generate the subroutine code. After the subroutine is defined, **YesNoFlag** is set to 1 so that **YesNo** won't expand the subroutine the next time the macro is invoked. Subsequent invocations of **YesNo** will generate but a single **call** instruction. For example, these two macro invocations:

```
YesNo
YesNo
```

expand to the following assembly language code:

```
; First invocation
  jmp Around
Proc GetYesNo
  ;
  ; Subroutine code here
  ;
  ret
Endp GetYesNo
Around:
  call GetYesNo
; second invocation
  call GetYesNo
```

Macros That Redefine Themselves

The only complaint that I have with the **YesNo** Macro in Listing 4.3 is the **YesNoFlag** variable that determines whether the macro should define the subroutine. I've never been a fan of using flag variables in my programs—they seem to indicate sloppy design work. But I needed some way to determine whether a macro had been invoked already, and for many years a flag variable was the only method I knew would work.

As I was ripping my hair out one day, looking for a bug, I stumbled on a very strange and wonderful feature of the assembler. I had been working on a macro that defined other macros and couldn't figure out why my programs weren't working. After spending several hours poring over the program listing, I discovered that I had inadvertently written a macro that redefined itself! What amazed me more than anything else was that the assembler actually let me get away with it.

Now I'm no expert on the inner workings of the assembler, so I can't tell you *how* the assembler handles this redefinition, but I can show you what we can do with it.

As a simple example, consider the **Greetings** macro that follows. The first time this macro is invoked, it uses **DosDisplayString** to define a greeting string and then display the greeting. Subsequent invocations of the macro generate only that code required to display the greeting.

```
; Display a greeting.
Macro Greetings
  ;;
  ;; First time through, define and display the string.
  ;;
  DosDisplayString <Hello, <"Hello, world",cr,lf>>
  ;;
  ;; Then, redefine the macro so that subsequent invocations
  ;; generate only that code required to display the string.
  ;;
  Macro Greetings
    DosDisplayString Hello
  Endm Greetings
Endm Greetings
```

The whole idea of a macro redefining itself reminds me of Earl Godwin's story *Daddy,* in which a woman gives birth to herself. It's a wonderfully strange story, really.

We can use a self-redefining macro to eliminate the **YesNoFlag** flag from our **YesNo** macro and similar flag variables that have bothered me so much over the years. A self-redefining version of **YesNo** is shown in Listing 4.4.

```
 1:   ; Listing 4.4--Self-redefining YesNo Macro
 2:   ;
 3:   ; YesNo
 4:   ; Wait for a 'Y' or 'N' response (upper- or lowercase).
 5:   ;
 6:   ; Sets Z flag if NO. Z flag is cleared if YES.
 7:   ;
 8:   Macro YesNo
 9:     Local Around
10:     jmp Around               ;; jump around procedure
11:     ;;
12:     ;; Define the GetYesNo subroutine
13:     ;;
14:     Proc GetYesNo
15:     @@GetKey:
16:       DosCall 8              ;; get character, no echo
17:       ToUpper al            ;; convert to uppercase
18:       sub al,'N'            ;; if smaller than 'N'
19:       jc @@GetKey           ;; try again
20:       jz @@Done             ;; if it was 'N', done
21:       sub al,'Y'-'N'        ;; check for 'Y'
22:       jnz @@GetKey
23:       inc al                ;; clear Z flag
24:     @@Done:
25:       ret
26:     Endp GetYesNo
27:     Around:                 ;; destination of jump around procedure
28:       call GetYesNo         ;; call the procedure
29:     ;;
30:     ;; The macro redefines itself!
31:     ;; Subsequent invocations of YesNo simply call
32:     ;; the GetYesNo subroutine.
33:     ;;
34:     Macro YesNo
35:       call GetYesNo
36:     Endm YesNo
37:   Endm YesNo
```

The first invocation of **YesNo** defines the **GetYesNo** subroutine and generates code to call it. The macro then redefines itself so that subsequent invocations simply call the **GetYesNo** subroutine. Strange? Yes, but wonderful as well.

I have purposely kept **YesNo** very simple in order to illustrate the idea of a macro calling a subroutine. We could make **YesNo** much more useful by adding parameters that specify the string to display and also the branches to take on positive or negative answers. If we were to make these additions to **YesNo**, this code fragment from DIDYOU.ASM:

```
DosDisplayString <<"Did you win? (Y/N) ">>
YesNo
jz DidntWin
```

would be rewritten like this:

```
YesNo <<"Did you win? (Y/N) ">>,,DidntWin
```

A good exercise to test your grasp of the techniques you've learned up to now would be to implement a **YesNo** macro with these features.

Disadvantages

Macros that define and use subroutines are fine for small code sequences, and for subroutines that don't exceed a few dozen lines of code. But as the subroutines get larger and the macros get more complex, our programs start taking longer to assemble. Worse yet, the assembler may run out of memory because it's storing all the subroutine code in a macro buffer waiting for expansion. As we continue to expand our macro library and write larger programs, this problem will only get worse.

What we need is a way to assemble the common subroutines separately but still reference them from within our programs. We do this using *object modules.*

4.2 Object Modules, an Overview

As you know, Turbo Assembler reads your source program and, assuming you didn't make any syntax errors, creates an object file that describes your program in a binary format. This object file is then processed by the linker and converted into an executable program. Figure 4.1 illustrates this sequence of events.

Figure 4.1. Assembling and linking

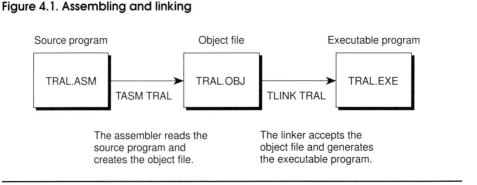

Especially with smaller assembly language programs, this process of creating an object file and then linking to create an executable program seems like a lot of extra work. But the link process is necessary in order to resolve any references to external symbols; symbols like subroutines and data that are contained in other modules.

ET, the Bloated Program

One of my pet projects that never gets finished is a combination text editor and terminal emulator. This is one of those programs that suffers from "creeping featureitis"—it just grows and grows. When ET grew to about 1,000 lines, I could no longer edit the thing because my editor (ET, of course) would only edit files up to 32K characters in length. Sure, I could have used WordStar, but it was a macho thing to have the editor edit itself—kind of like a surgeon performing an appendectomy on himself.

I initially broke the program up into three source files—a main module, the editor module, and the terminal module. The main module used **include** directives to bring in the source of the other two modules when the program was assembled. Figure 4.2 illustrates this structure.

Using **include** files helped keep things sane for a while, but as ET continued to grow it started to take a *long* time to assemble. Whenever I made the slightest change to any one module, I had to reassemble the entire program, which by now consisted of many, many different **include** files. I had to find a better way.

The answer was to use object modules. Rather than assemble all of the modules as a single file, I could assemble each module separately and then *link*

Figure 4.2. Assembling and linking with include files

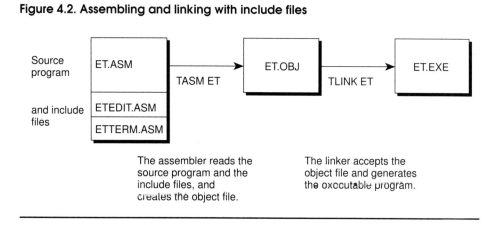

Figure 4.3. Assembling and linking with object modules

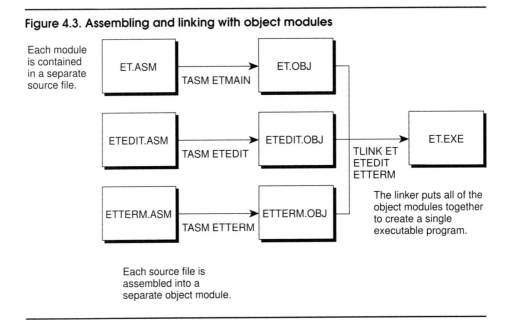

Each module is contained in a separate source file.

ET.ASM → ET.OBJ
TASM ETMAIN

ETEDIT.ASM → ETEDIT.OBJ
TASM ETEDIT

ETTERM.ASM → ETTERM.OBJ
TASM ETTERM

TLINK ET
ETEDIT
ETTERM

→ ET.EXE

The linker puts all of the object modules together to create a single executable program.

Each source file is assembled into a separate object module.

the resulting object modules together. Now when I make a change to a module, I need reassemble only that one module and then link all of the object modules together in order to create the executable program. This makes for *much* faster program development. Figure 4.3 illustrates this arrangement of ET's modules.

Amazingly enough, the actual mechanics of using object modules is almost as simple as Figure 4.3 suggests.

Public and External Declarations

Normally, the assembler will issue an error if you make reference to a subroutine that isn't defined in your source program. In order to reference an external subroutine, you need to tell the assembler about it. How? By declaring an external procedure using the **EXTRN** directive.

For example, suppose we were to move the **GetYesNo** subroutine to an external module rather than have the **YesNo** macro define the procedure as we did in Listings 4.3 and 4.4. The new **YesNo** macro simply generates a call to the **GetYesNo** subroutine. Because subroutine **GetYesNo** is not defined in our program, the assembler will display an error message unless we include this external declaration:

```
Extrn GetYesNo:Proc
```

This declaration tells the assembler that **GetYesNo** is a valid label name and that the address of the label will be provided at link time. The assembler accepts this bit of information and passes responsibility for this particular label on to the linker.

EXTRN, however, is only half of the equation. In the module that actually contains the **GetYesNo** subroutine, we have to tell the assembler that **GetYesNo** will be referenced externally. The assembler passes this information on to the linker (via the object module). In order to get the assembler to pass this information on, we declare **GetYesNo** as a **PUBLIC** procedure, like this:

```
Public GetYesNo:Proc
```

Think of **EXTRN** as a hook reaching out for an eyelet created by the **PUBLIC** directive. Figure 4.4 illustrates this concept.

Figure 4.4. EXTRN hooks and PUBLIC eyelets

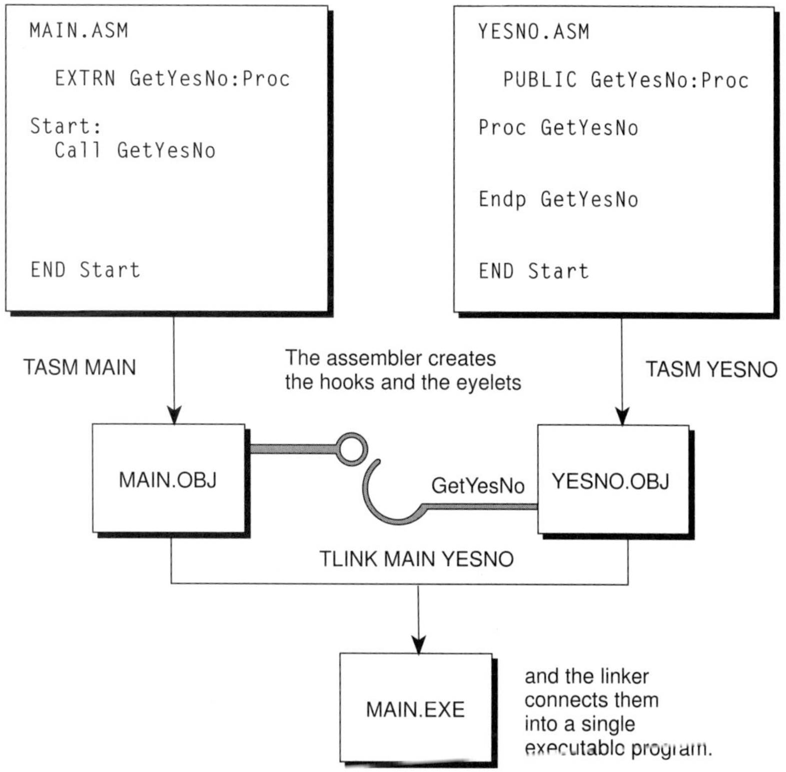

Using External Subroutines—An Example

Let's use our little DIDYOU program to illustrate the use of external subroutines. First, pull DOSMACS.INC up in your editor and delete the **YesNo** macro. We won't be using this version of the macro anymore, and we don't need it at all for this example.

After you've saved DOSMACS.INC, copy DIDYOU.ASM to a new file called DIDYOU2.ASM and add this line immediately after the **CodeSeg** directive:

```
Extrn GetYesNo:Proc
```

Then, replace the **YesNo** macro invocation with a line that reads

```
call GetYesNo
```

To build the external module, create a new file called YESNO.ASM, which contains the code shown in Listing 4.5.

```
 1:   ; Listing 4.5--YESNO.ASM
 2:   ;
 3:   ; GetYesNo subroutine.
 4:   ;
 5:     ideal
 6:  include "macros.inc"
 7:  include "dosmacs.inc"
 8:    model small
 9:    CodeSeg
10:  Public GetYesNo
11:  Proc GetYesNo
12:  GetKey:
13:    DosCall 8          ; get character, no echo
14:    ToUpper al         ; convert to uppercase
15:    sub al,'N'         ; if smaller than 'N'
16:    jc GetKey          ; try again
17:    jz @@Done          ; if it was 'N', done
18:    sub al,'Y'-'N'     ; check for 'Y'
19:    jnz GetKey
20:    inc al             ; clear Z flag
21:  @@Done:
22:    ret
23:  Endp GetYesNo
24:
25:    End
```

Note that the format for an external module is a bit different from the format for a main module. Specifically, there is no **Stack** directive in an external module, and the **End** directive does not specify a starting code address. These two items are handled by the main program and must not be included in an external module. If they are included in an external module, the linker will have trouble building your program and the resulting executable program will not work correctly.

Finally, to build the new program, DIDYOU2.EXE, enter the following commands at the DOS prompt:

```
tasm /m didyou2
tasm /m yesno
tlink didyou2 yesno
```

After TLINK has finished, you will have an executable program on disk named DIDYOU2.EXE, which behaves exactly like the original DIDYOU program from Listing 4.2.

Enhancing YesNo

At the end of the previous section, I mentioned some enhancements that would be convenient to have in macro **YesNo**. Let's take a few moments to add these enhancements.

We want the **YesNo** macro to accept three parameters: a message string (or label), a destination to branch to if the user answers Yes, and a different branch if the user answers No. In addition, our new **YesNo** macro will reference the **GetYesNo** external subroutine rather than defining the subroutine within the macro. If we use **DosDisplayString** to display the prompt, our new macro is very simple, as shown in Listing 4.6.

```
 1:   ; Listing 4.6--Enhanced YesNo macro
 2:   ;
 3:   ; YesNo <StringDef>,<YesBranch>,<NoBranch>
 4:   ;
 5:   ; Prompt user for YES or NO response and branch accordingly.
 6:   ;
 7:   Macro YesNo StringDef,YesBranch,NoBranch
 8:     DosDisplayString <StringDef>
 9:     extrn GetYesNo:Proc
10:     call GetYesNo          ;; get Yes or No answer
11:     ;;
12:     ;; Generate branching code if requested.
13:     ;;
14:     ifnb <YesBranch>
15:       jnz YesBranch
16:       ifnb <NoBranch>
17:         Jmp NoBranch
18:       endif
```

```
19:      elseifnb <NoBranch>
20:        jz NoBranch
21:      endif
22:    Endm YesNo
```

Notice that if you don't pass a **StringDef** parameter, macro **YesNo** still invokes **DosDisplayString**, assuming that the address of the prompt is already in the DX register. If you've already displayed a prompt and you just want to get a Yes or No answer, just call the **GetYesNo** subroutine without using **YesNo**.

Notice also that **YesNo** includes an **EXTRN** declaration. In this way, we don't have to remember to declare subroutine **GetYesNo** manually in every program that uses the **YesNo** macro.

We'll be using this new **YesNo** macro a little later, so you need to add Listing 4.6 to your DOSMACS.INC file.

Using Object Modules to Hold Global Data

Subroutines aren't the only items that can be placed in object modules. Data definitions that are common to many programs can also be defined in external modules and then linked with programs. For example, the character translation table is generated inside each program that uses the **XLAT** variant of our **ToLower** macro. We could save ourselves some assembly time and also simplify the **ToLower** macro if we placed the translation table in an external module as shown in Listing 4.7.

```
 1:   ; Listing 4.7--LOWERTBL.ASM
 2:   ;
 3:   ; External module holds the lowercase conversion table.
 4:   ;
 5:     ideal
 6:     model small
 7:     DataSeg
 8:
 9:   Public ??LcTable
10:
11:   Label ??LcTable Byte
12:     Char = 0                ; initialize count
13:     rept 256
14:       ;
15:       ; If Char is in the range of uppercase characters
16:       ; generate the lowercase equivalent. Otherwise,
17:       ; generate a byte with value of Char.
18:       ;
19:       if (Char ge 'A') and (Char le 'Z')
```

```
20:        db Char or 20h
21:      else
22:        db Char
23:      endif
24:      Char = Char + 1      ; go to next character
25:    endm
26:
27:   End
```

To build the external conversion table, create a new file called LOWERTBL.ASM and enter the code from Listing 4.7. Then assemble this new file by entering the following command at the DOS prompt.

```
tasm lowertbl
```

Assuming you got everything entered correctly, you should now have a new file on disk named LOWERTBL.OBJ, which is the linkable form of the lowercase conversion table.

In order to use this external conversion table, we need to modify our **ToLower** macro so that the macro knows that the conversion table is located in an external module. In addition, we can remove the part of **ToLower** that defines the conversion table, and delete the **MakeLcTable** macro and the **??LcFlag** variable. The new **ToLower** macro is shown in Listing 4.8.

```
 1:  ; Listing 4.8--ToLower Macro that references external conversion table
 2:  ;
 3:  ; ToLower Reg,<UseXlat>,<LoadBX>
 4:  ; Determine whether the contents of the specified register or
 5:  ; memory location is an uppercase alpha character (A..Z), and
 6:  ; if so, convert it to lowercase.
 7:  ;
 8:  ; Parameters
 9:  ;   Reg (Required)--register or memory reference
10:  ;   UseXlat (Optional)--meaningful only when Reg = AL
11:  ;   LoadBX (Optional)--meaningful only when Reg = AL and
12:  ; UseXlat is not blank.
13:  ;
14:  ; Returns
15:  ;   Reg converted to uppercase (if applicable)
16:  ;
17:  ; Preserves the contents of all registers but the one
18:  ; specified in the Reg parameter and BX if the third parameter
19:  ; is given.
20:  ;
21:  Macro ToLower Reg,UseXlat,LoadBX
22:    Local Around
```

```
23:    ifidni <Reg>,<al>
24:       ;;
25:       ;; If the requested register is AL and the second parameter
26:       ;; is nonblank, generate code to use xlat for the
27:       ;; conversion.
28:       ;;
29:       ifnb <UseXlat>
30:          DataSeg
31:          Extrn ??LcTable:Byte
32:          CodeSeg
33:          ;;
34:          ;; If the third parameter is not blank, load BX with the
35:          ;; address of the conversion table.
36:          ;;
37:          ifnb <LoadBX>
38:            mov bx,offset ??LcTable
39:          endif
40:          xlat                ;; do the conversion
41:          exitm
42:       endif
43:    endif
44:    ;;
45:    ;; If the macro executes to this point, generate code to
46:    ;; perform "compare and jump" translation.
47:    ;;
48:    IsUpper Reg              ;; see whether it's uppercase;
49:    jnz Around               ;; if not, ignore;
50:    or Reg,20h               ;; otherwise, convert to lowercase
51: Around:
52: Endm ToLower
```

Replace the **ToLower** macro in MACROS.INC with the new version in Listing 4.8. Once you do this, you're ready to test the new macro and the external conversion table.

For this test, I've selected an entirely useless program that displays a string, converts the string to lowercase, and then displays the converted string. This program, CONVERT.ASM, is shown in Listing 4.9.

```
1:  ; Listing 4.9 CONVERT.ASM
2:  ;
3:  ; Sample use of external conversion table.
4:  ;
5:    ideal
6:  include "macros.inc"
7:  include "dosmacs.inc"
8:    ProgramHeader small,0100h
9:
10:   CodeSeg
```

```
11:    Proc Main
12:      ExeStart
13:      DosDisplayString <<TheString>,<'CONVERT ME!',cr,lf>>
14:      ; Convert string to lowercase
15:      mov si,offset TheString
16:      mov bx,offset ??LcTable
17:    CvtLoop:
18:      lodsb                       ; get character
19:      cmp al,'$'                  ; if end of string,
20:      jz CvtDone                  ; done
21:      ToLower al,UseXlat          ; otherwise, convert to lowercase
22:      mov [si-1],al               ; and save
23:      jmp CvtLoop                 ; go to next character
24:    CvtDone:
25:      DosDisplayString <TheString>
26:      DosExitProgram 0
27:    Endp Main
28:
29:    End Main
```

To run the test program, create a new file called CONVERT.ASM that contains the code from Listing 4.9. Then assemble and link the file by entering the following commands at the DOS prompt:

```
tasm /m convert
tlink convert lowertbl
```

When you run it, CONVERT.EXE should display

```
CONVERT ME!
convert me!
```

and then return to the DOS prompt. Granted, it's not a very exciting program, but it illustrates the point without getting bogged down in little details like usefulness.

We can, of course, write a program that uses more than one external module. For example, we could use the **YesNo** macro to add some prompts to CONVERT and have the program display the messages only if we answered Yes to the prompts. If we were to make these enhancements to CONVERT.ASM, the linker command to build the executable program would become:

```
tlink convert lowertbl yesno
```

We can link as many modules as we like in order to build a single executable program. The number of modules we can specify on the command line is limited by the DOS 128-character command line buffer, but with a linker response file we could specify any number of object modules to be linked. (See the TLINK section of your *Turbo Assembler User's Guide* for more information on linker response files.) Even response files, however, require us to remember too much information.

Simple object modules are fine when you only have a handful of external subroutines, but as you start building larger programs and your subroutine library begins to grow, it becomes almost impossible to remember which modules to link with your program. When you find yourself spending as much time writing linker command lines as you spend writing your programs, you'll start wondering if there's a better way to go. There is, and it's really quite simple.

4.3 Object Module Libraries

Fortunately, we can combine our many different object modules into a single file, called an *object module library,* then instruct the linker to look in the library for the external subroutines. If we use an object module library, we can tell the linker, "find the external module in the library," rather than explicitly naming each module on the linker command line, as is necessary with simple object modules.

Logically, an object module library is simply a file that contains many different object modules all stuck together one after the other. Figure 4.5 illustrates the logical format of an object module library that contains two object modules: YESNO.OBJ and LOWERTBL.OBJ.

In reality, a library's structure is a little more complex, but we're not concerned with the internal structure. All we need to know is how to build a library and how to use it.

Building an Object Module Library

To build a library, we must assemble each module to be included and then use the TLIB program to create the library file. We're going to call our new library

---

Figure 4.5. Library containing YESNO.OBJ and LOWERTBL.OBJ

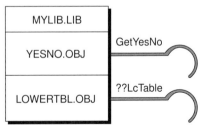

A single object module library can contain any number of object modules, each of which can have EXTRN or PUBLIC declarations.

MYLIB.LIB

YESNO.OBJ — GetYesNo

LOWERTBL.OBJ — ??LcTable

MYSTUFF.LIB, and include the two object modules we've constructed in this chapter: YESNO.OBJ and LOWERTBL.OBJ.

First, make sure you have the two object modules on disk. If they aren't there, build them by entering the following commands at the DOS prompt:

```
tasm /m yesno
tasm lowertbl
```

Now, to build the library, we invoke TLIB with this command:

```
tlib mystuff +yesno +lowertbl
```

When TLIB is finished, you should have a new file on disk called MYSTUFF.LIB, which contains the two object modules. We can now instruct TLINK to find our external modules in this library file.

Using an Object Module Library

Linking with an object module library is actually easier than linking with separate object modules, because we need remember only the library name, rather than the name of each module to be linked. For example, to link our CONVERT program, we would enter the following command:

```
tlink convert,,,mystuff
```

and if we were to make the changes to CONVERT that I mentioned earlier (having the program prompt before displaying the string), we would use the same linker command! We no longer need to tell the linker which modules to link. All we have to do is say "The modules are in the library; go look for them." The linker searches the library and loads the modules it needs from the library.

The last is an important point. When TLINK searches a library, the only modules that get placed in the executable file are those that are referenced by the program being linked. Modules that are not referenced are not included in the .EXE file. For example, DIDYOU2.ASM makes use of the YESNO external module, which is contained in MYSTUFF.LIB. When TLINK searches MYSTUFF.LIB, it finds YESNO and includes this module in the executable file. But LOWERTBL, which is also contained in MYSTUFF.LIB, is not placed in the executable program.

When searching a library, TLINK acts just as if you had explicitly told it which object modules to include, the only difference being that it extracts the modules from a library rather than from the individual object modules.

The only gripe I have with using object module libraries in this manner is that I forget how many commas to put on the command line. Fortunately, there is another, easier way to instruct the linker where to find the external modules.

Using the INCLUDELIB Directive

If you know, when you're writing your program, that the program will use modules that are contained in a library, you can tell the *assembler* where to find those modules. The assembler in turn tells the linker. We use the **includelib** directive to tell the assembler which library contains our external modules.

For example, CONVERT.ASM uses the **??LcTable** data that is defined in LOWERTBL.OBJ. Because we know that LOWERTBL.OBJ is contained in MYSTUFF.LIB, we can use an **includelib** directive to tell the assembler where to find **??LcTable**. Normally, I place the **includelib** directives in my programs directly after the **include** directives. So, in CONVERT.ASM, the first few lines of the program would be

```
; CONVERT.ASM--sample program using external ??LcTable
;
  ideal
include "macros.inc"
include "dosmacs.inc"
includelib "mystuff.lib" ;tell the linker to search MYSTUFF.LIB
  ProgramHeader small,0100h
```

If we make this addition to CONVERT.ASM, we can build CONVERT.EXE by issuing these two commands:

```
tasm /m convert
tlink convert
```

Notice that we didn't have to tell TLINK where to find the external modules. The **includelib** directive within CONVERT.ASM takes care of it for us.

There's only one (minor) problem. Now we have to remember the **includelib** directive whenever we build a program that uses routines from our library. And if we've got more than one library, we've got to remember an **includelib** directive for each library that we're going to use. Granted, it's easier to remember library names than individual module names, but why remember anything at all?

Normally, the subroutines and global data that I employ are used in conjunction with the macros from one of my standard include files. Rather than trying to remember to place the **includelib "mystuff.lib"** directive in each of my programs, I simply placed the directive at the beginning of my macro library file. That way, if I remember to **include** my macro libraries, the **includelib** directive is automatically included as well.

The first line of each of our include files (MACROS.INC and DOSMACS.INC), then, should be

```
includelib "mystuff.lib"
```

Using an object module library is actually easier than using separate object modules, and we don't need to change our programs in order to make use of the libraries. By placing the **includelib** directive in the macro **include** file, the fact that we're using a library is completely transparent.

There are, however, a couple of things we do have to worry about: maintaining the library and telling the linker where to find it.

Finding the Library

When I start a new programming project, I normally create a new directory on my disk to hold the files for the project. Because I don't want a separate copy of my standard libraries in each of my project directories, I need some way to tell TLINK where to find the libraries.

On my system, I have a top-level directory on my E: drive named LIB. This directory contains each of my standard libraries, and also a subdirectory for the source code for each of the libraries. Figure 4.6 shows this structure.

Figure 4.6. Structure of library directory E:\LIB

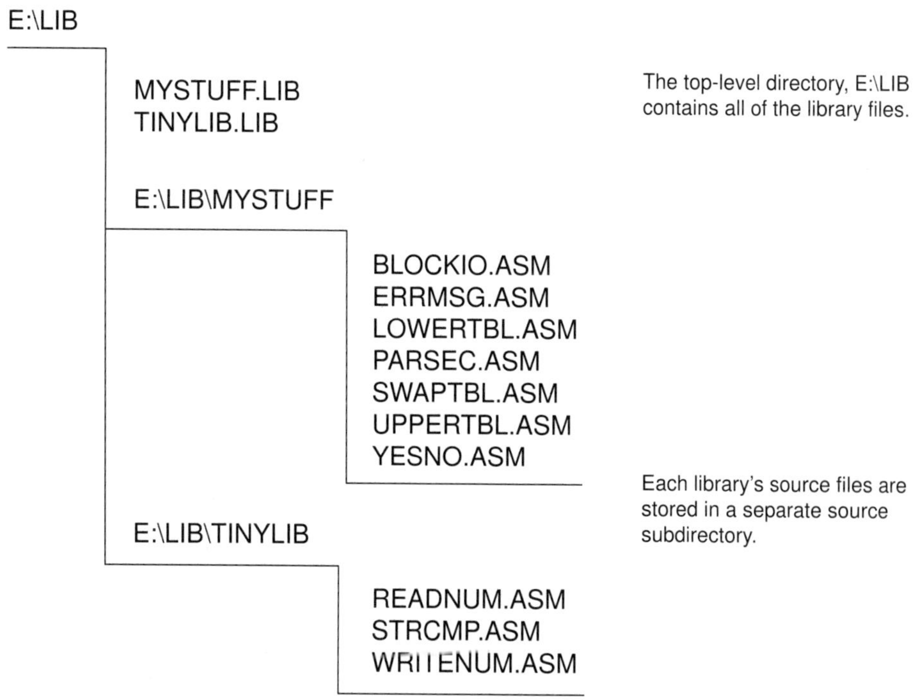

E:\LIB

MYSTUFF.LIB
TINYLIB.LIB

The top-level directory, E:\LIB contains all of the library files.

E:\LIB\MYSTUFF

BLOCKIO.ASM
ERRMSG.ASM
LOWERTBL.ASM
PARSEC.ASM
SWAPTBL.ASM
UPPERTBL.ASM
YESNO.ASM

Each library's source files are stored in a separate source subdirectory.

E:\LIB\TINYLIB

READNUM.ASM
STRCMP.ASM
WRITENUM.ASM

I could use the **includelib** directive in my macro library files to tell TLINK where to find the libraries, but then the program would link only on my system or a system structured in the same way. For example, if the **includelib** directive were

```
includelib "e:\lib\mystuff.lib"
```

and somebody tried to link the program on a computer that had no E: drive, TLINK would be unable to build the program.

Fortunately, we can use the TLINK configuration file to tell the linker where to find the libraries.

In the directory that contains TLINK.EXE, there is normally a file called TLINK.CFG. This is the linker configuration file. If this file does not exist, you can create a new one. TLINK.CFG contains a list of TLINK options that you wish set each time TLINK is executed. I won't get into each of the options here. To learn more about specific options, refer to the TLINK section in your *Turbo Assembler User's Guide*.

One TLINK option, -L, tells the linker where to look for library files. We can tell TLINK to always look in the E:\LIB directory by adding the line:

```
-LE:\LIB
```

to the existing TLINK.CFG file. If TLINK.CFG doesn't exist, create a file of that name that contains only the line just shown.

If TLINK.CFG already contains a -L command (mine did, the command was -LC:\BORLANDC\BIN), we can add our LIB directory to that command. For example, my TLINK.CFG file now contains a line that reads

```
-LC:\BORLANDC\BIN;E:\LIB
```

Once I modified TLINK.CFG and saved it, I no longer had to worry about where the libraries were.

4.4 Maintaining Object Module Libraries

Just like a car, house, boat, or anything else that gets used, a library requires maintenance. We may find a bug in one of the library routines, decide to add more features, or eliminate a function from the library. Once the library grows to more than just a handful of routines, rebuilding the entire library every time a simple change is made to one module is out of the question.

Fortunately, the TLIB program has commands that enable us to add, update, remove, and list library modules. Let's take a look at how each of these commands is used.

Adding a Library Module

As you saw when we first built MYSTUFF.LIB, the **+** command adds a module to a library. The **+** command can be used to create a new library, or to add a module to an existing library. For example, to create our library, we entered this command:

```
tlib mystuff +yesno +lowertbl
```

TLIB created MYSTUFF.LIB and added the modules YESNO.OBJ and LOWERTBL.OBJ to the library.

Now, suppose we have a new error message module, ERRMSG.OBJ, that we want to add to the library. Rather than rebuilding the entire library, we can add the new module by entering this command:

```
tlib mystuff +errmsg
```

Listing Library Modules

We can create a listing of the modules contained within a library by specifying a listing file on the TLIB command line. The resulting file shows the name of each module contained in the library, and each public symbol defined within each module. For example, to list the contents of MYSTUFF.LIB and create a file called MYSTUFF.LST, we would issue the following command at the DOS prompt:

```
tlib mystuff,mystuff
```

The resulting listing file, MYSTUFF.LST, is shown in Figure 4.7.

This file tells us that MYSTUFF.LIB contains two modules: LOWERTBL, consisting of 256 bytes; and YESNO, consisting of 31 bytes. In addition, LOWERTBL contains the PUBLIC symbol **??LcTable**, and YESNO contains the PUBLIC symbol **GetYesNo**.

I've not had to use a library listing file very often, but when I've had to have it, absolutely nothing else could provide me with the information I needed.

Figure 4.7. Library listing file, MYSTUFF.LST

```
Publics by module

LOWERTBL  size = 256
  ??LcTable

YESNO     size = 31
  GetYesNo
```

Removing a Library Module

At times, a library module becomes obsolete. In most cases this happens when I write a new module that includes the functions provided by an older module. Once all my programs have been modified to use the new module, I like to remove the old module from the library.

For example, if I were to build a new subroutine that accepted any character from a program-supplied list, the **GetYesNo** subroutine would no longer be needed. In this case, I would remove **GetYesNo** from MYSTUFF.LIB by entering this command:

```
tlib mystuff -yesno
```

Updating a Library Module

Suppose we wanted to change the **GetYesNo** subroutine so that it always displayed a message. Right now, the **YesNo** macro generates the code that displays the message prompt. **GetYesNo** just reads the YES or NO answer from the keyboard.

If we were to make this change to the subroutine, we'd need to update the library module—remove the old YESNO module from the library and add the new module. We could instruct TLIB to remove the old YESNO module and then add the new one by entering this command:

```
tlib mystuff -yesno +yesno
```

The people who designed TLIB, however, were bright enough to realize that updating modules within a library is done fairly often. As a result, they provided an update command: **-+**. Using this command, updating the YESNO module in MYSTUFF.LIB would be accomplished this way:

```
tlib mystuff -+yesno
```

Extracting Library Modules

In some cases, you may want to extract a module from the library to create an object module. In addition, you may want to remove the module from the library in the process.

In most cases, you will have the source code for the module you need to extract, but suppose you need a module from a vendor-supplied library for which you have no source code. For example, I wanted to include a **strlen** function in one of my libraries. Rather than having TLINK search the entire CS.LIB file supplied with Borland C++, I used TLIB to extract the module from CS.LIB and add it to my library. To extract the file from CS.LIB, I entered this command:

```
tlib c:\borlandc\lib\cs *strlen
```

which tells TLIB to create a file called STRLEN.OBJ from the STRLEN module in CS.LIB.

If I had wanted to remove the **strlen** module from CS.LIB and save a copy of it, I would have added the - flag to my command line, like this:

```
tlib c:\borlandc\lib\cs *-strlen
```

There are a few command line options that alter the way TLIB creates libraries, but we won't be using them in this book. To learn more about TLIB and the options we haven't covered, please see the TLIB section of your *Turbo Assembler User's Guide*.

4.5 Automating Library Maintenance with MAKE

When your library starts to grow and you start maintaining it on a regular basis, you'll find yourself forgetting to update the library after you've made changes to a number of the modules. Especially when you are making the same change to several modules, you can tend to edit each of the modules and then assemble all of the modified modules. The final step, of course, is to use TLIB to replace the library modules with the updated versions.

After making a change to about a dozen of my library modules, I proceeded to assemble each changed module and update the library. Now, I find it difficult to remember more than about a half-dozen things at once. As a result, I forgot to update one of the modules and spent over an hour trying to figure out why some of the changed modules weren't working. When I finally figured out where I had made the error, I went looking for a way to keep from making the same mistake again.

MAKE, supplied with Turbo Assembler, is a program that automates multimodule program development. (MAKE can be used for other tasks as well. A full discussion of MAKE would constitute a good-sized chapter.) To use MAKE, you create a "make file" that contains *dependency information* about the program you're building. MAKE reads this dependency information and performs the steps required to build the program.

Normally, MAKE is used to build executable programs, but it is equally useful in building an object module library.

MAKE Dependency Information

The dependency information that you supply in the make file tells MAKE about the library you're trying to build: what library you are building, what object modules make up the library, and what commands to execute in order to build the library and each of the object files.

The dependency information that you provide to MAKE is in the form of *rules*. The best way to illustrate how these rules work is through a small example. The make file that builds our library is shown in Listing 4.10.

```
 1:   # Listing 4.10--MYSTUFF.MAK
 2:   #
 3:   # MSTUFF.MAK--build library MYSTUFF.LIB
 4:   #
 5:
 6:   mystuff.lib: lowertbl.obj yesno.obj
 7:
 8:   lowertbl.obj: lowertbl.asm
 9:     tasm /m lowertbl
10:     tlib mystuff -+lowertbl
11:
12:   yesno.obj: yesno.asm
13:     tasm /m yesno
14:     tlib mystuff -+mystuff
```

Once we've created MYSTUFF.MAK, we can build our library by issuing this command at the DOS prompt:

```
make -fmystuff
```

Let's take a few moments to see how this works.

The lines in MYSTUFF.MAK that begin with **#** are comments. The **#** works just like the semicolon comment operator in assembly language—everything following a **#** on the line is considered a comment and is ignored by MAKE.

The first rule in MYSTUFF.MAK, shown here,

```
mystuff.lib: lowertbl.obj yesno.obj
```

is called an *explicit rule*. This rule tells MAKE that MYSTUFF.LIB depends on LOWERTBL.OBJ and YESNO.OBJ. If either LOWERTBL.OBJ or YESNO.OBJ has a DOS date and time stamp that is *newer* than the date and time stamp of MYSTUFF.LIB (or if the .OBJ file doesn't exist), MAKE must issue commands to add the new module to the library.

The next two rules, also explicit rules, tell MAKE that LOWERTBL.OBJ depends on LOWERTBL.ASM and YESNO.OBJ depends on YESNO.ASM. If the .ASM file has a date stamp that is newer than the .OBJ file (that is, the source has been modified), MAKE must reassemble the module and add the resulting object module to the library.

MYSTUFF.MAK, as shown in Listing 4.10, is fine if you've only got a few modules in the library. If you need to add a new file to the library, you simply add the file name to the first rule and build another explicit rule to handle the new file. For example, to add ERRMSG.OBJ to the list of library modules, you would change the first rule so that it reads:

```
mystuff.lib: lowertbl.obj yesno.obj errmsg.obj
```

and then add this new explicit rule to the bottom of the file:

```
errmsg.obj: errmsg.asm
  tasm /m errmsg
  tlib mystuff -+errmsg
```

As you can no doubt imagine, maintaining the make file for a large library gets quite involved. Fortunately, we can make one modification to MYSTUFF.MAK that makes it much easier to deal with.

Notice that the explicit rules for each of the modules are the same, with the exception of the filenames. Each of the rules says "Assemble the file and then add the object module to the library." We can create *implicit rules*, which tell MAKE how to build one file from another, based on the files' extensions. In the case of making a .OBJ file from a .ASM file, our implicit rule would be:

```
 .asm.obj:
   tasm /m $*
   tlib mystuff -+$*
```

which says "To make a .OBJ file from a .ASM file, issue the command **tasm /m $***. Then, issue the command **tlib mystuff -+$***, where **$*** is replaced with the name of the file being built."

Using this implicit rule, our make file, MYSTUFF.MAK is greatly simplified, as shown in Listing 4.11.

```
1:    # Listing 4.11--MYSTUFF.MAK
2:    #
3:    # MYSTUFF.MAK--build library MYSTUFF.LIB
4:    #
5:    .asm.obj:
6:      tasm /m $*
7:      tlib mystuff -+$*
8:
9:    mystuff.lib: lowertbl.obj yesno.obj
```

Now, if we want to add another module to the library, we need only add the object file name to the explicit rule and reissue this command:

```
make -fmystuff
```

MAKE is a very powerful and versatile tool that can save you hours of development time. The short examples just given barely scratch the surface of MAKE's capabilities. You can get a broader view by studying the description of MAKE in your *Turbo Assembler User's Guide* and by becoming familiar with all of the time-saving opportunities that are provided by this program.

4.6 Two More Case Conversions

Before we tackle a larger library module, let's round out our case conversion macros. In the previous sections, we created an object module for the lowercase conversion table and modified the **ToLower** macro to take advantage of the object module. It makes sense to do the same for **ToUpper**, and it also makes sense to add a new case conversion macro, **CaseSwap**, which converts lowercase characters to uppercase and uppercase characters to lowercase. There's really nothing new in these modifications and additions, so I'll introduce them with a minimum of discussion.

First, the new **ToUpper** and **CaseSwap** macros are shown in Listing 4.12. You should add these macros to MACROS.INC after you remove the existing version of **ToUpper**.

```
 1:   ; Listing 4.12--ToLower and CaseSwap macros
 2:   ;
 3:   ; ToUpper Reg,<UseXlat>,<LoadBX>
 4:   ; Determine whether the contents of the specified register or
 5:   ; memory location is a lowercase alpha character (a..z), and
 6:   ; if so, convert it to uppercase.
 7:   ;
 8:   ; Parameters
 9:   ;    Reg (Required)--register or memory reference
10:   ;    UseXlat (Optional)--meaningful only when Reg = AL
11:   ;    LoadBX (Optional)--meaningful only when Reg = AL and
12:   ; UseXlat is not blank.
13:   ;
14:   ; Returns
15:   ;    Reg converted to lowercase (if applicable).
16:   ;
17:   ; Preserves the contents of all registers but the one
18:   ; specified in the Reg parameter and BX if the third parameter
19:   ; is given.
20:   ;
21:   Macro ToUpper Reg,UseXlat,LoadBX
22:     Local Around
23:     ifidni <Reg>,<al>
24:        ;;
25:        ;; If the requested register is AL, and the second parameter
26:        ;; is nonblank, generate code to use xlat for the
```

```
27:          ;; conversion.
28:          ;;
29:       ifnb <UseXlat>
30:         DataSeg
31:         Extrn ??UcTable:Byte
32:         CodeSeg
33:           ;;
34:           ;; If the third parameter is not blank, load BX with the
35:           ;; address of the conversion table.
36:           ;;
37:         ifnb <LoadBX>
38:           mov bx,offset ??UcTable
39:         endif
40:         xlat                ;; do the conversion
41:         exitm
42:       endif
43:     endif
44:  ;;
45:  ;; If the macro executes to this point, generate code to
46:  ;; perform "compare and jump" translation.
47:  ;;
48:     IsLower Reg             ;; see whether it's lowercase;
49:     jnz Around              ;; if not, ignore;
50:     and Reg,0dfh            ;; otherwise, convert to uppercase
51:  Around:
52:  Endm ToUpper
53:
54:
55:  ; CaseSwap Reg,<UseXlat>,<LoadBX>
56:  ; Determine whether the contents of the specified register or
57:  ; memory location is a an alpha character (A..Z or a..z);
58:  ; if so, swap its case.
59:  ;
60:  ; Parameters
61:  ;   Reg (Required)--register or memory reference
62:  ;   UseXlat (Optional)--meaningful only when Reg = AL
63:  ;   LoadBX (Optional)--meaningful only when Reg = AL and
64:  ; UseXlat is not blank.
65:  ;
66:  ; Returns
67:  ;   Reg with case reversed (if applicable)
68:  ;
69:  ; Preserves the contents of all registers but the one
70:  ; specified in the Reg parameter and BX if the third parameter
71:  ; is given.
72:  ;
73:  Macro CaseSwap Reg,UseXlat,LoadBX
74:    Local Around,DoConvert
75:    ifidni <Reg>,<al>
```

```
 76:         ;;
 77:         ;; If the requested register is AL and the second parameter
 78:         ;; is nonblank, generate code to use xlat for the
 79:         ;; conversion.
 80:         ;;
 81:         ifnb <UseXlat>
 82:           DataSeg
 83:           Extrn ??CsTable:Byte
 84:           CodeSeg
 85:           ;;
 86:           ;; If the third parameter is not blank, load BX with the
 87:           ;; address of the conversion table.
 88:           ;;
 89:           ifnb <LoadBX>
 90:             mov bx,offset ??CsTable
 91:           endif
 92:           xlat              ;; do the conversion
 93:           exitm
 94:         endif
 95:       endif
 96:  ;;
 97:  ;; If the macro executes to this point, generate code to
 98:  ;; perform "compare and jump" translation.
 99:  ;;
100:       IsLower Reg          ;; see whether it's lowercase
101:       jz DoConvert         ;; if so, do conversion;
102:       IsUpper Reg          ;; otherwise, see whether uppercase
103:       jnz Around           ;; if not, ignore
104:  DoConvert:
105:       xor Reg,20h     ;; swap case
106:  Around:
107:  Endm CaseSwap
```

We need to create two new modules that will be included in our object module library. The first module, UPPERTBL.ASM (Listing 4.13) is a conversion table similar to LOWERTBL.ASM, but which converts uppercase letters to lowercase.

```
 1:   ; Listing 4.13--UPPERTBL.ASM
 2:   ;
 3:   ; UPPERTBL.ASM
 4:   ; External module holds the uppercase conversion table.
 5:   ;
 6:     ideal
 7:     model small
 8:     DataSeg
 9:
10:   Public ??UcTable
11:
```

```
12:    Label ??UcTable Byte
13:      Char = 0                ;; initialize count
14:      rept 256
15:        ;;
16:        ;; If Char is in the range of lowercase characters,
17:        ;; generate the uppercase equivalent. Otherwise,
18:        ;; generate a byte with value of Char.
19:        ;;
20:        if (Char ge 'a') and (Char le 'z')
21:          db Char and 0dfh
22:        else
23:          db Char
24:        endif
25:        Char = Char + 1     ;; go to next character
26:      endm
27:
28:    End
```

The second new external module, SWAPTBL.ASM, is very similar to LOWERTBL.ASM and UPPERTBL.ASM, but it converts lowercase characters to uppercase and vice-versa. This module is shown in Listing 4.14.

```
 1:    ; Listing 4.14—SWAPTBL.ASM
 2:    ;
 3:    ; SWAPTBL.ASM
 4:    ; External module holds the case-swap conversion table.
 5:    ;
 6:      ideal
 7:      model small
 8:      DataSeg
 9:
10:    Public ??CsTable
11:
12:    Label ??CsTable Byte
13:      Char = 0                ;; initialize count
14:      rept 256
15:        ;;
16:        ;; If Char is in the range of lowercase characters,
17:        ;; generate the uppercase equivalent.
18:        ;; If Char is in the range of uppercase characters,
19:        ;; generate the lowercase equivalent.
20:        ;; Otherwise, generate a byte with value of Char.
21:        ;;
22:        if (Char ge 'a') and (Char le 'z')
23:          db Char and 0dfh
24:        elseif (Char ge 'A') and (Char le 'Z')
25:          db Char or 20h
26:        else
```

```
27:        db Char
28:      endif
29:      Char = Char + 1    ;; go to next character
30:    endm
31:
32:  End
```

After you've added Listing 4.12 to your MACROS.INC file, and created new files UPPERTBL.ASM and SWAPTBL.ASM from Listings 4.13 and 4.14, respectively, change your MYSTUFF.MAK file so that it reads:

```
# MYSTUFF.MAK -- build library MYSTUFF.LIB
#
.asm.obj:
  tasm /m $*
  tlib mystuff -+$*

mystuff.lib: lowertbl.obj yesno.obj uppertbl.obj swaptbl.obj
```

and, finally, reconstruct your object module library by entering this command at the DOS prompt:

```
make -fmystuff
```

That's all we'll do with case conversions, for now. We'll come back to these subroutines in Chapter 6 when we build a case-conversion filter program.

4.7 DosErrMsg Revisited

At the beginning of the chapter, I pointed out that the **DosErrMsg** macro we developed at the end of Chapter 3 generates entirely too much code each time it's invoked. The code that **DosErrMsg** generates is not bad, it's just unnecessary. We would be much better off to modify this macro so that it calls an external subroutine to display error messages. The macro itself will simply set up the registers and make the subroutine call. This organization will save us a considerable amount of code space—at least 30 bytes per invocation. As a more concrete example of using object module libraries, let's make these changes to **DosErrMsg** and create the new object module.

In order to support both types of error message display, two subroutines are used. The first, **DosDispErrMsg**, simply displays the standard DOS error message identified by the value passed in AX. Calling **DosDispErrMsg** is equivalent to invoking the **DosErrMsg** macro with no parameters. The second subroutine, **DosDispInfoMsg**, first displays a user-defined error message and then calls **DosDispErrMsg** to display the standard DOS error message identified by the value passed in AX. Calling **DosDispInfoMsg** is equivalent to invoking **DosErrMsg** with one or two parameters.

If we place the error message table and the error message display code in an external module, our **DosErrMsg** macro becomes quite a bit simpler (although not trivial), as you can see from Listing 4.15.

```
 1:    ; Listing 4.15--DosErrMsg
 2:    ;
 3:    ; DosErrMsg <String>,<Arg2>
 4:    ; Write a user-defined error message and the standard DOS error
 5:    ; message corresponding to the value in AX to the standard
 6:    ; error device.
 7:    ;
 8:    ; Parameters
 9:    ;   String (Optional) - Either a text string or the label name
10:    ; of a string to display. If it's a text string, the string is
11:    ; defined in the data segment before displaying.
12:    ;   Arg2 (Optional) - If this parameter is given, the first
13:    ; parameter is assumed to be a label name, and Arg2 is assumed
14:    ; to be the string to define and display.
15:    ;
16:    ; If either or both of the parameters is given, CX and DX
17:    ; are loaded with the appropriate values. If DosErrMsg is
18:    ; invoked without parameters, only the DOS error message
19:    ; corresponding to the value in AX is written to StdErr.
20:    ;
21:    ; Before you invoke this macro, AX must hold an error value
22:    ; returned by a DOS function.
23:    ;
24:    ; This macro makes use of the subroutines DosDispErrMsg and
25:    ; DosDispInfoMsg that are defined in the ERRMSG.ASM module.
26:    ;
27:    ; AX, BX, CX, DX, and the flags are affected by the code created
28:    ; by this macro. All other registers are unaltered.
29:    ;
30:    Macro DosErrMsg String,Arg2
31:      Local ArgType,Temp
32:        ;;
33:        ;; Identify the external procedures used by this macro.
34:        ;;
35:      extrn DosDispInfoMsg:Proc
36:      extrn DosDispErrMsg:Proc
37:    ;;
38:    ;; If the first parameter is not blank, check the second
39:    ;; parameter and the first parameter's type to determine
40:    ;; what code to generate.
41:    ;;
42:      ifnb <String>
43:        ;;
```

```
44:        ;; If the second parameter is not blank, assume the first
45:        ;; parameter is a label name and define a string
46:        ;; with that name.
47:        ;;
48:      ifnb <Arg2>
49:        LenString String,<Arg2>
50:        mov cx,String&Len
51:        mov dx,offset String
52:      else
53:        ;;
54:        ;; The second parameter is blank. Check the type of
55:        ;; first parameter.
56:        WhatType <String>,ArgType
57:        ;;
58:        ;; If it's a string (ArgType = 0) or a constant
59:        ;; (ArgType = 24), define the data and generate
60:        ;; code to display it.
61:        ;;
62:        if (ArgType eq 0) or (ArgType eq 24h)
63:          LenString Temp,<String>
64:          mov cx,Temp&Len
65:          mov dx,offset Temp
66:        else
67:          ;;
68:          ;; Otherwise, just generate code to display it.
69:          ;;
70:          mov cx,String&Len
71:          mov dx,offset String
72:        endif
73:      endif
74:      call DosDispInfoMsg
75:    else
76:      call DosDispErrMsg
77:    endif
78:  Endm DosErrMsg
```

The two display subroutines and the definition of the error message table are left up to the external module ERRMSG.ASM, which is assembled separately and added to our object module library. Then, any program that needs to display error messages can link with this module. The source of ERRMSG.ASM is shown in Listing 4.16.

```
1:  ; Listing 4.16--ERRMSG.ASM
2:  ;
3:  ; Includes DosDispErrMsg and DosDispErrMsg1 procedures
4:  ; and the corresponding error table.
5:  ;
6:  ; These procedures are called by the DosErrMsg macro.
```

```
 7:   ;
 8:     ideal
 9:     model small
10:
11:   include "macros.inc"
12:   include "dosmacs.inc"
13:
14:   NErr = 90        ; through DOS 4 the highest error code is 90
15:
16:   ; ************************************************************
17:   ; *              Macros used in building the error table     *
18:   ; ************************************************************
19:
20:   ;
21:   ; MakeErrLbl
22:   ; Define a single error label that points to the
23:   ; "Unknown Error" message.
24:   ;
25:   Macro MakeErrLbl ErrNo
26:     Err&ErrNo = offset FileErrTable
27:   Endm MakeErrLbl
28:
29:   ;
30:   ; ErrDef ErrNo,String
31:   ; Define a preceding length string error message and set
32:   ; the corresponding error message pointer to point to
33:   ; the first byte of the string.
34:   ;
35:   Macro ErrDef ErrNo,String
36:     Local Temp
37:     dw Temp&Len
38:     Err&ErrNo = $
39:     LenString Temp,<String>
40:   Endm ErrDef
41:
42:   ;
43:   ; MakeErrPtr
44:   ; Define a word that contains a pointer
45:   ; to the specified error message.
46:   ;
47:   Macro MakeErrPtr ErrNo
48:     dw Err&ErrNo
49:   Endm MakeErrPtr
50:   ;
51:   ; ************************************************************
52:   ; *                End of macro definitions                  *
53:   ; ************************************************************
54:
55:     DataSeg
```

```
 56:    ;
 57:    ; Construct error message table and the pointer array.
 58:    ;
 59:    ; Initialize the error message pointers so that all point
 60:    ; to error message 0 (Unknown error).
 61:    ;
 62:      ErrNo = 0
 63:      rept NErr
 64:        MakeErrLbl %ErrNo
 65:        ErrNo = ErrNo + 1
 66:      endm
 67:    ;
 68:    ; Define the error messages.
 69:    ;
 70:      Label FileErrTable Byte
 71:      ErrDef 0,<"Unknown error">
 72:      ErrDef 1,<"Invalid function number">
 73:      ErrDef 2,<"File not found">
 74:      ErrDef 3,<"Path not found">
 75:      ErrDef 4,<"No handles available">
 76:      ErrDef 5,<"Access denied">
 77:      ErrDef 6,<"Invalid handle">
 78:      ErrDef 7,<"Memory control blocks destroyed">
 79:      ErrDef 8,<"Insufficient memory">
 80:      ErrDef 9,<"Invalid memory block address">
 81:      ErrDef 10,<"Invalid environment">
 82:      ErrDef 11,<"Invalid format">
 83:      ErrDef 12,<"Invalid access code">
 84:      ErrDef 13,<"Invalid data">
 85:      ErrDef 15,<"Invalid drive">
 86:      ErrDef 16,<"Attempt to remove current directory">
 87:      ErrDef 17,<"Not the same device">
 88:      ErrDef 18,<"No more files">
 89:      ErrDef 19,<"Disk write-protected">
 90:      ErrDef 20,<"Unknown unit">
 91:      ErrDef 21,<"Drive not ready">
 92:      ErrDef 22,<"Unknown command">
 93:      ErrDef 23,<"CRC error">
 94:      ErrDef 24,<"Bad request structure length">
 95:      ErrDef 25,<"Seek error">
 96:      ErrDef 26,<"Unknown media type">
 97:      ErrDef 27,<"Sector not found">
 98:      ErrDef 28,<"Out of paper">
 99:      ErrDef 29,<"Write fault">
100:      ErrDef 30,<"Read fault">
101:      ErrDef 31,<"General failure">
102:      ErrDef 80,<"File already exists">
103:      ErrDef 82,<"Cannot make directory entry">
104:      ErrDef 83,<"Fail on Int 24">
```

```
105:    ;
106:    ; Define the pointer table from the redefined message pointers.
107:    ;
108:      ErrNo = 0
109:      Label ErrPtrs Word
110:      rept NErr
111:        MakeErrPtr %ErrNo
112:        ErrNo = ErrNo + 1
113:      endm
114:
115:      LenString SpaceDashSpace,<" - ">
116:      LenString CRLF,<cr,lf>
117:
118:      CodeSeg
119:
120:    Public DosDispErrMsg1
121:    Public DosDispErrMsg
122:
123:    ;
124:    ; DosDispErrMsg1 is called when we need to display an
125:    ; informational message before we display the standard
126:    ; DOS error message. It falls through to DosDispErrMsg.
127:    ;
128:    ; Call with DX = address of message to display
129:    ;           CX = length of message in bytes
130:    ;           AX = DOS error code
131:    ;
132:    Proc DosDispErrMsg1
133:        push ax               ; save error code
134:        DosWriteFile StdErr   ; Write error message to StdErr
135:    ;
136:    ; Write the message separator (" - ").
137:    ;
138:        DosWriteFile StdErr,SpaceDashSpaceLen,<Offset SpaceDashSpace>
139:        pop ax                ; restore error code
140:    ;
141:    ; Notice the lack of a return instruction.
142:    ; This routine will fall through to DosDispErrMsg.
143:    ;
144:    Endp DosDispErrMsg1
145:
146:    ;
147:    ; DosDispErrMsg
148:    ; This routine is called to display a standard DOS
149:    ; error message.
150:    ;
151:    ; The DOS error number is passed in AX.
152:    ;
153:    Proc DosDispErrMsg
```

```
154:    ;
155:    ; Look up error code in table and display the error on StdErr.
156:    ;
157:      mov bx,offset ErrPtrs ; BX points to error message
158:                            ; pointer table
159:      cmp ax,NErr           ; if error code > number of error codes,
160:      jbe Around
161:      xor ax,ax             ; ...it's an unknown error
162:    Around:
163:      shl ax,1              ; error code * 2 for indexing
164:      add bx,ax             ; add to table base
165:      mov bx,[bx]           ; BX holds address of error message
166:      mov dx,bx             ; put in DX for write device function
167:      mov cx,[bx-2]         ; load message length in CX
168:      DosWriteFile StdErr
169:    ;
170:    ; Write a newline.
171:    ;
172:      DosWriteFile StdErr,CRLFLen,<offset CRLF>
173:      ret
174:    Endp DosDispErrMsg
175:
176:    End
```

In order to use the new **DosErrMsg** macro and the external subroutines, we need to replace the existing **DosErrMsg** macro in DOSMACS.INC with the new version shown in Listing 4.15. In addition, we need to add the error message display routines to our library, MYSTUFF.LIB. Making this addition is a simple matter of changing the explicit rule in MYSTUFF.MAK that reads

```
mystuff.lib: lowertbl.obj yesno.obj uppertbl.obj swaptbl.obj
```

so that it looks like this:

```
mystuff.lib: lowertbl.obj yesno.obj uppertbl.obj \
  swaptbl.obj errmsg.obj
```

We can then rebuild the library by entering this MAKE command at the DOS prompt:

```
make -fmystuff
```

In order to test the new **DosErrMsg** macro and its associated subroutines, I've created a small program, ERRTEST.ASM, which is shown in Listing 4.17.

```
1:  ; Listing 4.17--ERRTEST.ASM
2:  ;
```

```
 3:    ; Test the new DosErrMsg macro ERRTEST module.
 4:    ;
 5:      ideal
 6:    include "macros.inc"
 7:    include "dosmacs.inc"
 8:
 9:      ProgramHeader small,0100h
10:      CodeSeg
11:    Proc TestMsg
12:      ExeStart
13:      mov ax,4
14:      DosErrMsg <"First Message">
15:      mov ax,5
16:      DosErrMsg
17:      DosExitProgram 0
18:    Endp TestMsg
19:
20:      End TestMsg
```

Create a new file called ERRTEST.ASM and enter the code from Listing 4.17. After you save the file, assemble and link the program by entering the following commands at the DOS prompt:

```
tasm /m/l errtest
tlink errtest
```

You can execute the test program by entering the command

```
errtest
```

on the command line. Running the program should produce the output shown in Figure 4.8.

At something over 1,400 bytes, ERRTEST.EXE is much larger than it has to be in order to generate two simple error messages. The large code size is due to the error message table that is defined in ERRMSG.ASM and linked with the program. Any program that uses **DosErrMsg** will incur this overhead.

Figure 4.8. Output of ERRTEST.EXE

```
C:\MACROS>errtest
First Message - No handles available
Access denied

C:\MACROS>
```

The large size of the ERRMSG module is very noticeable in small programs like ERRTEST.EXE. In larger programs, however, which could easily be 10 times the size of ERRTEST.EXE, the size of the ERRMSG module would be much less noticeable.

Our new version of the **DosErrMsg** macro is much more space efficient than the version from Chapter 3, which generated at least 38 bytes of code for each invocation of the macro. Listing 4.16 generates at most 9 bytes of code for each invocation.

Generality is the key. The more general you make a macro or subroutine, the more memory it is likely to require. In the case of **DosErrMsg** and the ERRMSG module, the ability to easily display any of the DOS error messages is well worth the added code size.

4.8 Macro, Object Module, or Library?

We now have several ways that we can use macros to access subroutines. The most direct—having the macro define the subroutine on first use and then having the macro redefine itself—is all right for small subroutines with simple macro invocations. But if the subroutine is large or the macro's parameter processing is complex, this method becomes cumbersome.

You can use **include** files to hold common subroutines, but again, if the subroutines become large, you'll waste time assembling the subroutines for each program that uses them.

Using object modules is an ideal way to break large programs into more manageable chunks. Each module is assembled separately from the others, making program maintenance simpler and faster. For subroutines and data that are accessed by more than one program, however, object modules become unwieldy.

Object module libraries contain object modules that are common to many different programs. If we use the assembler's **includelib** directive and tell the linker where to find the library file, the use of object module libraries is transparent to the programmer.

Even object module libraries become difficult to maintain as they grow. The MAKE program can help us overcome much of this difficulty.

Which approach do you use? That's up to you. All of the techniques that we've seen in this chapter have their strengths and weaknesses. As you become more familiar with macros, subroutines, object modules, and library files, you'll begin to develop a feel for which tool is best suited to a particular job.

With all of these tools at your disposal, you'll never again be forced to hammer those screws into the wall.

Macro Libraries and Object Modules

Once more, we've made some additions to our macro libraries. In addition, we've created an entirely new object module library that we'll continue to expand and use in further chapters. What follows lists the contents of each of these files.

We've changed the **ToLower** macro in MACROS.INC and added two new macros: **ToUpper** and **CaseSwap**. To update your MACROS.INC file, replace the existing **ToLower** macro with Listing 4.8, and add Listing 4.12. In addition, be sure to add the **includelib "mystuff.lib"** directive at the beginning of the file.

DOSMACS.INC has also received a few changes. The following macros make up the newest version of this file:

Listing 2.21 Constant definitions
Listing 2.4 Macro **ExeStart**
Listing 2.5 Macro **DosCall**
Listing 2.7 Macro **DosExitProgram**
Listing 2.11 Macros **$String** and **zString**
Listing 2.22 Macro **DosOpenFile**
Listing 2.26 Macro **DosCloseFile**
Listing 3.4 Macros **CheckSeg** and **TermString**
Listing 3.5 Macro **WhatType**
Listing 3.9 Macro **CountArgs**
Listing 3.10 Macro **DosDisplayString**
Listing 3.11 Macros **DosReadFile**, **DosWriteFile**, **LenString** and **MakeString**
Listing 4.6 Macro **YesNo**
Listing 4.15 Macro **DosErrMsg**

Again, remember to add the **includlib "mystuff.lib"** directive to the top of DOSMACS.INC.

Finally, our new object module library, MYSTUFF.LIB, is made up of the following modules:

YESNO.ASM	Listing 4.5
LOWERTBL.ASM	Listing 4.7
UPPERTBL.ASM	Listing 4.13
SWAPTBL.ASM	Listing 4.14
ERRMSG.ASM	Listing 4.16

5

Optimization
and Flexibility

169

In the previous chapters, we've been more concerned with how to use macros than we have been with the quality of the code that our macros generate. We looked at some optimizations in Chapters 2 and 3, but for the most part we've been largely unconcerned with the speed or size of the generated code.

One of the primary reasons for writing in assembly language is that it enables us to get down to the bare metal; to create programs that are small and fast, and that make the best possible use of the hardware and operating system. Although "good enough" assembly language code is normally better than "real good" high-level language code, "good enough" just doesn't cut it when we're trying to squeeze bytes and shave cycles. When it comes down to sheer performance, nothing beats optimized assembly language.

There are many tricks to optimizing assembler programs, and try as I might I just can't keep all of that information in my head. What's worse, when I *do* remember a trick or two, it's usually an afterthought. I've spent entirely too much time going back to optimize parts of programs that could have been tighter to begin with. There's simply too much to remember.

That's where macros come in. Why try to remember these code sequences when we can write macros that take care of most of the routine details for us? We can build a set of macros that enable us to quickly generate efficient code sequences for common operations. These macros won't replace hand-optimized assembly language in critical sections of a program, but they will help to keep the program small and fast, and also reduce the amount of time we spend optimizing noncritical parts of the program.

In this chapter, we'll take another look at some of the macros we've created and make them generate better code. In addition, we'll examine some optimization tricks that become much easier to implement when coded in macros.

5.1 IsRange Revisited

I find the **IsRange** macro that was introduced in Chapter 1 to be among the most generally (and genuinely!) useful macros in my collection. It is relatively simple as macros go and, better yet, it contains many features of much more involved and complex macros. All in all, **IsRange** is an excellent tool for experimentation and instruction.

For discussion purposes, I've duplicated the **IsRange** macro from Chapter 1, and **IsUpper**—one of the macros that uses **IsRange**—in Listing 5.1.

```
1:   ; Listing 5.1--IsRange and IsUpper macros
2:   ;
3:   Macro IsUpper Reg
4:     IsRange <Reg>,'A','Z'
5:   Endm IsUpper
6:
```

```
 7:    Macro IsRange Reg,Lower,Upper
 8:      Local Around
 9:    ;;
10:    ;; Check for required parameters.
11:    ;;
12:      ifb <Reg>
13:        err
14:        Display "Register or memory reference must be specified"
15:        exitm
16:      elseifb <Lower>
17:        err
18:        Display "Lower boundary must be specified"
19:        exitm
20:      elseifb <Upper>
21:        err
22:        Display "Upper boundary must be specified"
23:        exitm
24:      endif
25:    ;;
26:    ;; All parameters exist. Generate code to perform the tests.
27:    ;;
28:      cmp Reg,Lower
29:      jbe Around
30:      cmp Reg,Upper
31:      ja Around
32:      test Reg,0
33:    Around:
34:    Endm IsRange
```

Using these macros, code that determines whether the character in AL is an uppercase letter and branches accordingly, would be written like this:

```
  IsUpper al
  jz IsUpperCase
NotUpperCase:
```

and the code generated by this macro would be

```
; IsUpper al
  cmp al,'A'       ;if <= 'A',
  jbe ??0000       ;then done
  cmp al,'Z'       ;if > 'Z',
  ja ??0000        ;then done
  test al,0        ;otherwise, set flags
??0000:
  jz IsUpperCase       ;branch accordingly
NotUpperCase:
```

which is clearly not optimal. How so? If we were to write the code by hand, we'd end up with this:

```
cmp al,'A'      ;if < 'A'
jb NotUpperCase      ;branch false
cmp al,'Z'      ;if <= 'Z'
jna IsUpperCase      ;branch true
NotUpperCase:
```

"What's the difference?" you ask. Using the Zen Timer from Michael Abrash's *Zen of Assembly Language*, I timed 1,000 iterations of each code fragment using 4 different values in the AL register. The results are shown in Figure 5.1.

As you can see in Figure 5.1, the hand-optimized code is anywhere from 8 to 60 percent faster than the code generated by **IsUpper**. Obviously, if we're going to be using macros in real programs, we've got to make them generate much better code. And we can! Let's see how.

Figure 5.1. Instruction timings, IsUpper versus hand code

Value in AL	1,000 IsUpper	1,000 Hand code	Difference
0	1,009 µs	930 µs	7.83%
'A'	1,730 µs	1,200 µs	30.64%
'Z'	1,466 µs	1,200 µs	18.14%
'Z'+1	1,334 µs	533 µs	60.04%

Testing performed on a noncached 386SX running at 20MHz

Speeding Up IsRange

The secret to speeding up **IsRange** is to add branching parameters so that the generated code can branch earlier depending on what it determines about the value it's testing. Properly written, we can make **IsRange** generate code that's exactly like we'd write by hand. In addition, by adding the branching parameters to **IsRange**, we make the macro much more flexible, as we'll see later.

The new **IsRange** macro, with branching parameters, is shown in Listing 5.2. Also shown are new **IsUpper**, **IsLower**, **IsDigit**, and **IsAlpha** macros that accept the branching parameters.

```
1:   ; Listing 5.2--New IsRange and associated macros
2:   ;
3:   ; IsRange Reg,Lower,Upper,<IsInRange>,<NotInRange>
4:   ;   Determines whether the contents of the specified register or
5:   ; memory location is within the boundaries specified by Lower
```

```
 6:    ; and Upper, inclusive, and branches to the proper address
 7:    ; if requested.
 8:    ;
 9:    ; Parameters
10:    ;   Reg (Required) - Register or memory reference
11:    ;   Lower (Required) - Lower range boundary
12:    ;   Upper (Required) - Upper range boundary
13:    ;   IsInRange (Optional) - Branch address for TRUE comparison
14:    ;   NotInRange (Optional) - Branch address for FALSE comparison
15:    ;
16:    ; Returns
17:    ;   If the branching parameters are not given:
18:    ;     Z flag set if value is within range
19:    ;     Z flag clear if value is not within range
20:    ;   If one or both branching parameters is given, the destination
21:    ;   address indicates the value.
22:    ;
23:    ; Preserves the contents of all registers except the flags.
24:    ;
25:    Macro IsRange Reg,Lower,Upper,IsInRange,NotInRange
26:      Local Done
27:    ;;
28:    ;; Check for required parameters
29:    ;;
30:      ifb <Reg>
31:        err
32:        Display "Register or memory reference must be specified"
33:        exitm
34:      elseifb <Lower>
35:        err
36:        Display "Lower boundary must be specified"
37:        exitm
38:      elseifb <Upper>
39:        err
40:        Display "Upper boundary must be specified"
41:        exitm
42:      endif
43:    ;;
44:    ;; All parameters exist. Generate code to perform the tests.
45:    ;;
46:      cmp Reg,Lower
47:      ifnb <NotInRange>
48:        jc NotInRange
49:      elseifb <IsInRange>
50:        jbe Done
51:      else
52:        jc Done
53:      endif
```

```
54:    ;; End of lower bound checking. Test upper bound.
55:    cmp Reg,Upper
56:    ifnb <NotInRange>
57:      ja NotInRange
58:      ifnb <IsInRange>
59:        jmp IsInRange
60:      endif
61:    elseifb <IsInRange>
62:      ja Done
63:      test Reg,0
64:    else
65:      jbe IsInRange
66:    endif
67: ifb <NotInRange>
68:    Label Done Near
69: endif
70: Endm IsRange
71:
72: Macro IsUpper Reg,YesBranch,NoBranch
73:    IsRange <Reg>,'A','Z',<YesBranch>,<NoBranch>
74: Endm IsUpper
75:
76: Macro IsLower Reg,YesBranch,NoBranch
77:    IsRange <Reg>,'a','z',<YesBranch>,<NoBranch>
78: Endm IsUpper
79:
80: Macro IsDigit Reg,YesBranch,NoBranch
81:    IsRange <Reg>,'0','9',<YesBranch>,<NoBranch>
82: Endm IsUpper
83:
84: Macro IsAlpha Reg,YesBranch,NoBranch
85:    Local Done
86:    ifnb <YesBranch>
87:      IsUpper <Reg>,<YesBranch>
88:    else
89:      IsRange <Reg>,Done
90:    endif
91:    IsLower <Reg>,<YesBranch>,<NoBranch>
92:  Done:
93: Endm IsUpper
```

Let's take a look at some of the code that this new **IsRange** macro generates.

If we use the old invocation sequence with **IsUpper**, as shown in the following example, the code generated by the new **IsRange** macro is identical to what the previous version generated. This is called "backward compatibility"—old code will work fine with the new macro. For example, this invocation of **IsUpper**:

```
IsUpper al
```

still generates:

```
  cmp al,'A'
  jbe Done
  cmp al,'Z'
  ja Done
  test al,0
Label Done Near
```

However, the generated code is greatly improved if we specify at least one branch parameter. Examine the macro invocations in Listing 5.3 and the code that is generated for each:

```
 1:    ; Listing 5.3
 2:    ; Sample uses of the new IsUpper macro
 3:
 4:    ; Branch to label ItsUpper if AL contains an uppercase
 5:    ; alpha character.
 6:    ;   IsUpper al,ItsUpper
 7:      cmp al,'A'
 8:      jc Done
 9:      cmp al,'Z'
10:      jbe ItsUpper
11:    Label Done Near
12:    ; If we get here, AL does not contain an uppercase character.
13:
14:
15:    ; Branch to label NotUpper if AL does not contain an
16:    ; uppercase alpha character.
17:    ;   IsUpper al,,NotUpper
18:      cmp al,'A'
19:      jc NotUpper
20:      cmp al,'Z'
21:      ja NotUpper
22:    ; If we get here, the character in AL is uppercase.
23:
24:
25:    ; Branch to label ItsUpper if AL contains an uppercase
26:    ; alpha character. Branch to NotUpper if not.
27:    ;   IsUpper al,ItsUpper,NotUpper
28:      cmp al,'A'
29:      jc NotUpper
30:      cmp al,'Z'
31:      ja NotUpper
32:      jmp ItsUpper
```

By adding the branching parameters, we cause our macros to generate better code—code equivalent to what we'd write by hand. Using this new **IsRange** macro, we can optimize our **ToUpper** and **ToLower** macros as well. Figure 5.2 shows the changes required to make **ToUpper** and **ToLower** use the new **IsRange** macro for "compare and jump" code generation. This figure assumes that your **IsUpper** and **IsLower** macros are using the new branching parameters, as shown in Listing 5.2.

Figure 5.2. Modifying ToUpper and ToLower

ToLower:

Old Code	New Code
| ```
IsUpper Reg
jnz Around
or Reg,20h
Around:
Endm ToLower
``` | ```
IsUpper Reg,,Around
or Reg,20h

Around:
Endm ToLower
``` |

ToUpper:

Old Code	New Code
| ```
IsLower Reg
jnz Around
and Reg,0dfh
Around:
Endm ToUpper
``` | ```
IsLower Reg,,Around
and Reg,0dfh

Around:
Endm ToUpper
``` |

And Flexibility as Well

Faster code is only one of the benefits provided by adding branching parameters to **IsRange**. With the new parameters come new capabilities—specifically the ability to perform and branch using the common conditionals less than, less than or equal to, greater than or equal to, and greater than.

The easy part is adding the new macros, which are shown in Listing 5.4. Notice that these macros use only one of the bounds parameters that **IsRange** accepts.

```
1:    ; Listing 5.4--Conditional macros
2:    ;
3:    ; These are conditional macros that take advantage of
4:    ; the new IsRange macro.
5:    ;
6:    Macro IsLess Reg,Val,Yep,Nope
```

```
 7:        IsRange <Reg>,,<Val>,<Nope>,<Yep>
 8:     Endm IsLess
 9:
10:     Macro IsLessEqual Reg,Val,Yep,Nope
11:        IsRange <Reg>,<Val>,,<Yep>,<Nope>
12:     Endm IsLessEqual
13:
14:     Macro IsGreaterEqual Reg,Val,Yep,Nope
15:        IsRange <Reg>,,<Val>,<Yep>,<Nope>
16:     Endm IsGreaterEqual
17:
18:     Macro IsGreater Reg,Val,Yep,Nope
19:        IsRange <Reg>,<Val>,,<Nope>,<Yep>
20:     Endm IsGreater
```

As you can see in Listing 5.5, the difficult part is getting all of the conditionals right in **IsRange**. In a nutshell, we've made all of the parameters optional, although there are some restrictions pointed out in the comments at the top of the macro. We won't go into a step-by-step discussion, but I suggest that you study Listing 5.5 until you understand exactly how this final version of **IsRange** works.

```
 1:    ; Listing 5.5--IsRange
 2:    ;
 3:    ; New IsRange macro that supports IsLess, IsLessEqual,
 4:    ; IsGreater and IsGreaterEqual
 5:    ;
 6:    ; IsRange Reg,Lower,Upper,<IsInRange>,<NotInRange>
 7:    ;   Determines whether the contents of the specified register or
 8:    ; memory location is within the boundaries specified by Lower
 9:    ; and Upper, inclusive, and branches to the proper address
10:    ; if requested.
11:    ;
12:    ; Parameters
13:    ;   Reg (Optional) - Register or memory reference
14:    ;   Lower (Optional) - Lower range boundary
15:    ;   Upper (Optional) - Upper range boundary
16:    ;   IsInRange (Optional) - Branch address for TRUE comparison
17:    ;   NotInRange (Optional) - Branch address for FALSE comparison
18:    ;
19:    ; If the Reg parameter is not specified, IsRange assumes
20:    ; that the flags are set from a previous comparison. In
21:    ; this case, the macro will generate branching code based
22:    ; on the value of the Z flag. At least one of the two
23:    ; branching parameters (IsInRange or NotInRange) must
24:    ; be specified.
25:    ;
26:    ; Except when Reg is blank, at least one of the bounds
```

```
27:    ; parameters (Lower or Upper) must be specified.
28:    ;
29:    ; Except when Reg is blank, the IsInRange and NotInRange
30:    ; parameters are always optional.
31:    ;
32:    ; Returns
33:    ;   If the branching parameters are not given:
34:    ;     Z flag set if value is within range
35:    ;     Z flag clear if value is not within range
36:    ;   If one or both branching parameters is given, the destination
37:    ;   address indicates the value.
38:    ;
39:    ; Preserves the contents of all registers except the flags.
40:    ;
41:    Macro IsRange Reg,Lower,Upper,IsInRange,NotInRange
42:      Local Done
43:      ;;
44:      ;; If the <Reg> parameter is not specified, generate code
45:      ;; based on the values of the <IsInRange> and <NotInRange> parameters.
46:      ;; The resulting code uses the existing values in the Flags register.
47:      ;; If neither of the two branches is specified, a message
48:      ;; is displayed and no code is generated.
49:      ;;
50:      ifb <Reg>
51:        ifb <IsInRange>
52:          ifb <NotInRange>
53:            Err
54:            Display "Blank IsRange Macro"
55:          else
56:            jne NotInRange       ;; only <NotInRange> is specified
57:          endif
58:        elseifb <NotInRange>
59:          je IsInRange           ;; only <IsInRange> is specified
60:        else
61:          jne NotInRange         ;; both <IsInRange> and <NotInRange>
62:          jmp IsInRange          ;; are specified
63:        endif
64:        exitm
65:      endif
66:      ;;
67:      ;; At this point, we know that <Reg> was specified.
68:      ;; At least one of <Upper> or <Lower> must be specified.
69:      ;;
70:      ifb <Lower>
71:        ifb <Upper>
72:          Err
73:          Display "One of <Upper> or <Lower> must be specified"
74:          exitm
```

```
 75:        endif
 76:      endif
 77:    ;;
 78:    ;; Check for lower bound. If lower bound specified,
 79:    ;; generate code to test/branch on combination of lower
 80:    ;; and upper bounds.
 81:    ;;
 82:     ifnb <Lower>                    ;; lower bound has been specified
 83:       cmp Reg,Lower                 ;; test lower bound
 84:    ;;
 85:    ;; If no upper bound was specified, treat this as a
 86:    ;; LessEqual or GreaterEqual, depending upon IsInRange and NotInRange
 87:    ;;
 88:       ifb <Upper>                   ;; no upper bound specified
 89:         ifnb <IsInRange>            ;; if a "true" branch specified
 90:           jbe IsInRange             ;; then treat it as a LessEqual
 91:           ifnb <NotInRange>
 92:             jmp NotInRange
 93:           endif
 94:         elseifnb <NotInRange>       ;; otherwise...
 95:           ja NotInRange             ;; treat it as a Greater
 96:         endif
 97:       else                     ;; upper bound IS specified
 98:         ifnb <NotInRange>      ;; then branch
 99:           jc NotInRange        ;; to specified address if not in range
100:         elseifb <IsInRange>
101:           jbe Done
102:         else
103:           jc Done
104:         endif
105: ;; end of lower bound checking. Test upper bound.
106:         cmp Reg,Upper
107:         ifnb <NotInRange>
108:           ja NotInRange
109:           ifnb <IsInRange>
110:             jmp IsInRange
111:           endif
112:         elseifb <IsInRange>
113:           ja Done
114:           test Reg,0
115:         else
116:           jbe IsInRange
117:         endif
118:         ifb <NotInRange>
119:           Label Done Near
120:         endif
121:       endif
122:       exitm                    ;; exit the macro--nothing else to do
```

```
123:     endif
124:  ;;
125:  ;; If the macro expansion gets to this point, the lower bound
126:  ;; has not been specified. We know that the upper bound has
127:  ;; been specified because we tested for it previously.
128:  ;; Proceed with upper bound checking.
129:  ;;
130:    cmp Reg,Upper                  ;; test upper bound
131:    ifnb <IsInRange>               ;; if IsInRange specified
132:      jae IsInRange                ;; then treat it as a greater equal
133:      ifnb <NotInRange>
134:        jmp NotInRange
135:      endif
136:    elseifnb <NotInRange>          ;; otherwise,
137:      jb NotInRange                ;; treat it as a less than
138:    endif
139:  Endm IsRange
```

Other Considerations

The final version of **IsRange** shown in Listing 5.5 generates much better code than the version we originally developed in Chapter 1. In addition, it is more flexible in that it can generate code to check for several common conditions. However, **IsRange** still generates nonoptimum code when the **Reg** parameter is a memory reference. For instance, this invocation:

```
IsRange <[word ptr PayRate]>,MinPay,MaxPay,GoodPay
```

will check the value at the memory location addressed by **[DS:PayRate]** and branch to the label **GoodPay** if the value is within the bounds of **MinPay** and **MaxPay**. The code generated by this macro invocation would be:

```
;IsRange <[word ptr PayRate],MinPay,MaxPay,GoodPay>
  cmp [word ptr PayRate],MinPay
  jc ??0000
  cmp [word ptr PayRate],MaxPay
  jna GoodPay
??0000:
```

Although this code appears optimum at first glance, it requires 4 byte-sized memory references on an 8088 (2 word-sized memory references on an 8086, 80286, or later processor), and a total of 16 bytes of code.

One of the best optimizations possible is to reduce memory accesses. If we were to load the **PayRate** value into AX and test it from there, we can reduce the number of memory accesses to one and the code size to 13 bytes. How? Consider the following code fragment:

```
mov ax,[PayRate]
IsRange ax,MinPay,MaxPay,GoodPay
```

which will expand to

```
  mov ax,[PayRate]
;IsRange ax,MinPay,MaxPay,GoodPay
  cmp ax,MinPay
  jc ??0000
  cmp ax,MaxPay
  jbe GoodPay
??0000:
```

How much faster is the second version? On my 20-MHz 386SX system, the version that loads AX with the value executes almost 13 percent faster than the version that does direct comparisons of the **[PayRate]** value. On an 8088 system, this difference would be even greater.

So, although **IsRange** *helps* you to produce better code, the final responsibility is yours. Our macros have been designed to help generate code, not to relieve us of the responsibility of thought. The best optimizer is still right between your ears. As with any other language, it's quite possible to generate bad code using our macros, but with a little thought these macros can help you to generate very tight, very fast code in a fraction of the time it would take you to write all of the code by hand.

5.2 Lists of Values and IsIn

As useful as it is, **IsRange** is entirely powerless when it comes to determining whether a register matches a nonsequential list of values. For example, in the **ParseCommandLine** subroutine in the next chapter, we need to determine whether the character in AL is one of the command-line whitespace characters. Traditional assembly language code to perform this test would be written like this:

```
cmp al,' '
jz SkipSpaces              ;skip spaces, tabs, and commas
cmp al,tab
jz SkipSpaces
cmp al,','
jz SkipSpaces
```

Although you may not think anything of writing three sets of **cmp...jz** instructions, imagine having to check a list of 10 characters. Would you want to write *that* list by hand? Is it possible that you could make a mistake while doing it? Yeah, me too.

As with any other repetitive task, it's fairly simple to create a macro, **IsIn**, that, given sufficient information, can generate these instructions for us. Our first implementation of this macro is shown in Listing 5.6.

```
 1:    ; Listing 5.6--IsIn
 2:    ;
 3:    ; IsIn Reg,Values,YesBranch
 4:    ; Branch to YesBranch if the value in Reg matches one
 5:    ; of the items in the list of Values.
 6:    ;
 7:    ; Parameters
 8:    ;   Reg (Required) - Register or memory reference
 9:    ;   Values (Required) - Comma-separated list of values
10:    ;   YesBranch (Optional) - Label to branch to if match found
11:    ;   NoBranch (Optional) - Label to branch to if no match found
12:    ;
13:    Macro IsIn Reg,Values,YesBranch,NoBranch
14:      Local Done
15:      ifb <Reg>
16:        err
17:        Display "<Reg> parameter required in macro IsIn"
18:        exitm
19:      elseifb <Values>
20:        err
21:        Display "<Values> parameter required in macro IsIn"
22:        exitm
23:      endif
24:      irp V,<Values>
25:        cmp Reg,V
26:        ifnb <YesBranch>
27:          jz YesBranch
28:        else
29:          jz Done
30:        endif
31:      endm
32:      ifnb <NoBranch>
33:        jmp NoBranch
34:      endif
35:      ifb <YesBranch>
36:        Label Done Near
37:      endif
38:    Endm IsIn
```

Using the new **IsIn** macro, the 6 lines of code above can be exactly duplicated by using this single macro invocation:

```
IsIn al,<' ',tab,','>,SkipSpaces
```

There are, however, two situations in which this version of **IsIn** does not generate optimum code. Although neither of the situations is very common, they both *can* occur, so it would be best for us to provide for them.

The first example of nonoptimum code appears when both of the branching parameters are blank. For example, if we just wanted to set the Z flag to indicate if the character in AL matched a list of values, we would write the macro invocation as shown:

```
IsIn al,<'/','-'>
```

and the generated code would look like this:

```
  cmp al,'/'
  jz ??0000
  cmp al,'-'
  jz ??0000
??0000:
```

which contains a JZ instruction that really doesn't need to be there.

The second example is similar to the first and occurs when the **YesBranch** parameter is blank and the **NoBranch** parameter is specified. Consider this macro invocation:

```
IsIn <'/','-'>,,DoFileName
```

which generates this code:

```
  cmp al,'/'
  jz ??0000
  cmp al,'-'
  jz ??0000
  jmp DoFileName
??0000:
```

The last two instructions could be changed to a single **jnz DoFileName**.

Considering that the current version of **IsIn** generates good code for my most common uses, I was tempted to leave it as it stands and not worry about the few extra cycles in a code sequence that I don't use very often. But, one day I might just decide to use one of these other invocations and need it to be as fast as possible. So . . .

The problem is that the **irp** loop generates the **jz** instruction automatically—without regard to whether it's working on the last item. This makes sense, considering that **irp** has absolutely no idea of the position in the list of the item that is currently being worked on. But we need to have the **irp** loop *not* generate the **jz** instruction for the last item in the list.

How do we do that? By using a flag variable and generating the **jz** instruction at the *top* of the loop when the counter variable is not 0. The new **IsIn** macro that uses this technique is shown in Listing 5.7. Again, I suggest that you study this macro closely until you understand how it works.

```
1:   ; Listing 5.7--Optimized IsIn Macro
2:   ;
3:   ; IsIn Reg,Values,YesBranch
4:   ; Branch to YesBranch if the value in Reg matches one
5:   ; of the items in the list of Values.
6:   ;
7:   ; Parameters
8:   ;   Reg (Required) - Register or memory reference
9:   ;   Values (Required) - Comma-separated list of values
10:  ;   YesBranch (Optional) - Label to branch to if match found
11:  ;   NoBranch (Optional) - Label to branch to if no match found
12:  ;
13:  Macro IsIn Reg,Values,YesBranch,NoBranch
14:    Local Done,Counter
15:    ifb <Reg>
16:      err
17:      Display "<Reg> parameter required in macro IsIn"
18:      exitm
19:    elseifb <Values>
20:      err
21:      Display "<Values> parameter required in macro IsIn"
22:      exitm
23:    endif
24:    Counter = 0
25:  ;;
26:  ;; Generate the compare and jump instructions.
27:  ;; The first time through the loop, Counter will be 0,
28:  ;; so no branching instruction will be generated.
29:  ;; Subsequent iterations will generate the branching
30:  ;; instruction for the previous comparison.
31:  ;;
32:    irp V,<Values>
33:      if Counter eq 0
34:        Counter = 1
35:      elseifnb <YesBranch>
36:        jz YesBranch
37:      else
38:        jz Done
39:      endif
40:      cmp Reg,V
41:    endm
42:  ;;
43:  ;; All of the comparisons have been generated. Now
```

```
44:    ;; generate code for the final branch, depending on
45:    ;; the values of YesBranch and NoBranch.
46:    ;;
47:    ;; If YesBranch is nonblank, generate a 'jz' to that
48:    ;; label and a 'jmp' to NoBranch if the second branching
49:    ;; parameter is given.
50:    ;;
51:      ifnb <YesBranch>
52:        jz YesBranch
53:        ifnb <NoBranch>
54:          jmp NoBranch
55:        endif
56:    ;;
57:    ;; If YesBranch is not specified, generate a 'jnz' to
58:    ;; NoBranch if the second branching parameter is given.
59:    ;; Because no YesBranch is given, we must generate a label
60:    ;; for the positive matches to branch to.
61:    ;;
62:      else
63:        ifnb <NoBranch>
64:          jnz NoBranch
65:        endif
66:        Label Done Near
67:      endif
68:    Endm IsIn
```

Efficiency Considerations

In addition to testing values in any of the general-purpose registers, it is possible to use **IsIn** to test the contents of a memory location against a list of values. Doing so, however, is not recommended, for the same reasons that I pointed out in the section on **IsRange**.

Even with the optimizations that we made to the last branch instruction, **IsIn** generates a fairly large amount of code—two instructions per item to be checked—and the generated code is not what anybody would term highly efficient. Unfortunately, "test and branch" is not something that the 80x86 series of processors does quickly. The speed of the generated code is highly dependent on the order in which items are checked, so it's a good idea to place the most commonly selected values at the head of the list of items to be checked.

5.3 Generating Processor-Specific Code

As Intel continues to develop its microprocessor line, what used to be a "high-end" computer becomes more affordable. For example, it is now possible to purchase a 16-MHz 80386SX-based computer for less than a similarly equipped 8088-based computer cost only two years ago. Even today, the 80386SX-based

---

Table 5.1. Ideal mode processor directives

Directive	Enables Assembly of
P8086	8086 instructions only
P186	80186 instructions
P286	All 80286 instructions
P286N	Nonprivileged 80286 instructions
P286P	Priviliged 80286 instructions
P386	All 80386 instructions
P386N	Nonprivileged 80386 instructions
P386P	Priviliged 80386 instructions
P486	All 80486 instructions
P486N	Nonprivileged 80486 instructions
P486P	Priviliged 80486 instructions
P287	80287 coprocessor instructions
P387	80387 coprocessor instructions
P8087	8087 coprocessor instructions

---

computers are considered "low-end" business machines, and much software is written that *requires* an 80386 processor; the code won't run on anything less. This trend will undoubtedly continue, but you will frequently be required to write code that will run on an 8088.

Turbo Assembler has directives that enable you to tell it which processor to generate code for. With these directives, you can selectively enable or disable processor-specific instructions. For example, if you're writing a program that will run in 80286 protected mode, the **P286** directive tells the assembler to enable assembly of all 80286 instructions. Without this directive, the assembler will issue an error message whenever it encounters an 80286-specific instruction.

Table 5.1 lists all of the processor directives available in Turbo Assembler Ideal mode.

As an example of generating processor-specific code, consider the **LShift** macro that we developed in Chapter 1. This macro (which I've duplicated in Listing 5.8) generates code to shift the requested register left the number of places specified by the second parameter.

```
1:   ; Listing 5.8--LShift Macro
2:   ;
3:   ; LShift Reg,<Num>
4:   ; Shift the specified register or memory location left the
5:   ; number of bit positions specified by the Num parameter.
6:   ; If Num is not specified, perform a one-bit shift.
7:   ;
8:   ; Parameters
```

```
 9:    ;    Reg (Required) - Register or memory reference
10:    ;    Num (Optional) - Number of bits to shift
11:    ;
12:    ; Returns
13:    ;    Nothing
14:    ;
15:    ; Preserves the contents of all registers except the one
16:    ; specified in the Reg parameter.
17:    ;
18:    Macro LShift Reg,Num
19:      ;;
20:      ;; Check parameters
21:      ;;
22:      ifb <Reg>
23:        err
24:        Display "Register or memory reference must be specified"
25:        exitm
26:      elseifb <Num>
27:        ;;
28:        ;; If Num is blank, generate code
29:        ;; to do only a single shift.
30:        ;;
31:        shl Reg,1
32:      else
33:          ;;
34:          ;; Otherwise, generate code to do the specified number of shifts.
35:          ;;
36:        rept Num
37:          shl Reg,1
38:        endm
39:      endif
40:    Endm LShift
```

LShift, when invoked like this:

```
LShift ax,4
```

will generate the following code:

```
;LShift ax,4
  shl ax,1
  shl ax,1
  shl ax,1
  shl ax,1
```

which is all well and good but for two things. First of all, shifting a register left four times can be accomplished more quickly using this code sequence:

```
mov cl,4
shl ax,cl
```

Secondly, on the 80286 and later processors, a register can be shifted multiple times with a single instruction. For example, on an 80286, you can shift the AX register left four times using this one instruction:

```
shl ax,4
```

Actually, I left one other thing out of the **LShift** macro shown in Listing 5.8. If you invoke the macro with this line:

```
shl ax,cl
```

the assembler will generate an "Illegal use of register" error when it attempts to expand the macro. Fortunately, fixing this little problem was a simple matter of adding an **ifidni <Num>,<cl>** directive and handling this form of the **shl** instruction separately.

The first problem—shifting using the CL register—can be handled with a third macro parameter, **UseCL**, in much the same way that we handled the **UseXlat** parameter in our case-conversion macros. This is a straightforward modification of the **LShift** macro, and I will not discuss it here, although I've implemented it in the new version of **LShift**.

The second item, however, requires a bit of study. How do we determine what instructions to generate? If the **P286** directive is in effect, we can use the 80286-specific form of **shl**, but if we're generating 8088 code, using 80286 instructions will cause an error.

Fortunately, Turbo Assembler provides a numeric equate, **@Cpu**, that returns information about the currently selected processor. The information returned by **@Cpu** is encoded as shown in Table 5.2.

Table 5.2. Encoding of @Cpu information

Bit	Description
0	8086 instructions enabled
1	80186 instructions enabled
2	80286 instructions enabled
3	80386 instructions enabled
4	80486 instructions enabled
7	Privileged instructions enabled (80286, 386, 486)
8	8087 instructions enabled
10	80287 instructions enabled
11	80387 instructions enabled
	The bits not defined here are reserved for future use.

There are two very important things to remember when you use **@Cpu**. First, because the 8086 family is upward compatible, when you enable 80386 instructions using **P386**, all of the processor instructions below it (80286, 80186, and 8086) will be enabled as well. Secondly, **@Cpu** *only provides information about the processor you've selected at assembly time*. **@Cpu** does not tell you what kind of processor your program is running on.

Using **@Cpu**, we can build text equates that enable us to determine which processor is currently selected so that we can generate the most appropriate code. These text equates are shown in Listing 5.9.

```
 1:    ; Listing 5.9--Text equates for testing @Cpu
 2:
 3:    Cpu86    equ <1 and @Cpu>
 4:    Cpu186   equ <2 and @Cpu>
 5:    Cpu286   equ <4 and @Cpu>
 6:    Cpu386   equ <8 and @Cpu>
 7:    Cpu486   equ <10h and @Cpu>
 8:    CpuPriv  equ <80h and @Cpu>
 9:    Cpu87    equ <0100h and @Cpu>
10:    Cpu287   equ <0400h and @Cpu>
11:    Cpu387   equ <0800h and @Cpu>
```

These macros should be added at the top of your MACROS.INC file.

More Assembler Quirks

Chapter 1 discussed the differences between constants defined with the = operator and text equates defined with the **EQU** directive. That discussion pointed out that text equates are evaluated *when they are used*. Unfortunately, there is one exception to this rule.

For some reason, when Turbo Assembler encounters an **EQU** directive in which the first operand is a defined constant or a text macro, the result is a defined constant. For example, in Listing 5.9, the definition for **Cpu86** was originally written like this:

```
Cpu86 equ @Cpu and 1
```

But when the file was assembled, Turbo Assembler assigned a value of 0101H to **Cpu86**. *The assembler created a defined constant instead of a text equate.* The strange thing is that any of the following will cause the assembler to correctly create a text equate:

```
Cpu86 equ 1 and @Cpu
Cpu86 equ <@Cpu and 1>
Cpu86 equ <1 and @Cpu>
```

It appears that TASM always correctly handles equates that are enclosed in angle brackets. Therefore, in order to avoid confusion, I suggest that you always bracket your equates as just shown.

Using the CPU Identification Macros

In order to make the **LShift** macro processor aware, we must add another conditional test that identifies the currently enabled processor and generates appropriate code. The new **LShift** macro shown in Listing 5.10 includes processor checking as well as the new third parameter. This parameter allows the macro to generate more efficient code by using the CL register if requested. Study this macro carefully until you understand it completely.

```
 1:   ; Listing 5.10--New "processor-aware" LShift macro
 2:
 3:   ; LShift Reg,<Num>,<UseCL>
 4:   ; Shift the specified register or memory location left the
 5:   ; number of bit positions specified by the Num parameter.
 6:   ; If Num is not specified, perform a 1-bit shift.
 7:   ;
 8:   ; Parameters
 9:   ;   Reg (Required)--Register or memory reference
10:   ;   Num (Optional)--Number of bits to shift.
11:   ;   UseCL (Optional) - If specified, Num is loaded into CL and
12:   ; a "shl Reg,cl" instruction is used.
13:   ;
14:   ; Returns
15:   ;   Nothing
16:   ;
17:   ; Preserves the contents of all registers except the one
18:   ; specified in the Reg parameter. When UseCL is specified, CL
19:   ; will contain the Num parameter.
20:   ;
21:   Macro LShift Reg,Num,UseCL
22:   ;;
23:   ;; Check parameters
24:   ;;
25:     ifb <Reg>
26:       err
27:       Display "Register or memory reference must be specified"
28:       exitm
29:     elseifidni <Num>,<cl>
30:       shl Reg,cl
31:     elseifnb <UseCL>
32:   ;;
33:   ;; If UseCL is specified, load CL with the Num parameter
34:   ;; and shift using "shl Reg,cl"
35:   ;;
```

```
36:       ifb <Num>
37:         mov cl,1
38:       else
39:         mov cl,Num
40:       endif
41:       shl Reg,cl
42:    elseifb <Num>
43:       ;;
44:       ;; If Num is blank, generate code to do a single shift.
45:       ;;
46:       shl Reg,1
47:    else
48:       if Cpu186
49:         ;;
50:         ;; If 80186 instructions are enabled, use the extended
51:         ;; form of the shift instruction.
52:         ;;
53:         shl Reg,Num
54:       else
55:         ;;
56:         ;; Otherwise, generate code to do the specified number of shifts.
57:         ;;
58:         rept Num
59:            shl Reg,1
60:         endm
61:       endif
62:    endif
63:  Endm LShift
```

Using the new LShift macro, this code fragment:

```
P8086
  LShift ax,4
  LShift ax,4,UseCL
P286
  LShift ax,4
  LShift ax,4,UseCL
```

will generate the following code:

```
;P8086
;  LShift ax,4
  shl ax,1
  shl ax,1
  shl ax,1
  shl ax,1
;  LShift ax,4,UseCL
  mov cl,4
  shl ax,cl
```

```
;P286
;   LShift ax,4
    shl ax,4
;   LShift ax,4,UseCL
    mov cl,4
    shl ax,cl
```

5.4 A Generalized Shift and Rotate Macro

If you study the **LShift** and **RShift** macros presented in Chapter 1, you'll notice that they are almost identical—the only difference being that **LShift** generates **shl** instructions and **RShift** generates **shr** instructions. Once again, we see a case where we could save ourselves quite a bit of typing if we were to create a more general macro, **ShiftRot**, that can be used to define the **LShift** and **RShift** macros. When you consider that there are 8 instructions with the same syntax as **shl** (**rcl**, **rcr**, **rol**, **ror**, **shl**, **shr**, **sal**, and **sar**), you'll quickly see that a "helper" macro of this type would be very useful indeed. Listing 5.11 shows this new **ShiftRot** macro.

```
 1:   ; Listing 5.11--ShiftRot Macro
 2:   ;
 3:   ; ShiftRot Inst,Reg,<Num>,<UseCL>
 4:   ; Perform the specified Instruction on the given Register or memory
 5:   ; location the number of times specified by <Num>. If <Num> isn't
 6:   ; specified, perform a one-bit shift/rotate.
 7:   ;
 8:   ; This macro is not intended to be used in-line, but as a "helper"
 9:   ; macro for the shift and rotate macros.
10:   ;
11:   ; Parameters
12:   ;   Inst (Required) - Instruction to perform
13:   ;   Reg (Required) - Register or memory reference
14:   ;   Num (Optional) - Number of bits to shift.
15:   ;   UseCL (Optional) - If specified, Num is loaded into CL and
16:   ; the "shl <Reg>,cl" form of the instruction is used.
17:   ;
18:   ; Returns
19:   ;   Nothing
20:   ;
21:   ; Preserves the contents of all registers except the one
22:   ; specified in the Reg parameter. When UseCL is specified, CL
23:   ; will contain the Num parameter.
24:   ;
25:   Macro ShiftRot Inst,Reg,Num,UseCL
26:   ;;
27:   ;; Check parameters
28:   ;;
29:     ifb <Inst>
```

```
30:      err
31:      Display "Instruction must be specified"
32:      exitm
33:    elseifb <Reg>
34:      err
35:      Display "Register or memory reference must be specified"
36:      exitm
37:    elseifnb <UseCL>
38:    ;;
39:    ;; If UseCL is specified, load CL with the Num parameter
40:    ;; and shift using the "shl Reg,cl" form.
41:    ;;
42:      ifb <Num>
43:        mov cl,1
44:      else
45:        mov cl,Num
46:      endif
47:      Inst Reg,cl
48:    elseifb <Num>
49:    ;;
50:    ;; If Num is blank, generate code to do a single shift.
51:    ;;
52:      Inst Reg,1
53:    else
54:      if Cpu186
55:      ;;
56:      ;; If 80186 instructions are enabled, use the extended
57:      ;; form of the shift instruction.
58:      ;;
59:        Inst Reg,Num
60:      else
61:      ;;
62:      ;; Otherwise, generate code to do the specified number of shifts.
63:      ;;
64:        rept Num
65:          Inst Reg,1
66:        endm
67:      endif
68:    endif
69:   Endm ShiftRot
```

Using the new **ShiftRot** macro, we could easily proceed to create the eight shift and rotate macros that correspond with the eight shift and rotate instructions that are available on the 8088. Two sample macros of this type are shown in Listing 5.12.

```
1:  ; Listing 5.12--Sample macros that use ShiftRot
2:
3:  Macro LShift Reg,Num,UseCL
```

```
4:      ShiftRot <shl>,<Reg>,<Num>,<UseCL>
5:    Endm LShift
6:
7:    Macro RRotc Reg,Num,UseCL
8:      ShiftRot <rcr>,<Reg>,<Num>,<UseCL>
9:    Endm RRotc
```

I was pretty impressed with myself when I finished **ShiftRot** and the eight related macros. I now had the ability to generate the most efficient shift or rotate code with a single instruction. It wasn't until I actually started using the macros that I noticed the problem. *I couldn't remember the macro names!* I'd been using **shl** for so long that my fingers would start to type it before I realized that I really wanted to use **LShift**. At first I thought it was just a case of resistance to change, but the more I worked with the new macros, the more I began to realize that I had made a mistake—the new macros were harder to use than the old mnemonics. There had to be a better way.

Redefining Assembler Instructions

A little-known feature of the assembler is that you can redefine assembler mnemonics. For example, it's quite legal to use the mnemonic **shl** as a label, as shown here:

```
Proc Something
  or ax,ax
  jnz shl
    ...
    ...
Label shl Near
  shl ax,1
  ret
Endp Something
```

When Turbo Assembler encounters this code, it will issue a warning similar to this:

```
*Warning* TEST.ASM(8) Reserved word used as symbol: SHL
```

but the program will work as expected.

Combined with the ability to write self-redefining macros, the ability to use assembler mnemonics as symbols enables us to write macros that redefine standard assembler mnemonics. We can write a **shl** macro that works just like the **LShift** macro shown in Listing 5.12; the advantage is that all we have to learn is the extended syntax rather than the new macro name.

Writing the macro that performs this bit of trickery is a lot easier than explaining how it works. Listing 5.13 introduces **MakeShiftRot**, a helper macro that handles all of the details for us.

```
 1:    ; Listing 5.13--MakeShiftRot macro
 2:    ;
 3:    ; MakeShiftRot Inst
 4:    ; Helper macro that generates a redefined shift or rotate
 5:    ; macro with extended syntax.
 6:    ; The single parameter is required and must be one of these:
 7:    ; shl, shr, sal, sar, rol, ror, rcl, rcr
 8:    ;
 9:    Macro MakeShiftRot Inst
10:      Macro Inst Reg,Num,UseCL
11:        Purge Inst
12:        ShiftRot Inst,<Reg>,<Num>,<UseCL>
13:        MakeShiftRot Inst
14:      Endm Inst
15:    Endm MakeShiftRot
```

MakeShiftRot doesn't actually generate any executable code, it simply creates a macro that knows how to replicate itself. Let's take a look at how **MakeShiftRot** is used to build and use the **shl** macro.

First, **MakeShiftRot** is invoked to create the new macro, as shown here:

```
MakeShiftRot <shl>
```

The code generated from this invocation is

```
;MakeShiftRot <shl>
Macro shl Reg,Num,UseCL
  Purge shl
  ShiftRot shl,<Reg>,<Num>,<UseCL>
  MakeShiftRot <shl>
Endm shl
```

Now, when the **shl** macro is invoked, it purges itself, invokes **ShiftRot** to generate the requested code, and then invokes **MakeShiftRot** to re-create the **shl** macro. *The macro commits suicide and then re-creates itself.* For example, the code generated by this assembler statement:

```
shl al,4,UseCl
```

would be

```
;   shl al,4,UseCL
  Purge shl
```

```
mov cl,4
shl al,cl
Macro shl Reg,Num,UseCL
   Purge shl
   ShiftRot shl,<Reg>,<Num>,<UseCL>
   MakeShiftRot <shl>
Endm shl
```

Macro **shl** purges itself from the assembler's symbol table so that subsequent uses of **shl** refer to the standard assembler mnemonic. **ShiftRot** is used to generate the proper code, just as it was used in the **LShift** macro in Listing 5.12. Then, **MakeShiftRot** is invoked to regenerate the the **shl** macro.

Using **ShiftRot**, we can redefine all eight of the shift and rotate instructions so that they all accept the extended syntax. These new macros are shown in Listing 5.14.

```
 1:   ; Listing 5.14--Redefining the shift and rotate instructions
 2:
 3:      MakeShiftRot <shl>
 4:      MakeShiftRot <shr>
 5:      MakeShiftRot <sal>
 6:      MakeShiftRot <sar>
 7:      MakeShiftRot <rcl>
 8:      MakeShiftRot <rcr>
 9:      MakeShiftRot <rol>
10:      MakeShiftRot <ror>
```

We now have the best of both worlds: extended-syntax shift and rotate instructions using the standard mnemonics. The only catch is that Turbo Assembler will issue a "Reserved word used as symbol" warning for each mnemonic that we redefine in this way. Fortunately, the message is only a warning, not a fatal error.

Extended Shifts with TASM 3.0

Turbo Assembler 3.0 supports some of the new syntax that we've added to the shift and rotate instructions. For example, when TASM 3.0 encounters this instruction:

```
shl ax,4
```

while 8086 code generation is enabled, the instruction will automatically be converted to four individual **shl ax,1** instructions.

At first glance this new feature of the assembler appears to make our **MakeShiftRot** macro obsolete, but the extended shift instruction does not support the **UseCL** parameter. If you want to use CL for the shift count, you still have to load the CL register before issuing the **shl** instruction.

Furthermore, earlier versions of Turbo Assembler don't support the extended syntax, so **MakeShiftRot** is still a useful tool.

If you have TASM 3.0 and you're going to write code that is specific to that version of the assembler, you might want to replace this processor-checking code in **ShiftRot**:

```
if Cpu186
;;
;; If 80186 instructions are enabled, use the extended
;; form of the shift instruction.
;;
  Inst Reg,Num
else
;;
;; Otherwise, generate code to do the specified number of shifts.
;;
  rept Num
    Inst Reg,1
  endm
endif
```

with this one instruction:

```
Inst Reg,Num
```

5.5 Wrapping Up

As *Zen of Assembly Language* shows, the list of possible code optimizations is much longer than what I could possibly cover in this chapter. We've explored only a handful of representative cases. As with the previous chapters, the point of this chapter is to show you what is possible—how macros can be used to help you generate smaller, faster code.

Macros *can* be used to generate optimized code. As you have seen, creating these macros takes quite a bit of thought and may require some obscure tricks. But the benefits are well worth the effort. Once you have created the macros, you can use them with the assurance that the code you generate will be as good as what you would write by hand.

Macro Library Files

In this chapter, we've only changed a couple of the macros in our macro library. **IsRange** and its related macros have received quite a facelift, we've added **IsIn**, and the **LShift** and **RShift** macros have been replaced with

MakeShiftRot, **ShiftRot**, and the eight redefined assembler mnemonics. As before, I've refrained from listing the entire contents of MACROS.INC and have instead simply shown which of the listings are used to make up this file.

The contents of the new MACROS.INC, then, are

Listing 1-15 Original macro include file
Listing 2-2 Macro **ProgramHeader**
Listing 4-8 Macro **ToUpper** (replaces original)
Listing 4-12 Macro **CaseSwap**
Listing 5.2 Macros **IsUpper**, **IsLower**, **IsDigit**, and **IsAlpha** (replace originals)
Listing 5.4 Macros **IsLess**, **IsLessEqual**, **IsGreaterEqual**, and **IsGreater**
Listing 5.5 Macro **IsRange** (replaces original)
Listing 5.7 Macro **IsIn**
Listing 5.9 CPU identification macros
Listing 5.11 Macro **ShiftRot**
Listing 5.13 Macro **MakeShiftRot**
Listing 5.14 Redefining the shift instructions

In addition, remember to make the modifications to **ToUpper** and **ToLower** that are shown in Figure 5.2.

6

A General-Purpose
Filter Shell

Remember sitting in your high school chemistry class studying chemical equations, electron orbitals, heats of fusion, and other mysterious incantations that somebody decided every well-rounded high school student should be familiar with? I found the classroom theory interesting enough, but *hearing* that a certain mixture of chemicals releases some specific number of kilocalories of heat is nothing like going into the chemistry lab and actually *seeing* what happens when you drop a few ccs of glycerine onto a pile of potassium permanganate.

The last five chapters remind me of my high school chemistry class. We've spent a lot of time developing your understanding of macros, include files, object modules, and other advanced assembly language topics. Although we have seen some interesting demonstrations along the way, there has been nothing quite like the miniature volcano I remember from that chemistry lab experiment. Nothing to say, "*This* is the power of macros."

In this chapter, I intend to change that.

The vast majority of the programs I write, either at home or at work, fall into the broad category known as *filters*. We saw a typical (albeit stripped-down) filter in Chapter 2 when we studied TRAL.ASM. Filter programs typically read an input file, perform some processing, and write an output file. Filters can be as simple as TRAL or as complex as a high-level language compiler. Source code formatters, file search utilities, program listers, and even Turbo Assembler fall into this category.

Every filter program I've ever written can be loosely described by this pseudocode:

```
Initialize
Repeat
  Process a character
Until there are no more characters to process
Deinitialize
Exit Program
```

Granted, there is more to even the simplest filter program than a half-dozen lines of pseudocode, but *all* filter programs fall into this general mold.

The problem is, we spend a large amount of time on things that should be done automatically: parsing the command line, allocating memory, opening files, reading characters, and so on. These tasks are the same for *every* filter program, yet we spend time writing a customized command-line parsing procedure when we should be concentrating on the crux of the problem: the processing routine.

After about the hundredth time I chopped up an existing program to build yet another filter, I sat down to write a set of macros and subroutines that handle virtually all of the common filter code. These new tools that handle the drudgery of building assembly language filter programs freed me to expend my efforts on the processing routines at the heart of my filter programs.

In this chapter, we'll develop macros and subroutines for command-line parsing and buffered file I/O. Finally, we'll build a filter "shell" that serves as a template for quickly building fast, efficient assembly language filter programs.

In the last four chapters we've studied all of the concepts we need in order to implement the macros in this chapter. With all the ground we have to cover, we will be moving along quite a bit faster in this chapter than we have done previously.

Before we begin writing our filter program shell, we need to make a couple of enhancements to our **ExeStart** program initialization macro.

Let's get started!

6.1 Memory Allocation and ExeStart

When I introduced the **ExeStart** macro in Chapter 2, I mentioned that most programs perform much more initialization than simply setting up a single segment register. Right now, that's all **ExeStart** does. It initializes the DS register so that our programs reference the proper data segment. This simple initialization is fine for toy programs like HELLO and TRAL, but *real* programs need a little more preparation before they can do anything useful.

When DOS loads a program for execution, the program is normally given all available memory, the only catch being that the program doesn't know how much memory is available to it. Although it's possible for a program to figure out how much memory is available, it's much easier for the program to determine how much memory it *needs* in order to start up and then release everything else to DOS. The program can then request any additional memory from the DOS memory manager.

With the growing popularity of Microsoft Windows and other multitasking environments that can make use of free memory, it is a good idea for us to write programs that release to DOS any memory that is not required. In an attempt at peaceful coexistence, we'll place the memory-releasing code in the **ExeStart** macro so that all of our programs will be neighborly and use only the amount of memory that they absolutely must have.

Figure 6.1 shows how DOS allocates memory and also shows an exploded view of how one of our programs is laid out in memory. Take a moment to study this figure before moving on to the following discussion.

As the exploded view shows, the program's code segment begins directly after the Program Segment Prefix (PSP) and is followed by the data and stack segments, in that order. The PSP, along with the code, data, and stack segments compose the program's static memory requirements. Any memory beyond the end of the stack is unused and can be released to DOS.

Figure 6.1. DOS memory map and program memory map

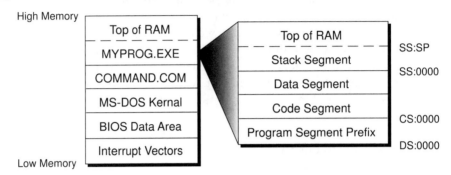

Application programs are loaded into memory after the DOS
and BIOS code, and are given all remaining memory.

A program's static memory requirements, then, can be determined by this formula:

```
Required Memory = PSP + Code + Data + Stack
```

When an .EXE program is loaded, the ES and DS registers are pointing to the PSP. The CS register is of course pointing to the code segment, and SS, as you would expect, points to the stack segment. The segment registers are *always* initialized this way, making it fairly easy for a program to determine its own memory requirements by performing this calculation:

```
Required Memory (in bytes) = 16*(SS - DS) + SP
```

Remember that each memory segment (or paragraph) is 16 bytes long, so to determine the number of bytes contained in a range of paragraphs, we must multiply the number of paragraphs by 16.

The DOS memory allocation routines, however, require that we allocate and release memory in paragraph-sized chunks. In order to provide the DOS routines with a required size in paragraphs, rather than bytes, we'll use this formula:

```
Required Memory (in paragraphs) = (SS - DS) + Round Up(SP / 16)
```

The size of the stack is rounded up to the next whole paragraph so we don't inadvertently chop off part of the stack when we ask DOS to release the memory.

Once a program has determined how much memory it needs, all remaining memory can be released to DOS by calling INT 21h function 4Ah (Modify

Memory Allocation). This function requires ES to hold the address of a previously allocated memory block (in this case, the Program Segment Prefix) and BX to hold the new size of the block, given in paragraphs.

The code that determines the program's memory requirements and releases the rest of the memory to DOS is shown in Listing 6.1.

```
 1:    ; Listing 6.1
 2:    ;
 3:    ; Determine a program's memory requirements and release
 4:    ; all other memory to DOS.
 5:    ;
 6:        mov ax,ss
 7:        mov dx,ds
 8:        sub ax,dx      ;; AX holds required paragraphs
 9:        mov bx,sp
10:        shr bx,1       ;; convert stack size (in bytes) to paragraphs
11:        shr bx,1
12:        shr bx,1
13:        shr bx,1
14:        inc bx         ;; and add 1 paragraph just in case
15:        add bx,ax      ;; add size of rest of program
16:        mov ah,4ah
17:        int 21h        ;; and release all other memory to DOS
```

Before we add this code to our **ExeStart** macro, we need to discuss one other initialization task that makes our programs more efficient and easier to write.

Addressing the Stack with DS

You'll recall from your assembler basics that the BP register indexes memory relative to the SS register, and that the other index registers (BX, DI, and SI) index relative to DS. There are a few exceptions to this rule, the most notable being that DI indexes relative to ES in the context of string instructions.

As a result of this index/segment register mapping, we must specify a segment override whenever we access stack parameters with BX, DI, or SI, or when we access data segment variables with BP. If, however, we make SS and DS the same, any of the index registers can be used to index into either the stack or the data segment.

Because the stack segment always follows the data segment (at least in *our* programs!), making the stack DS-relative is a simple matter of setting SS equal to the data segment address and adding the size of the data segment to the initial stack pointer. Figure 6.2(a) illustrates the default segment register assignments, and Figure 6.2(b) shows the segment registers after the stack has been made relative to DS.

Figure 6.2. Data segment and stack segment register mappings (all numbers shown in hexadecimal)

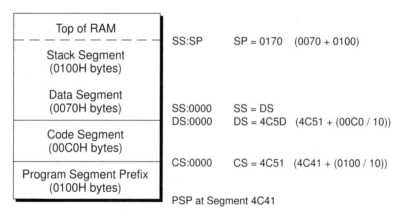

(a) Sample program laid out in memory. The register values are computed based on the location of the PSP and the size of the individual segments.

(b) The sample program after adjusting the stack segment register and the stack pointer. The stack is now addressable as part of the data segment.

Modifying the stack pointer in this manner reduces the maximum data segment size by the size of the stack. Because the stack is contained within the data segment, this technique cannot be used in programs in which the combined size of the stack and static data is more than 64K of memory. Fortunately, assembly language programs of this type are few and far between.

The new **ExeStart** macro shown in Listing 6.2 uses the code from Listing 6.1 to determine a program's memory requirements. Once the remaining memory has been released, **ExeStart** modifies the SS register and moves the stack pointer as required so that the stack can be addressed relative to the data segment.

```
 1:    ; Listing 6.2--New ExeStart macro
 2:    ;
 3:    ; ExeStart--Perform program startup processing:
 4:    ; (1) Release all excess memory.
 5:    ; (2) Set DS to point to default data segment.
 6:    ; (3) Make stack DS-relative.
 7:    ;
 8:    Macro ExeStart
 9:       ;;
10:       ;; Release excess memory.
11:       ;;
12:       mov ax,ss
13:       mov dx,ds
14:       sub ax,dx       ;; AX holds required paragraphs
15:       mov bx,sp
16:       shr bx,4        ;; compute stack size in paragraphs
17:       inc bx          ;; and add 1 paragraph just in case
18:       add bx,ax       ;; add size of rest of program
19:       DosCall 4ah     ;; and release all other memory to DOS
20:       ;;
21:       ;; Set up DS.
22:       ;;
23:       mov dx,DGROUP
24:       mov ds,dx       ;; DS now points to data segment
25:       ;;
26:       ;; Generate code to make stack DS-relative.
27:       ;;
28:       mov bx,ss
29:       sub bx,dx       ;; BX holds size of data segment (in paragraphs)
30:       shl bx,4        ;; converts to bytes
31:       cli             ;; interrupts off to manipulate stack
32:       mov ss,dx       ;; makes SS = DS
33:       add sp,bx       ;; and adds size of data to stack pointer
34:       sti
35:    Endm ExeStart
```

The programs we develop from this point on will assume that **ExeStart** has been used to release memory and modify the stack pointer, so you'll have to replace the current version of **ExeStart** in DOSMACS.INC with the code shown in Listing 6.2.

6.2 Defining the Program Shell

Before we go charging headlong into writing a set of macros and subroutines, it's a good idea to sit down and define what it is that we want the macros and subroutines to do. If we go off half-cocked, we'll end up with an entirely useless set of tools that do nothing well and everything poorly.

In order to keep from confusing myself, I long ago standardized a command-line format for all of my filter programs. Every one of my programs expects a command line in the following format:

```
FILTER [[{-|/}option]...] [<infile> [<outfile>]]
```

The option list consists of switches and/or parameters, each of which is preceded by a dash (-) or slash (/) character. The input and output filenames are optional. If the input filename is not given on the command line, the filter gets its input from **StdIn**. Similarly, if the output filename is not specified, the program sends its output to **StdOut**. In addition, every program supports the **/?** command-line switch that displays information about how to use the program.

For example, one of my filter programs, CASE.ASM, performs case conversations in much the same manner as does TRAL.ASM. This program supports these four options:

/? displays a program help message

/l converts all characters to lowercase

/u converts all characters to uppercase

/x swaps case of all characters

The help message displayed by the **/?** switch consists of a single-line description of the program, the command-line format, a list of the program's options, and any other pertinent information about the program. The help message displayed by CASE is shown in Figure 6.3.

In addition to a standard command-line format and help message, we'd like our filter programs to be as efficient as possible, within reason. "Within reason"

Figure 6.3. Sample filter program help message

```
CASE -- Perform case conversations on text files

Usage: CASE [[{/|-}option]...] [infile [outfile]]

Valid options
  ? - display this help message
  l - convert all characters to lowercase
  u - convert all characters to uppercase
  x - swap case of all characters

Only one of /l, /u, or /x may be specified.
If infile is not specified, STDIN is used.
If outfile is not specified, STDOUT is used.
```

means that we'd like the programs to be fast, but we don't want to expend an extraordinary amount of effort on each filter program that we write.

The ideal filter shell would automatically include those parts that don't change from program to program, leaving us free to concentrate on the few important items that *do* change. For example, every filter program must parse the command line, provide some error detection and reporting, and perform efficient input and output operations.

The only items that change in my filter programs are the program name and description, the specific command-line parameters accepted (and their associated descriptions), and the processing routine that actually performs the work. All the other parts are the same! If we were to construct a system of macros and subroutines that handles the grunt work (option parsing, opening files, initializing memory, and so on), we would be free to spend more time on the filter's processing routine—the part of the program that requires the most attention.

After much study and experimentation, I identified the following as what would be most helpful and time-saving in writing filter programs:

- A program initialization macro
- A macro that simplifies definition of the program name and description
- A macro that simplifies option definition
- A subroutine that parses the command line in accordance with the defined options
- Macros and subroutines that provide efficient character input and output
- A macro and subroutines that provide generalized error reporting
- A macro that generates program exit code

Of this list, we have already written the program initialization macro (**ExeStart**) and the error-reporting routines (**DosErrMsg** macro and ERRMSG.ASM). The most difficult item on the list—parsing the command line—is very dependent on the macros that define the program options, so let's start with option definition.

6.3 Parsing the Command Line

As I pointed out when introducing TRAL.ASM in Chapter 2, most filter programs (indeed, most programs in general) look to the command line for filenames and option switches that modify the program's default behavior.

In itself, parsing the command line is not overly difficult. However, without a standard subroutine to handle all of the mundane details, you're likely to spend entirely too much time writing code that gets filenames and options from the command line. The difficulty lies not in reading characters from the command line but in properly processing the information that is read.

The actual work of parsing the command line and displaying the help message when requested is done by a subroutine called **ParseCommandLine**, which reads the command line and calls the proper parsing routine for each specific option. In order to do this, the program that calls **ParseCommandLine** must provide some information about valid options and filenames.

Data Structures for Command-line Parsing

Look again at Figure 6.3, which shows the help message displayed when CASE.EXE is invoked with this command:

```
case /?
```

Of all the information shown in Figure 6.3, only the program name and description, and the descriptions of the particular options are specific to CASE.ASM. All the other information is common to all filter programs. If we provide just the program-specific information to **ParseCommandLine**, the subroutine is able to properly parse the command line and display the program help message when necessary. Listing 6.3 shows the program and option description information specific to CASE.ASM.

```
 1:   ; Listing 6.3
 2:   ;
 3:   ; Program and option description information for CASE.ASM.
 4:   ;
 5:      DataSeg
 6:
 7:   ; Program name.
 8:      dw ProgramNameLen
 9:   Label ProgramName Byte
10:      db "CASE"
11:   ProgramNameLen = $ - ProgramName
12:
13:   ; Program description.
14:      dw ProgramDescLen
15:   Label ProgramDesc Byte
16:      db "Perform case conversions on text files",cr,lf
17:   ProgramDescLen = $ - ProgramDesc
18:
19:   ; Option 'l' information
20:   Label OptionL Word
21:      dw Offset ProcessOptionL     ; address of processing routine
22:      dw OptlDescLen               ; length of description
23:   Label OptlDesc Byte             ; option description
24:      db "convert all characters to lowercase",cr,lf
25:   OptlDescLen = $ - OptlDesc
```

```
26:
27:    ; Option 'u' description.
28:    Label OptionU Word
29:      dw Offset ProcessOptionu      ; address of processing routine
30:      dw OptuDescLen                ; length of description
31:    Label OptuDesc Byte             ; option description
32:      db "convert all characters to uppercase",cr,lf
33:    OptuDescLen = $ - OptuDesc
34:
35:    ; Option 'x' description
36:    Label OptionX Word
37:      dw Offset ProcessOptionX      ; address of processing routine
38:      dw OptxDescLen                ; length of description
39:    Label OptxDesc Byte             ; option description
40:      db "swap case of all characters",cr,lf
41:      OptxDescLen = $ - OptxDesc
42:
43:    ; Additional usage information
44:      dw UsageInfoLen
45:    Label UsageInfo Byte
46:      db "Only one of /l, /u or /x may be specified",cr,lf
47:    UsageInfoLen = $ - UsageInfo
48:
49:    ; Options pointer table.
50:    Label OptPtrTable Word
51:      dw 0ffffh      ; Option A--not used
52:      dw 0ffffh      ; Option B--not used
53:      dw 0ffffh      ; Option C--not used
54:      dw 0ffffh      ; Option D--not used
55:      dw 0ffffh      ; Option E--not used
56:      dw 0ffffh      ; Option F--not used
57:      dw 0ffffh      ; Option G--not used
58:      dw 0ffffh      ; Option H--not used
59:      dw 0ffffh      ; Option I--not used
60:      dw 0ffffh      ; Option J--not used
61:      dw 0ffffh      ; Option K--not used
62:      dw OptionL
63:      dw 0ffffh      ; Option M--not used
64:      dw 0ffffh      ; Option N--not used
65:      dw 0ffffh      ; Option O--not used
66:      dw 0ffffh      ; Option P--not used
67:      dw 0ffffh      ; Option Q--not used
68:      dw 0ffffh      ; Option R--not used
69:      dw 0ffffh      ; Option S--not used
70:      dw 0ffffh      ; Option T--not used
71:      dw OptionU
72:      dw 0ffffh      ; Option V--not used
73:      dw 0ffffh      ; Option W--not used
```

```
74:        dw OptionX
75:        dw 0ffffh     ; Option Y--not used
76:        dw 0ffffh     ; Option Z--not used
77:
78:    ;
79:    ; Options record structure used by ParseCommandLine.
80:    ;
81:    Label ProgOptions Word
82:        ProgNameAddr   dw ProgramName   ; pointer to program name
83:        ProgDescAddr   dw ProgramDesc   ; pointer to program desc
84:        UsageInfoAddr  dw UsageInfo     ; pointer to usage info
85:        OptTableAddr   dw OptPtrTable   ; pointer to options table
86:        PostProcess    dw ValidateOptions     ; pointer to options
87:                                        ; post-processing routine
88:        InputFilePtr  dw 0              ; pointer to input file name
89:        OutputFilePtr dw 0              ; pointer to output file name
```

Let's take a few moments to study Listing 6.3 in detail.

The program name and description that make up the first line of the help message are simple strings with preceding length words. In the past, we've used the **LenString** macro to define these strings, and that's what we'll use again.

The next two structures are descriptions for each of the options that CASE recognizes. The **/?** option is not defined here. **ParseCommandLine** treats **/?** as a special case and handles it internally. Each of the option descriptions is in this form:

Word	Address of processing routine
Word	Length of option description
String	Option description

For each option, we must define a routine that processes that option. Normally this routine simply sets a flag to indicate that the option has been selected, although much more involved option processing may be necessary. In some cases, you'll want to follow an option character with a parameter such as a number or filename. For example, the MAKE program uses the **-f** option to define the name of a make file. We saw this in Chapter 4 when we used MAKE to assemble our external modules and create MYSTUFF.LIB by entering this command:

```
make -fmystuff
```

The option processing routines used with **ParseCommandLine** can be written to accept command-line parameters in this format.

Following the option definitions is a string that contains additional usage information. This information is normally used to point out option conflicts or other information that is essential to running the program. Because all filters expect the same type of command line, the information about input and output files is not defined here but is provided automatically by **ParseCommandLine** for every program.

OptPtrTable, which follows the additional usage information, contains pointers to the description record of each of the 26 possible options. Those options that are not used have a value of 0ffffh in this table. An attempt to use one of the undefined options will result in an error message. In the case of CASE.ASM, only options **/l**, **/u**, and **/x** are defined.

Finally, a structure containing pointers to all of the option description information is defined. A pointer to this structure is passed as a parameter to **ParseCommandLine**, which uses the information in order to make sense out of the command-line parameters.

The **PostProcess** pointer in the **ProgOptions** structure is a near pointer to a subroutine that performs options validation after the **ParseCommandLine** subroutine has finished reading the command line. This subroutine typically makes sure that any required options have been specified and that there are no conflicts among the selected options. If there are any errors in the selected options, the postprocessing routine returns with the carry flag set and the DX and CX registers containing the address and length, respectively, of an error message. In the case of an error, **ParseCommandLine** will display an error message and terminate the program.

The two filename pointers in the **ProgOptions** structure are initialized to 0 to indicate that the filename has not been found on the command line. When **ParseCommandLine** finds a filename, the subroutine will parse the filename into a data area, then place the address of that data area in the proper memory location (either **InputFilePtr** or **OutputFilePtr**). An attempt to supply more than two filenames on the command line will result in an error.

In addition to the option description data, any program that calls **ParseCommandLine** must also supply subroutines that process each option character. For example, in CASE.ASM, there are three option-processing routines: **ProcessOptionL**, **ProcessOptionU**, and **ProcessOptionX**. Each of these subroutines sets a flag in memory to indicate that the corresponding option flag was found on the command line. A postprocessing routine determines whether there are any conflicts in the selected options.

Although it's true that **ParseCommandLine** is somewhat limited in the types of command lines that it can handle, you'll be surprised at how many programs' command lines fit this format. The consistency provided by a standard command-line format, however, outweighs any small limitation on the types of command lines supported.

Using Macros to Define the Command-line Parameters

As you know, I'm not one to enter all of those data definitions by hand for every filter program that I write. I've developed a small set of macros that makes defining this option data very easy and also eliminates most of the possible errors into the bargain.

The option definition macros are shown in Listing 6.4. Also included are the **OptRec** structure passed to **ParseCommandLine** and a **GetOptions** macro that is used to call **ParseCommandLine** with the required parameters. A description of each of the macros follows the listing.

```
 1:   ; Listing 6.4--Option Definition Macros
 2:   ;
 3:   ; Options record structure used by ParseCommandLine.
 4:   ;
 5:   Struc OptRec
 6:     ProgNameAddr   dw ?    ; pointer to program name
 7:     ProgDescAddr   dw ?    ; pointer to program description
 8:     UsageInfoAddr  dw ?    ; pointer to additional usage info
 9:     OptTableAddr   dw ?    ; pointer to options table
10:     InputFilePtr   dw 0    ; pointer to input file name
11:     OutputFilePtr  dw 0    ; pointer to output file name
12:   Ends OptRec
13:
14:   ; ProgName Name,Desc
15:   ; Define program name and program description strings.
16:   ;
17:   Macro ProgName Name,Desc
18:     dw ProgramNameLen
19:     LenString ProgramName,<Name>
20:     dw ProgramDescLen
21:     LenString ProgramDesc,<Desc,cr,lf>
22:   Endm ProgName
23:
24:   ;
25:   ; Option OptChar,Descrip
26:   ; Define information for one option.
27:   ;
28:   ; The option description structure is
29:   ;
30:   ; Word--Address of processing routine
31:   ; Word--Length of message
32:   ; Text--Text of option description message
33:   ;
34:   Macro Option OptChar,Descrip
35:     Local OptSize
36:     ?Opt&OptChar& = $              ;; make pointer to this option
```

```
37:        dw Offset ProcessOption&OptChar&  ;; address of processing routine
38:        dw Opt&OptChar&DescLen
39:        LenString Opt&OptChar&Desc,<&Descrip&,cr,lf>
40:     Endm Option
41:
42:     ;
43:     ; EndOptions <PPRtn>
44:     ; Build the Options structure and the options pointer table.
45:     ;
46:     ; The optional PPRtn parameter specifies the address of
47:     ; an options post-processing routine that validates the
48:     ; selected program options.
49:     ;
50:     Macro EndOptions PPRtn
51:       Local TempUsage,TempPtr
52:       ;;
53:       ;; Set TempUsage to indicate whether any
54:       ;; additional usage info was defined
55:       ;;
56:       ifdef UsageInfo
57:         TempUsage = UsageInfo
58:       else
59:         TempUsage = 0ffffh
60:       endif
61:
62:       ;; Set TempPtr to indicate whether the postprocessing
63:       ;; routine was specified.
64:       ;;
65:       ifnb <PPRtn>
66:         TempPtr = offset PPRtn
67:       else
68:         TempPtr = 0ffffh
69:       endif
70:       ;;
71:       ;; Construct the Options structure. Define only the first five
72:       ;; fields. Allow the two filename pointers to default to 0.
73:       ;;
74:       ProgOptions OptRec <ProgramName,ProgramDesc,TempUsage,\
75:          OptPtrTable,TempPtr>
76:       ;;
77:       ;; Loop through each of the 26 option characters and place the
78:       ;; address of the processing routine for each valid option in the
79:       ;; jump table. Nonspecified options will be directed to the "bad
80:       ;; option" routine
81:       ;;
82:       Label OptPtrTable Word
83:       irpc Oc,<abcdefghijklmnopqrstuvwxyz>
84:          ifndef ?Opt&&Oc&
```

```
85:          dw 0ffffh
86:        else
87:          dw ?Opt&&Oc&
88:        endif
89:     Endm
90:  Endm EndOptions
91:
92:  ;
93:  ; GetOptions
94:  ; Call ParseCommandLine after setting up parameters.
95:  ;
96:  Macro GetOptions
97:     extrn ParseCommandLine:Proc
98:     mov dx,offset ProgOptions
99:     call ParseCommandLine
100:    Purge GetOptions
101: Endm GetOptions
```

ProgramName accepts two parameters—the program name and program description—and then invokes the **LenString** macro to allocate space for the **ProgName** and **ProgDesc** strings.

The **Option** macro also accepts two parameters—the option letter and a short description of the option. This macro sets a variable to indicate the start of the information for this option. This variable is then used by the **EndOptions** macro to create the options pointer table, in much the same way that the **BuildErrTable** macro in Chapter 3 constructed the error message pointer table. The **Options** macro also allocates space for the option description. The option processing routine is named **ProcessOption*x***, where *x* is replaced by the letter of the option that this routine processes.

Finally, the **EndOptions** macro builds the **OptPtrTable** and the **ProgOptions** structure from the information provided by the **ProgName** and **Option** macros, and by the **PPRtn** parameter.

So, how do we use these macros? Add Listing 6.4 to your DOSMACS.INC file and then enter the beginnings of CASE.ASM from Listing 6.5 into a new file. We'll be able to assemble this program and examine the listing file, but we won't be able to link or execute it until we get the **ParseCommandLine** subroutine working.

```
1:  ; Listing 6.5--Start of CASE.ASM
2:  ;
3:  ; CASE.ASM
4:  ; Will soon be a case-conversion program.
5:  ; Right now it's a testbed for the option description macros.
6:  ;
7:    ideal
8:  include "macros.inc"
```

```
 9:    include "dosmacs.inc"
10:
11:      ProgramHeader Small,0100h
12:
13:      DataSeg
14:    ;
15:    ; Set up the program description and options information.
16:    ;
17:    ProgName "CASE",<"Perform case conversions on text files">
18:
19:    Option l,<"convert all characters to lowercase">
20:    Option u,<"convert all characters to uppercase">
21:    Option x,<"swap case of all characters">
22:
23:      dw UsageInfoLen
24:    LenString UsageInfo, \
25:      <"Only one of /l, /u or /x may be specified",cr,lf>
26:
27:    EndOptions OptPostProcess
28:
29:      CodeSeg
30:
31:    Proc Main
32:      ExeStart            ; initialize program
33:      GetOptions          ; process the command line
34:      call DoFilter       ; do filter processing
35:      mov al,0
36:      adc al,0            ; set return code
37:      DosExitProgram      ; exit program
38:    Endp Main
39:
40:      DataSeg
41:    ;
42:    ; Options flags.
43:    ; If nonzero, the option was selected on the command line.
44:    ;
45:    FlagL db 0
46:    FlagU db 0
47:    FlagX db 0
48:
49:      CodeSeg
50:
51:    ;
52:    ; Process the /l command line option.
53:    ;
54:    Proc ProcessOptionL
55:      mov [FlagL],1
56:      ret
```

```
57:    Endp ProcessOptionL
58:
59:    ;
60:    ; Process the /u command line option.
61:    ;
62:    Proc ProcessOptionU
63:      mov [FlagU],1
64:      ret
65:    Endp ProcessOptionU
66:
67:    ;
68:    ; Process the /x command line option.
69:    ;
70:    Proc ProcessOptionX
71:      mov [FlagX],1
72:      ret
73:    Endp ProcessOptionX
74:
75:    ;
76:    ; Validate the selected options.
77:    ;
78:    Proc OptPostProcess
79:      mov al,[FlagL]          ; determine how many options were selected
80:      add al,[FlagU]
81:      add al,[FlagX]
82:      dec al                  ; if only one option,
83:      jz @@Done               ; everything's OK
84:    BadCmdLine:
85:      LenString OptInfo,<"Must specify one and only one option",cr,lf>
86:      mov dx,offset OptInfo
87:      mov cx,OptInfoLen
88:      stc
89:    @@Done:
90:      ret
91:    Endp OptPostProcess
92:
93:    ;
94:    ; Perform the filter processing.
95:    ; Right now, all it does is display a message indicating
96:    ; that the selected options are okay.
97:    ;
98:    Proc DoFilter
99:      DosDisplayString <<"Valid command line",cr,lf>>
100:     clc                    ; clear error flag
101:     ret
102:    Endp DoFilter
103:
104:    End Main
```

Save Listing 6.5 in a file called CASE.ASM and assemble it by entering this command:

```
tasm /m/l case
```

If you examine the listing file (CASE.LST), you'll see that the data definitions are equivalent to those in Listing 6.3.

With the options data defined, all we need is a subroutine that can read the data structures and parse the options and filenames as required.

Using the Option Data—ParseCommandLine

All the mechanics of parsing the command line (calling the program-specific, option-processing subroutines, and reading the filenames) are handled by the **ParseCommandLine** subroutine. **ParseCommandLine** also displays the program help message when requested by the **/?** command-line switch and provides error reporting when an invalid command line is entered.

PARSEC.ASM, the module that contains **ParseCommandLine** and associated subroutines, is shown in Listing 6.6. In a nutshell, this module reads the command line character by character and calls the processing routine for each option character it finds. In addition, input and output filenames are parsed into a save area, and pointers to the filenames are placed in the **Options** structure. A more detailed description of the module's operation follows the code.

```
 1:    ; Listing 6.6--PARSEC.ASM
 2:    ;
 3:    ; PARSEC.ASM--command-line parsing subroutines.
 4:    ; Use in conjunction with ProgName, Option, EndOptions, and
 5:    ; GetOptions macros from DOSMACS.INC.
 6:    ;
 7:       ideal
 8:       model small
 9: include "macros.inc"
10: include "dosmacs.inc"
11:
12:    ;
13:    ; Process any command-line options and get the input and output
14:    ; filenames. Options are preceded by either - or /.
15:    ;
16:    ; Call with DX pointing to the options data structure. This
17:    ; routine assumes that DS is addressing the default data segment.
18:    ;
19:    ; If this routine returns, the command line was parsed successfully.
20:    ; On error, this routine writes an error message to the STDERR device
21:    ; and exits the program with an error code of 1.
22:    ;
```

```
23:    ; This routine saves DS, BP, SI and DI.
24:    ; All other registers are destroyed.
25:    ;
26:        DataSeg
27:    OptsPointer dw ?   ; pointer to options structure
28:        CodeSeg
29:
30:    Public ParseCommandLine
31:    Proc ParseCommandLine
32:        pushregs <ax,bx,cx,dx,bp,si,di,ds,es> ; save registers
33:        mov [OptsPointer],dx
34:        cld
35:        mov ah,62h
36:        int 21h                     ; get PSP address in BX
37:        mov es,bx
38:    NextArg:
39:        mov si,0081h                ; first character in command line
40:    SkipSpaces:
41:        lods [byte es:si]           ; get next character
42:        IsIn al,<' ',tab,','>,SkipSpaces  ; skip white space
43:        IsIn al,<0,cr>,@@Done       ; if end of line, done
44:        IsIn al,<'-','/'>,DoOption  ; if option character, process option
45:        call DoFileName             ; otherwise, process filename
46:        jbe @@Done                  ; if end of line, done
47:        jmp SkipSpaces              ; else go get next option
48:    ;
49:    DoOption:
50:        lods [byte es:si]           ; get next character
51:        IsIn al,<0,cr>,@@Done       ; check for end of line
52:        mov dl,al                   ; save original character
53:        cmp al,'?'                  ; if option is /?
54:        jz DoUsage                  ; display usage info
55:        mov bx,[OptsPointer]        ; get pointer table address in BX
56:        mov bx,[(OptRec ptr bx).OptTableAddr]
57:        ToLower al                  ; convert option char to lowercase
58:        IsLower al                  ; and make sure it's a-z
59:        jnz @@2                     ; if not a-z, skip
60:    ;
61:    ; Set up to call the processing routine for this particular option.
62:    ;
63:        xor ah,ah                   ; convert character in AL
64:        sub ax,'a'
65:        shl ax,1                    ; to offset in AX
66:        add bx,ax                   ; and add to BX for index into table
67:    @@2:
68:        mov al,dl                   ; restore original option character
69:        mov bx,[bx]                 ; get pointer to routine address
70:        inc bx                      ; if pointer = FFFFh,
```

```
 71:     jz BadOption                    ; it's an invalid option
 72:     call [word bx-1]                ; call the processing routine
 73:     jnbe SkipSpaces                 ; if no error and not end of line
 74:                                     ; get next option
 75:     jz @@Done                       ; if end of line, exit
 76:   ;
 77:   ; Carry set indicates that there was an error in parsing the option.
 78:   ; DX points to the error message and CX holds the message length.
 79:   ;
 80:     call DispNameMessage      ; display program name & error message
 81:     jmp DoUsage               ; and go to usage routine
 82:
 83: @@Done:                        ; no more options
 84:   ;
 85:   ; Done parsing command line. Call postprocessing routine
 86:   ; if it was defined.
 87:   ;
 88:     mov bx,[OptsPointer]           ; pointer table address in BX
 89:     cmp [(OptRec ptr bx).PostProcess],-1 ; if address of PP rtn is...
 90:     jz @@AllDone                        ; ...0ffffh, all done
 91:     call [(OptRec ptr bx).PostProcess] ; otherwise, do postprocessing
 92:     jnc @@AllDone                       ; if carry clear, all okay
 93:   ;
 94:   ; If the options postprocessing routine returns with carry set,
 95:   ; some combination of options was invalid.  DX will contain the
 96:   ; address of an error message and CX will hold the message length.
 97:   ;
 98:     call DispNameMessage          ; display program name & message
 99:     jmp DoUsage                   ; and branch to usage routine
100: @@AllDone:
101:     popregs <es,ds,di,si,bp,dx,cx,bx,ax>  ; restore registers
102:     ret
103:   Endp ParseCommandLine
104:
105:   ;
106:   ; DoFileName
107:   ; Copy a filename parameter from the command line into the
108:   ; data area. This routine assumes that the first filename will
109:   ; be the input filename and the second is the output filename.
110:   ; If more than 2 filenames are entered on the command line,
111:   ; this routine will display a message and exit with an error.
112:   ;
113:     DataSeg
114:   LenString TooManyFiles,<"Too many filenames on command line",cr,lf>
115:   InputFileName  db 64 dup (0)
116:   OutputFileName db 64 dup (0)
117:     CodeSeg
118:
```

```
119:    Proc DoFileName
120:      mov bx,[OptsPointer]              ; BX points to options structure
121:      lea cx,[(OptRec ptr bx).InputFilePtr] ; CX = input filename
122:                                       ; pointer address
123:      mov di,offset InputFileName
124:      cmp [byte di],0                  ; Input filename defined?
125:      jz @@OK                          ; nope, continue
126:      lea cx,[(OptRec ptr bx).OutputFilePtr] ; CX = output filename
127:                                       ; pointer address
128:      mov di,offset OutputFileName
129:      cmp [byte di],0                  ; Output filename defined?
130:      jz @@OK                          ; nope, continue
131:    ;
132:    ; Too many file names on command line.
133:    ; Exit with error message.
134:    ;
135:      mov dx,offset TooManyFiles
136:      mov cx,TooManyFilesLen
137:      call DispNameMessage             ; write program name & error message
138:      jmp DoUsage                      ; and go to usage routine
139:    ;
140:    ; Copy filename from command line into save area.
141:    @@OK:
142:      mov bx,cx                 ; BX now holds filename pointer address
143:      mov [bx],di               ; save start of filename in options struc
144:    @@CharLoop:
145:      ToUpper al                       ; convert filename to uppercase
146:      mov [byte di],al                 ; store character in filename
147:      inc di
148:      lods [byte es:si]                ; and read next char
149:      IsIn al,<0,cr>,@@Done            ; check for end of line
150:      IsIn al,<' ',Tab,','>,,@@CharLoop
151:    @@AlmostDone:
152:      or al,al                         ; clears z and c flags
153:    @@Done:
154:      mov [byte di],0
155:      ret
156:    Endp DoFileName
157:
158:    ;
159:    ; BadOption
160:    ;
161:    ; Display the "Invalid option" message and branch to DoUsage.
162:    ;
163:      DataSeg
164:    LenString InvOptChar,<"Invalid option character (?)",cr,lf>
165:    BadOptChar = $ - 4              ; pointer to '?' in error message
166:      CodeSeg
```

```
167:    Proc BadOption
168:      mov [byte ptr BadOptChar],dl  ; save option character in message
169:      mov dx,offset InvOptChar      ; DX = message address
170:      mov cx,InvOptCharLen          ; CX = message length
171:      call DispNameMessage          ; display the message
172:      jmp DoUsage                   ; and then display usage info
173:    Endp
174:
175:    ;
176:    ; DoUsage
177:    ; Write usage information to STDERR.
178:    ;
179:      DataSeg
180:    LenString Sep,<"--">
181:    LenString CRLF,<cr,lf>
182:    LenString Usage,<cr,lf,"Usage: ">
183:    LenString UseMsg,<" [{/|-}options] [infile [outfile]]",cr,lf, \
184:                      lf,"Valid options",cr,lf>
185:    LenString HelpOpt,<"  ? - displays this help message",cr,lf>
186:    LenString OptOut,<"  ! - ">
187:
188:    Label Use1 Byte
189:      db "If infile is not specified, STDIN is used",cr,lf
190:      db "If outfile is not specified, STDOUT is used",cr,lf
191:      db lf
192:    Use1Len = $ - Use1
193:      CodeSeg
194:
195:    Proc DoUsage
196:      mov si,[OptsPointer]           ; SI = address of options info
197:      mov si,[(OptRec ptr si).ProgDescAddr]
198:      mov dx,si                      ; DX points to program description
199:      mov cx,[si-2]                  ; CX is length
200:      call DispNameMessage           ; write program name & description
201:
202:      DosWriteFile StdErr,UsageLen,<offset Usage>    ; "Usage: "
203:      mov di,[(OptRec ptr si).ProgNameAddr]
204:      DosWriteFile StdErr,[di-2],di                  ; program name
205:      DosWriteFile StdErr,UseMsgLen,<offset UseMsg>  ; command line format
206:    ;
207:    ; Now write each option description to StdErr.
208:    ;
209:      DosWriteFile StdErr,HelpOptLen,<offset HelpOpt> ; help option
210:      mov al,'a'
211:      mov si,[(OptRec ptr si).OptTableAddr]
212:    @@OptLoop:
213:      mov di,[si]                    ; next option address in DI
214:      inc di                         ; see whether this option is used
```

```
215:      jz @@NxtOpt                       ; if not, go to next option
216:      mov [OptOut+2],al                 ; put option character here
217:      push ax                           ; save character
218:      push di                           ; save option address
219:      DosWriteFile StdErr,OptOutLen,<offset OptOut>
220:      pop di
221:      lea dx,[di+3]               ; DX holds address of option description
222:      DosWriteFile StdErr,[di+1]
223:      pop ax                            ; restore character
224:   @@NxtOpt:
225:      inc si                            ; bump to next option address
226:      inc si
227:      inc al                            ; next option character
228:      cmp al,'z'
229:      jbe @@OptLoop
230:   ;
231:   ; Output the other usage information.
232:   ;
233:      DosWriteFile StdErr,CRLFLen,<offset CRLF>       ; newline
234:      mov si,[OptsPointer]
235:      mov di,[(OptRec ptr si).UsageInfoAddr] ; usage message address in DI
236:      inc di                         ; if no additional usage information,
237:      jz @@Around                    ; output final info and exit
238:      lea dx,[di-1]
239:      DosWriteFile StdErr,[di-3]     ; additional usage info
240:   @@Around:
241:      DosWriteFile StdErr,Use1Len,<offset Use1>   ; and final notes
242:      DosExitProgram 1                            ; and exit with error
243:   Endp DoUsage
244:
245:   ;
246:   ; Write program name and error message to StdOut.
247:   ; Message address in DX, message length in CX.
248:   ;
249:      DataSeg
250:   LenString ColonSpace,<": ">
251:      CodeSeg
252:   Proc DispNameMessage
253:      push dx
254:      push cx
255:      DosWriteFile StdErr,CRLFLen,<Offset CRLF>
256:      mov si,[OptsPointer]
257:      mov di,[(OptRec ptr si).ProgNameAddr]
258:      DosWriteFile StdErr,[di-2],di              ; output the filename
259:      DosWriteFile StdErr,ColonSpaceLen,<offset ColonSpace>
260:      pop cx
261:      pop dx
262:      DosWriteFile StdErr                        ; write the error message
263:      ret
```

```
264:    Endp DispNameMessage
265:
266:    End
```

After saving all the registers and storing the address of the options structure passed in DX, **ParseCommandLine** obtains the address of the calling program's Program Segment Prefix using INT 21h function 62h. The command-line buffer occupies the 128 bytes starting at address 0080h in this segment.

The loop starting at the **SkipSpaces** (line 40) label reads each character from the command-line buffer and identifies it as one of the following:

• a white space character (space, tab, or comma)

• an option switch (/ or -)

• an end-of-line character (CR or 0)

• something else

Space characters are ignored, and end-of-line characters cause a branch to the **@@Done** label, where the registers are restored and control returns to the calling program.

When an option switch (/ or -) is encountered, control branches to **DoOption** (line 49). This routine reads the next command-line character and branches to the proper processing routine if the character is one of the valid command-line switches defined by the calling program. If the character is a question mark (?), control passes to the **DoUsage** routine (line 195), which writes the usage information to the StdErr device and terminates the program. If the character is not a valid command-line switch, control passes to **BadOption** (line 167), which displays an error message and then branches to **DoUsage**.

When **DoOption** finds a valid command-line option character, control is passed to the routine in the calling program that processes that option. The option-processing routine can access the command line to read parameters if it obeys the rules set down by **ParseCommandLine**. Once the option-processing routine is finished, it sets the carry and zero flags to indicate status. Carry is set if an error occurred and zero is set if the end of the command line was reached by the option-processing routine. If no error occurred and there are more characters on the command line, we branch back to **SkipSpaces** to pick up the next command-line parameter.

When **ParseCommandLine** identifies a character other than space, end-of-line, or option, it assumes that the character is the beginning of a filename and calls **DoFileName** (line 119), which copies the filename into the proper data area.

DoFileName is a simple-minded subroutine, in that it performs no validation on the filenames that it reads from the command line. As a result, it is possible to have invalid filenames returned by the **ParseCommandLine** subroutine, which will cause a file-open attempt to fail in the calling program.

DoFileName knows that the first file it reads will be the input filename and the second filename it reads will be the output filename. If it encounters more than two filenames, **DoFileName** writes an error message to StdErr and branches to the **DoUsage** subroutine. If no error occurs, **DoFileName** returns to **ParseCommandLine**. If the end of the command line was reached, the zero flag will be set.

BadOption is very simple. It simply displays a message indicating which option switch was invalid and then branches to **DoUsage**.

DoUsage is the most difficult of all the subroutines that make up PARSEC.ASM, and is most responsible for the layout of the options structures. If I had chosen not to include usage information in my standard filter program, the options structure and the **ParseCommandLine** subroutine would have been much simpler.

Briefly, **DoUsage** writes the program name, description, and the standard usage information to StdErr. In addition, it writes the descriptions of each of the option characters defined by the calling program. This last part—writing the option descriptions—is the most involved. If you're interested in exactly how this is accomplished, I suggest that you study the **DoUsage** routine very closely.

In order to use **ParseCommandLine**, create a new file called PARSEC.ASM and enter the code from Listing 6.6. Because we'll use **ParseCommandLine** in many of our programs, we'll add the PARSEC module to our standard library, MYSTUFF.LIB. To accomplish this, modify MYSTUFF.MAK so that it reads:

```
# MSTUFF.MAK -- build library MYSTUFF.LIB
#
.asm.obj:
  tasm /m $*
  tlib mystuff -+$*
mystuff.lib: lowertbl.obj yesno.obj uppertbl.obj swaptbl.obj \
            errmsg.obj parsec.obj
```

and then rebuild the library by entering this command:

```
make -fmystuff
```

Assuming that there were no errors in the construction of the library, module PARSEC is now contained in MYSTUFF.LIB and we can link it with our test program.

Using ParseCommandLine

CASE.ASM (Listing 6.5) uses the options description macros and calls the **ParseCommandLine** subroutine. If you haven't built CASE.ASM from Listing 6.5, do so now. After you've saved the file, assemble CASE.ASM and build the executable CASE.EXE by entering the following commands:

```
tasm /m case
tlink case
```

If you got everything right, you should have a new file on disk called
CASE.EXE, which we can now use to test our new **ParseCommandLine**
subroutine.

First, let's see whether we got the **/?** option correct. Enter this command:

```
case /?
```

at the DOS prompt and verify that the information displayed is the same as
shown in Figure 6.3.

Try CASE with several different command lines to see how it works. Any
invalid command line should result in an error message and then the usage
information display. A valid command line will cause CASE to display "Valid
command line". Some sample command lines and their expected results are
shown:

```
case                    ;invalid (no option specified)
case /?                 ;valid
case /x infile outfile  ;valid
case -l infile          ;valid (output will go to StdOut)
case -u >outfile        ;valid (input from StdIn, output to outfile)
case /u x1 x2 x3        ;invalid (too many filenames)
case /x /u              ;invalid (only one option may be used)
```

ParseCommandLine is by no means the most generalized command-line
parsing routine that we could write. A truly general parsing subroutine, however, would require much more code than we have space for here.

Even with its restrictions, **ParseCommandLine** provides a flexible standard command-line format that can be easily used by any program that must
obtain information from the DOS command line. Using the **ProgName**, **Option**, **EndOptions**, and **GetOptions** macros in conjunction with
ParseCommandLine makes defining and using command-line options much
easier than if we were to write a customized command-line parser for each
program.

6.4 Buffered File I/O

I pointed out in Chapter 2 that TRAL.ASM (the program that converted its
source to lowercase) was slow because we used single-character file I/O in
order to keep the program simple. Granted, the program *was* simple, but about
as quick as a snake crawling out of a refrigerator. If we want people to use the
programs we create, those programs not only have to work but work quickly.

The easiest way to speed up our filter programs is to remove the I/O bottleneck by adding buffered file operations to our repertoire of tricks.

Conceptual Overview

Single-character I/O is slow because each time the program needs to read or write a character, it must set up registers and call DOS through INT 21h. DOS itself spends a considerable amount of time just figuring out what service was requested and how to process it, and then spends even *more* time extracting a single character from (or placing a single character in) the small buffer that it keeps for each open file. All of this DOS processing takes lots and lots of time.

In order to cut down on the number of calls we make to the DOS Read function, we allocate a large memory buffer and then have DOS read enough characters from the file to fill this buffer. Characters are extracted from the buffer by our program, which we can ensure uses the fastest possible code. DOS is accessed only infrequently—only when we've exhausted the characters in the buffer. By reducing the number of DOS accesses (and the corresponding overhead), we can dramatically improve the performance of our filter programs.

The algorithms for implementing buffered input and output are very simple, as shown by the pseudocode in Figure 6.4. The only tricks to these algorithms lie in detecting and correctly processing the "read buffer empty" and "write buffer full" conditions. As you will shortly see, even those parts of the code are very straightforward.

Figure 6.4. Pseudocode for buffered I/O routines

```
; Pseudocode for buffered input.
;
While not end of file
  If at end of buffer
    Read from file into buffer
  End If
  Read character from buffer
End While

; Pseudocode for buffered output.
;
While there are characters to output
  Put a character in buffer
  If Buffer is full
    Write Buffer to file
  End If
End While
Write Final Partial Buffer
```

As with most projects I've worked on, the greatest difficulty in implementing a general buffered I/O package lies in designing the programming interface. So, before we get started on the code that actually reads and writes characters (and handles the buffers), let's take a look at how we're going to initialize and use the files.

Variables for Buffered I/O

In order to implement buffered input and output, we've got to keep track of some information about the file we're accessing. We need to know the name of the file, the size and location of the buffer, and the address of the next character to be read from (or written to) the buffer. We also need to save the file handle returned by the DOS open file function. One other item, the number of characters in the buffer, is only required for input files. The **FileDef** structure that contains all of this information is shown in Listing 6.7.

```
 1:   ; Listing 6.7--File definition structure
 2:   ;
 3:   Struc FileDef
 4:     BuffSize dw ?          ; file buffer size
 5:     FNamePtr dw 0          ; pointer to filename string
 6:     Handle   dw 0          ; file handle
 7:     BuffSeg  dw 0          ; buffer starting segment
 8:     BuffPtr  dw 0          ; current position in buffer
 9:     NChars   dw 0          ; number of characters in buffer
10:                           ; (input files only)
11:   Ends FileDef
```

Of course, before we can use any of the information in the **FileDef** structure, we need to open the file, save the returned file handle, allocate space for the buffer, and initialize the other variables. The algorithm for initializing a file is shown in the pseudocode below.

```
; Initializing a file for buffered operations.
;
FileDef.BufferSize = Size of Buffer
FileDef.FNamePtr = Pointer to File Name
Allocate memory for buffer
FileDef.BuffSeg = Segment of allocated memory block
FileDef.BuffPtr = 0
Open file with proper Open Mode and Share Mode.
FileDef.Handle = handle returned from open
```

This initialization is the same for every file, be it input or output, regardless of the buffer size. As you've probably guessed, I've created a macro, **InitFile**

(Listing 6.8) that performs all of the initialization steps provided we give it
sufficient information.

```
 1:    ; Listing 6.8--InitFile
 2:    ;
 3:    ; InitFile LblName,FNamePtr,BuffSize,OpenMode,ShareMode,<ErrExit>
 4:    ;
 5:    ; Initialize a file for buffered operations.
 6:    ;   Allocates a FileDef structure in the data segment.
 7:    ;   Allocates memory for the buffer.
 8:    ;   Opens the file.
 9:    ;   Initializes all FileDef variables.
10:    ;
11:    Macro InitFile LblName,FName,BuffSize,OpenMode,ShareMode,ErrExit
12:      Local YesNo,Done,DoFile
13:
14:      DataSeg
15:      ;; Define the file in the data segment.
16:      LblName FileDef <BuffSize>
17:
18:      CodeSeg
19:      ;;
20:      ;; It is necessary to use AX as an intermediate variable here
21:      ;; in order to handle all possible FName parameters, because
22:      ;; SymType and WhatType are not able to correctly identify
23:      ;; all symbol types.
24:      ;;
25:      ifdifi <FName>,<AX>
26:        push ax
27:        mov ax,FName                ;; get filename pointer in AX
28:      endif
29:      mov [&LblName&.FNamePtr],ax   ;; and save in FileDef structure
30:      ifdifi <FName>,<AX>
31:        pop ax
32:      endif
33:      ;;
34:      ;; Compute buffer size in paragraphs.
35:      ;;
36:      BuffRem = BuffSize and 0fh
37:      BuffSizeAlloc = BuffSize shr 4
38:      if (BuffRem ne 0)
39:        BuffSizeAlloc = BuffSizeAlloc + 1
40:      endif
41:      mov bx,BuffSizeAlloc          ;; BX = # of paragraphs requested
42:      DosCall 48h                   ;; get the memory from DOS
43:      ;;
44:      ;; Generate code to branch on error. If an error occurs,
45:      ;; BX will hold the number of paragraphs available and
```

```
46:    ;; AX will contain the standard DOS error code.
47:    ;;
48:    ifnb <ErrExit>
49:      jc ErrExit
50:    else
51:      jc Done
52:    endif
53:    mov [&LblName&.BuffSeg],ax      ;; save buffer segment
54:    ;;
55:    ;; Open file.
56:    ;; If FnamePtr is 0, use StdIn or StdOut, depending
57:    ;; on value of OpenMode.
58:    ;;
59:    cmp [&LblName&.FNamePtr],0      ;; if filename specified
60:    jnz DoFile                      ;; open the file
61:    ;;
62:    ;; Otherwise, use the standard input or output handle.
63:    ;;
64:    if OpenMode eq omRead
65:      mov [&LblName&.Handle],StdIn
66:    else
67:      mov [&LblName&.Handle],StdOut
68:    endif
69:    jmp Done
70:  DoFile:
71:    DosOpenFile [&LblName&.FNamePtr],<OpenMode>,<ShareMode>, \
72:                [&LblName&.Handle],ErrExit
73:  Done:
74:    Endm InitFile
```

If the **FName** parameter is 0, **InitFile** determines which of the standard file handles (**StdIn** or **StdOut**) to use, depending on the open mode parameter. This flexibility is necessary because we may want a filter program to read from **StdIn** or write to **StdOut**.

InitFile handles memory allocation, opening the file, and initializing all **FileDef** variables. In addition, if an error occurs during initialization, **InitFile** will branch to a user-specified address for further action. Using this macro in our programs is very simple, as illustrated by the code fragment from CASE.ASM shown in Listing 6.9.

```
1:  ; Listing 6.9--Using InitFile
2:  ;
3:  ; Code fragment from CASE.ASM illustrating the use
4:  ; of macro InitFile.
5:
6:  ;
7:  ; Program header and data definitions above.
8:  ;
```

```
 9:    Proc Main
10:      ExeStart
11:      GetOptions
12:      ;
13:      ; Initialize the input and output files.
14:      ;
15:      InitFile Infile,[ProgOptions.InputFilePtr],16384,omRead,\
16:            smCompat,DoError
17:      InitFile OutFile,[ProgOptions.OutputFilePtr],16384,omCreate,\
18:            faNormal,DoError
19:      call DoFilter
```

If we were to modify CASE.ASM so that it includes the code in Listing 6.9, the code generated for the first **InitFile** macro invocation would be that shown in Listing 6.10. (I've added some comments and reformatted the listing file in order to make it more readable.) The code for the second **InitFile** invocation would be similar. You should study this code until you understand exactly how **InitFile** works.

```
 1:    ; Listing 6.10--Code generated by InitFile invocation
 2:
 3:      ; Initialize the input and output files.
 4:      ;
 5:      InitFile Infile,[ProgOptions.InputFilePtr],16384,\
 6:            omRead,smCompat,DoError
 7:
 8:      DataSeg
 9:      Infile FileDef <16384>   ; define FileDef structure for input file
10:
11:      CodeSeg
12:      ;
13:      ; Save FName parameter in the FileDef structure.
14:      ;
15:      push ax
16:      mov ax,[ProgOptions.InputFilePtr]
17:      mov [Infile.FNamePtr],ax
18:      pop ax
19:      ;
20:      ; Compute buffer size in paragraphs and allocate memory.
21:      ;
22:      BuffRem = 16384 and 0fh       ; BuffRem = 0
23:      BuffSizeAlloc = 16384 shr 4   ; BuffSizeAlloc = 0400h
24:      mov bx,BuffSizeAlloc
25:      ; DosCall 48h
26:      mov ah,48h
27:      int 21h
28:      jc DoError                    ; branch if error
29:      mov [Infile.BuffSeg],ax       ; save buffer starting segment
```

```
30:       cmp [Infile.FNamePtr],0      ; if the input filename was given
31:                                     ; on the command line
32:       jnz ??000B                    ; branch to file opening routine
33:       mov [Infile.Handle],StdIn     ; otherwise, use StdIn
34:       jmp ??000A                    ; and branch to end of routine
35:       ;
36:       ; Need to open a file for input.
37:       ;
38:    ??000B:
39:       ; DosOpenFile [Infile.FNamePtr],<omRead>,<smCompat>,\
40:       ;            [Infile.Handle],DoError
41:       mov dx,[Infile.FNamePtr]
42:       mov al,omRead+smCompat
43:       DosCall 3Dh
44:       mov ah,3Dh
45:       int 21h
46:       jc DoError
47:       mov [Infile.Handle],ax
48:    ??000A:
49:       ;
50:       ; End of input file initialization.
```

InitFile is yet another excellent illustration of the power that macros provide and why I make extensive use of macros in my everyday programming. Without **InitFile**, I'd have to write those 50 lines of code by hand every time I needed to open a file in one of my programs. The single-line **InitFile** invocation

• Is much easier to type

• Is self-documenting

• Reduces the chance for errors

• Concentrates on *what* rather than *how*

Believe it or not, we're almost ready to put our new buffered I/O routines to the test. The hard part—initializing the files—is out of the way. All we have to do now is create the macros and subroutines that access the files.

Implementing Buffered Input

The algorithm for buffered input, as you recall from Figure 6.4, can be described by this pseudocode:

```
; Pseudocode for buffered input.
;
While not end of file
  If at end of buffer
    Read from file into buffer
  End If
```

```
    Read character from buffer
End While
```

If we assume that the input file has been defined and opened using the **InitFile** macro, the code that extracts a character from the input buffer can be enclosed in a macro called **GetCh** as shown in Listing 6.11.

```
 1:    ; Listing 6.11--GetCh macro
 2:    ;
 3:    ; GetCh--Read a character from an input buffer.
 4:    ;
 5:    Macro GetCh LblName
 6:       Local Around,Done
 7:       Extrn ReadBuffer:Proc
 8:       mov es,[&LblName&.BuffSeg]      ;; ES = file buffer segment
 9:       push si
10:       mov si,[&LblName&.BuffPtr]      ;; address of next character in SI
11:       cmp si,[&LblName&.NChars]       ;; check for end of buffer
12:       jnz Around                      ;; if not end of buffer, continue
13:       push bp                         ;; otherwise, refill the buffer
14:       mov bp,offset &LblName&         ;; BP = address of FileDef structure
15:       call ReadBuffer                 ;; fill buffer from file
16:       pop bp
17:       jbe Done                        ;; if error (Carry set),
18:                                       ;; or end of file (Z set)
19:                                       ;; branch around
20:    Around:
21:       mov al,[es:si]                  ;; get character in AL
22:       inc si                          ;; bump pointer
23:       mov [&LblName&.BuffPtr],si      ;; and save it
24:    Done:
25:       pop si
26:    Endm GetCh
```

If you study Listing 6.11 closely, you'll notice that I'm especially careful to save the SI and BP registers, but ES is guaranteed to be destroyed whenever this code is executed. Let me explain why.

As you know, the 8086 has only four segment registers. Of these registers, CS and SS are dedicated to specific tasks and are therefore unavailable for general-purpose usage. Of the remaining two, the DS register is normally used to access global data, leaving only ES to point to "other things"—in this case, the input and output buffers. Because ES is the only available register, we're going to have to reload it each time we read or write, so there's no point in saving it beforehand. If, at some point, we need to depend on the value of ES, we can hand-code a PUSH before and a POP after the input routine.

Speaking of dedicating registers, many simple filter programs can afford to dedicate the SI register to the input buffer and the DI register to the output buffer. Doing so will eliminate the need to reload the index register each time a character is read or written. As you will see, making allowance within the macro for this special case is really very easy.

The final version of **GetCh**, shown in Listing 6.12, accepts four parameters, rather than the single parameter accepted by the version in Listing 6.11. In addition to the **LblName** parameter that tells which file is being accessed, the new version of **GetCh** in Listing 6.12 adds the following:

• **EofJmp**, the address to branch to when the input file is exhausted

• **ErrJmp**, the address to branch to if an error occurs

• **LoadSi**, a flag variable that instructs the macro to generate code that saves and restores SI if the register can't be dedicated to reading the input buffer

```
 1:    ; Listing 6.12--GetCh macro
 2:    ;
 3:    ; GetCh LblName,<EofJmp>,<ErrJmp>,<LoadSi>
 4:    ; Read character from input buffer into AL.
 5:    ;
 6:    ; On exit, Carry = 1 if error
 7:    ;          Zero  = 1 if end-of-file
 8:    ;
 9:    ; On error, AX will hold the DOS error code.
10:    ;
11:    ; If LoadSi is specified, this macro preserves all registers
12:    ; except AL, ES and the flags.
13:    ; If LoadSi is not given, the SI register is assumed to
14:    ; be dedicated to indexing the input buffer and should
15:    ; not be used for any other purpose in the program.
16:    ;
17:    Macro GetCh LblName,EofJmp,ErrJmp,LoadSi
18:      Local Around,Done
19:      extrn ReadBuffer:Proc
20:      mov es,[&LblName&.BuffSeg]     ;; ES = buffer segment
21:      ;;
22:      ;; If SI not dedicated to buffer, we must save it
23:      ;; and load the buffer pointer from the FileDef structure.
24:      ;;
25:      ifnb <LoadSi>
26:        push si
27:        mov si,[&LblName&.BuffPtr]
28:      endif
29:      cmp si,[&LblName&.NChars]      ;; check for end of buffer
30:      jnz Around                     ;; branch if not end of buffer
31:      ;;
32:      ;; We've read the last character from the buffer.
33:      ;; Call ReadBuffer to refill the buffer.
34:      ;;
```

```
35:        push bp
36:        mov bp,offset LblName        ;; BP points to FileDef structure
37:        call ReadBuffer              ;; and ReadBuffer fills the buffer
38:        pop bp
39:        ;;
40:        ;; Generate branch to error or end-of-file routine if required.
41:        ;;
42:        ifb <ErrJmp>
43:          ifb <EofJmp>
44:            jbe Done
45:          else
46:            jc Done
47:            jz EofJmp
48:          endif
49:        else
50:          jc ErrJmp
51:          ifb <EofJmp>
52:            jz Done
53:          else
54:            jz EofJmp
55:          endif
56:        endif
57:        ;;
58:        ;; If no errors occurred, we end up here.
59:        ;;
60:        Around:
61:          mov al,[es:si]             ;; get character from buffer into AL
62:          inc si                     ;; and bump buffer pointer
63:        Done:
64:          ;;
65:          ;; If SI not dedicated to buffer,
66:          ;; save buffer pointer and restore SI.
67:          ;;
68:          ifnb <LoadSi>
69:            mov [&LblName&.BuffPtr],si
70:            pop si
71:          endif
72:        Endm GetCh
```

Notice that if you do not specify the **LoadSi** parameter, **GetCh** assumes that SI already points to the next character to be read from the input file. In addition, the **BuffPtr** variable is not updated after each read, so you must be sure to update it if you use SI for something other than indexing the input buffer.

When the code generated by **GetCh** discovers that it has read the last character in the input buffer, it places the address of the input file's **FileDef** structure in BP and calls **ReadBuffer** to refill the input buffer from the input file. If **ReadBuffer** returns with the Z flag set, there are no more characters available in the input file. If the Carry flag is set on return, then **ReadBuffer** encountered an error in attempting to read from the input file. In case of end-of-file or error, **GetCh** branches to the user-defined error-handling routine.

If no errors occur in refilling the input buffer, **ReadBuffer** updates the **FileDef** structure and returns with SI pointing to the first available character in the input buffer.

Macro **GetCh**, then, defines how we want the **ReadBuffer** subroutine to interact with the outside world. With **GetCh** providing the blueprint, we can easily implement the **ReadBuffer** subroutine shown in Listing 6.13.

```
 1:   ; Listing 6.13--ReadBuffer Subroutine
 2:   ;
 3:   ; ReadBuffer--Read a buffer full from a file.
 4:   ; BP points to a record of type FileDef.
 5:   ;
 6:   ; Returns:
 7:   ;    Z flag set if end-of-file
 8:   ;    Carry flag set if error and AX contains error code
 9:   ;    Z and C cleared if successful
10:   ;
11:   ; On successful completion, SI will point to the beginning of
12:   ; the input buffer and [(FileDef ptr bp).NChars] is updated to
13:   ; reflect the number of characters actually read from the file.
14:   ;
15:   ; If no errors occur, all registers except SI and the flags are saved.
16:   ;
17:   Public ReadBuffer
18:   Proc ReadBuffer
19:     PushRegs <ax,bx,cx,dx,ds>
20:     mov cx,[(FileDef ptr bp).BuffSize]  ; CX = # of characters to read
21:     mov bx,[(FileDef ptr bp).Handle]    ; BX = file handle
22:     xor si,si                           ; SI = buffer start
23:     mov [(FileDef ptr bp).BuffPtr],si   ; save at BuffPtr
24:     mov ds,[(FileDef ptr bp).BuffSeg]   ; DS = buffer segment
25:     DosReadFile ,,0,,@@ReadErr
26:     mov [(FileDef ptr bp).NChars],ax    ; store # bytes read
27:     PopRegs <ds,dx,cx,bx,ax>
28:     ret
29:   @@ReadErr:                            ; read error routine
30:     PopRegs <ds,dx,cx,bx>               ; restore these 4
31:     ret 2                               ; AX is set by DosReadFile
32:   Endp ReadBuffer
```

Before we try to use the new **GetCh** macro in our programs, let's take a look at the other half of the equation: buffered output with **PutCh**.

Implementing Buffered Output

The algorithm for buffered output, as you saw in Figure 6.4, is quite similar to the buffered input algorithm. I've duplicated the buffered output algorithm from Figure 6.4.

```
; Pseudocode for buffered output
;
While there are characters to output
  Put a character in buffer
  If Buffer is full
    Write Buffer to file
  End If
End While
Write Final Partial Buffer
```

The only significant difference between the input and output algorithms is that the output algorithm must explicitly test for and properly handle the "partial buffer" condition, which will occur at the end of a program. As a result, implementing buffered output requires two macros: **PutCh**, which places a character in the buffer and calls the **WriteBuffer** subroutine when the buffer fills; and **FinalWrite**, which writes the final partial buffer. These two macros are shown in Listing 6.14.

```
 1:   ; Listing 6.14--PutCh and FinalWrite macros
 2:   ;
 3:   ; PutCh LblName,<ErrJmp>,<LoadDi>
 4:   ; Write character from AL to output buffer.
 5:   ;
 6:   ; On exit, Carry = 1 if error
 7:   ;
 8:   ; On error, AX will hold the DOS error code.
 9:   ;
10:   ; If LoadDi is specified, this macro preserves all registers
11:   ; except ES and the flags.
12:   ;
13:   ; If LoadDi is not given, the DI register is assumed to
14:   ; be dedicated to indexing the input buffer and should
15:   ; not be used for any other purpose in the program.
16:   ;
17:   Macro PutCh LblName,ErrJmp,LoadDi
18:     Local Around,Done
19:     extrn WriteBuffer:Proc
20:     mov es,[&LblName&.BuffSeg]     ;; ES = buffer segment
21:     ;;
22:     ;; If DI is not dedicated to the output buffer, then
23:     ;; save DI and load the buffer pointer.
```

```
24:        ;;
25:        ifnb <LoadDi>
26:          push di
27:          mov di,[&LblName&.BuffPtr]
28:        endif
29:        stosb                    ;; put character in buffer and bump pointer
30:        cmp di,[&LblName&.BuffSize]    ;; check for full buffer
31:        jnz Around                ;; if not full, continue
32:        ;;
33:        ;; We've filled the buffer.
34:        ;; Call WriteBuffer to empty buffer to file.
35:        ;;
36:        mov [&LblName&.BuffPtr],di    ;; store buffer pointer
37:        push bp
38:        mov bp,offset LblName        ;; BP = FileDef structure
39:        call WriteBuffer            ;; WriteBuffer does the output
40:        pop bp
41:        ;;
42:        ;; Generate the proper error branch.
43:        ;;
44:        ifb <ErrJmp>
45:          jc Done
46:        else
47:          jc ErrJmp
48:        endif
49:      ;;
50:      ;; If no errors occurred, we'll end up here.
51:      ;;
52:      Around:
53:        ;;
54:        ;; If DI not dedicated to the output buffer,
55:        ;; save buffer pointer and restore DI.
56:        ;;
57:        ifnb <LoadDi>
58:          mov [&LblName&.BuffPtr],di
59:          pop di
60:        endif
61:      Done:
62:      Endm PutCh
63:
64:      ;
65:      ; FinalWrite LblName,<StoreDi>
66:      ;
67:      ; Write the last buffer to the output file.
68:      ; If StoreDi is nonblank, store DI to [FileDef.BuffPtr]
69:      ;
70:      ; Returns:
71:      ;   Carry flag set if error.  AX will hold DOS error code.
```

```
72:    ;
73:    ; On success, the carry flag will be cleared and DI will
74:    ; point to the beginning of the output buffer.
75:    ;
76:    ; This macro saves all registers except DI and Flags.
77:    ;
78:    Macro FinalWrite LblName,StoreDi
79:      Local Around
80:      ;;
81:      ;; See whether buffer is empty.
82:      ;;
83:      ifnb <StoreDi>
84:        mov [&LblName&.BuffPtr],di
85:        or di,di
86:      else
87:        cmp [&LblName&.BuffPtr],0
88:      endif
89:      jz Around                       ;; if buffer not empty
90:      push bp
91:      mov bp,offset LblName            ;; setup
92:      call WriteBuffer                 ;; and write the buffer
93:      pop bp
94:    Around:
95:    Endm FinalWrite
```

You'll notice that **PutCh** accepts only three parameters: the name of the file being accessed, an address to branch to on error, and **LoadDi**, a flag that works in much the same way as the **LoadSi** flag accepted by macro **GetCh**. If **LoadDi** is blank, the macro assumes that DI has been dedicated to indexing the output buffer, and the register will not be saved by **PutCh**.

There aren't any surprises in the code for **WriteBuffer**, either. As you can see in Listing 6.15, **WriteBuffer** is almost a carbon copy of **ReadBuffer**.

```
1:    ; Listing 6.15--WriteBuffer Subroutine
2:    ;
3:    ; WriteBuffer--Write buffer to output file.
4:    ; BP points to a record of type FileDef.
5:    ;
6:    ; On exit, DI will point to the beginning of the output buffer.
7:    ; On error, the carry flag will be set and AX will hold
8:    ; the DOS error code.
9:    ;
10:   Public WriteBuffer
11:   Proc WriteBuffer
12:     PushRegs <ax,bx,cx,dx,ds>
13:     mov bx,[(FileDef ptr bp).Handle]     ; BX = file handle
14:     mov cx,[(FileDef ptr bp).BuffPtr]    ; CX = # bytes to write
```

```
15:    xor di,di                              ; DI = buffer pointer
16:    mov [(FileDef ptr bp).BuffPtr],di      ; save at BuffPtr
17:    mov ds,[(FileDef ptr bp).BuffSeg]      ; DS = buffer segment
18:    DosWriteFile ,,0,@@WriteErr,<<"Write error",cr,lf>>, \
19:                              <<"Disk full",cr,lf>>
20:    PopRegs <ds,dx,cx,bx,ax>
21:    ret
22:  @@WriteErr:
23:    PopRegs <ds,dx,cx,bx>             ; restore these 4
24:    ret 2                             ; AX is set by DosWriteFile
25:  Endp WriteBuffer
```

Using the Buffered I/O Routines

Before we can use the buffered input and output routines in our programs, we've got to add the macros to DOSMACS.INC, and build an object module for the **ReadBuffer** and **WriteBuffer** subroutines.

First, add the following listings to the end of your DOSMACS.INC file:

• Listing 6.7—**FileDef** structure

• Listing 6.8—**InitFile** macro

• Listing 6.12—**GetCh** macro

• Listing 6.14—**PutCh** and **FinalWrite** macros

Then, create a new file called BLOCKIO.ASM, and insert the **ReadBuffer** and **WriteBuffer** subroutines (Listings 6.13 and 6.15) as shown in Listing 6.16.

```
 1:   ; Listing 6.16--Building BLOCKIO.ASM
 2:   ;
 3:   ; BLOCKIO.ASM--Buffered input and output subroutines.
 4:   ;
 5:   ; Use in conjunction with GetCh and PutCh macros.
 6:   ;
 7:     ideal
 8:     model small
 9:     jumps
10:   include "macros.inc"
11:   include "dosmacs.inc"
12:
13:     CodeSeg
14:
15:   ; Insert Listing 6.13 (ReadBuffer) here.
16:   ; Insert Listing 6.15 (WriteBuffer) here.
17:
18:   End
```

Finally, modify MYSTUFF.MAK, the "make" file that builds our object module library, so that it will assemble BLOCKIO.ASM and place the resulting object module in our library. The new version of MYSTUFF.MAK is shown here:

```
# MSTUFF.MAK -- build library MYSTUFF.LIB
#
.asm.obj:
  tasm /m $*
  tlib mystuff -+$*
mystuff.lib: lowertbl.obj yesno.obj uppertbl.obj swaptbl.obj \
          errmsg.obj parsec.obj blockio.obj
```

Finally, rebuild the library by entering this command at the DOS prompt:

```
make -fmystuff
```

We're now ready to add buffered input and output operations to our programs.

6.5 Putting It All Together

We've already got the beginnings of a working filter program in CASE.ASM (Listing 6.5). We've got to add the processing routine, but that's relatively minor compared to what we've already done. With the exception of the processing routine, all of the pieces of our filter are written and waiting for us to glue them together.

The processing routine for CASE.ASM is really very simple. Prior to beginning our processing loop, we simply identify which conversion (lower, upper, or swap) was selected from the command line, load the address of the corresponding table into BX, and then use XLAT within the processing loop. It's easier than it sounds, really. Take a look at Listing 6.17.

```
 1:   ; Listing 6.17--CASE.ASM
 2:   ;
 3:   ; CASE.ASM--Case conversion utility.
 4:   ; Demonstration of the general-purpose filter shell.
 5:   ;
 6:       ideal
 7:   include "macros.inc"
 8:   include "dosmacs.inc"
 9:
10:       ProgramHeader Small,0100h
11:
12:       CodeSeg
13:
14:   Proc Main
15:       ExeStart                ; initialize program
```

```
16:      GetOptions              ; process the command line
17:      ;
18:      ; Initialize the input and output files.
19:      ;
20:      InitFile Infile,[ProgOptions.InputFilePtr],16384,omRead,\
21:               smCompat,DoError
22:      InitFile OutFile,[ProgOptions.OutputFilePtr],16384,omCreate,\
23:               faNormal,DoError
24:      call DoFilter           ; do filter processing
25:      jnc @@Done
26:   DoError:
27:      DosErrMsg               ; write error message
28:      DosExitProgram 1        ; and exit with error
29:   @@Done:
30:      DosCloseFile [InFile.Handle]
31:      DosCloseFile [OutFile.Handle]
32:      DosExitProgram 0        ; exit program
33:   Endp Main
34:
35:   ;
36:   ; ********************************************************
37:   ; *        Nothing above this point should change.       *
38:   ; ********************************************************
39:   ;
40:      DataSeg
41:   ;
42:   ; Set up the program description and options information.
43:   ;
44:   ProgName "CASE",<"Perform case conversions on text files">
45:
46:   Option l,<"convert all characters to lowercase">
47:   Option u,<"convert all characters to uppercase">
48:   Option x,<"swap case of all characters">
49:
50:      dw UsageInfoLen
51:   LenString UsageInfo, \
52:      <"Only one of /l, /u, or /x may be specified",cr,lf>
53:   EndOptions OptPostProcess
54:
55:   ;
56:   ; Options flags.
57:   ; If nonzero, the option was selected on the command line.
58:   ;
59:   FlagL db 0
60:   FlagU db 0
61:   FlagX db 0
62:
63:   ;
```

```
64:  ; Because we don't use the macros that define these external
65:  ; tables, we'll have to do the definition manually.
66:  ;
67:  Extrn ??LcTable:Byte,??UcTable:Byte,??CsTable:Byte
68:
69:     CodeSeg
70:
71:  ;
72:  ; Process the /l command-line option.
73:  ;
74:  Proc ProcessOptionL
75:     mov [FlagL],1
76:     ret
77:  Endp ProcessOptionL
78:
79:  ;
80:  ; Process the /u command-line option.
81:  ;
82:  Proc ProcessOptionU
83:     mov [FlagU],1
84:     ret
85:  Endp ProcessOptionU
86:
87:  ;
88:  ; Process the /x command-line option.
89:  ;
90:  Proc ProcessOptionX
91:     mov [FlagX],1
92:     ret
93:  Endp ProcessOptionX
94:
95:  ;
96:  ; Validate the selected options.
97:  ;
98:  Proc OptPostProcess
99:     mov al,[FlagL]         ; determine how many options were selected
100:    add al,[FlagU]
101:    add al,[FlagX]
102:    dec al                 ; if only one option
103:    jz @@Done              ; everything's okay
104: BadCmdLine:
105:    LenString OptInfo,<"Must specify one and only one option",cr,lf>
106:    mov dx,offset OptInfo
107:    mov cx,OptInfoLen
108:    stc
109: @@Done:
110:    ret
111: Endp OptPostProcess
112:
```

```
113:    ;
114:    ; Perform the filter processing.
115:    ;
116:    Proc DoFilter
117:       ;
118:       ; First determine which of the options was selected and
119:       ; place the address of the proper conversion table in BX.
120:       ;
121:       mov bx,offset ??LcTable
122:       cmp [FlagL],1                  ; lowercase selected?
123:       jz DoIt                        ; okay, do lowercase
124:       mov bx,offset ??UcTable
125:       cmp [FlagU],1                  ; uppercase selected?
126:       jz DoIt                        ; okay, do uppercase
127:       mov bx,offset ??CsTable        ; alright, then; swap 'em!
128:    DoIt:
129:       xor si,si                      ; initialize buffer pointers
130:       xor di,di
131:       ;
132:       ; NOTE: SI and DI are dedicated to the buffers!
133:       ; Be sure to save these registers if you're going
134:       ; to use them for something else.
135:       ;
136:    FilterLoop:
137:       GetCh InFile,@@Done,@@AllDone
138:       xlat
139:       PutCh OutFile,@@Done
140:       jmp FilterLoop
141:    @@Done:                           ; all done (or error occurred)
142:       FinalWrite OutFile,StoreDi     ; otherwise, do the final write
143:    @@AllDone:                        ; and exit the program
144:       ret
145:    Endp DoFilter
146:
147:    End Main
```

At about 150 lines of code, CASE.ASM is actually smaller than the original version of TRAL.ASM and a lot easier to understand. CASE.ASM is larger than the final version of TRAL (TRALM.ASM Listing 2.27), but CASE provides more features than TRAL: two more case conversions, command-line parsing, and buffered I/O are the most noticeable ones.

Most importantly, CASE is orders of magnitude faster than TRAL in processing the file. For example, on my system, with all files contained on a RAM disk, the version of TRALM.ASM shown in Listing 2.27 executes in about 4.5 seconds. CASE, on the other hand, invoked with this command line:

```
case /l tral.asm lowcase
```

executes in about 0.10 second! The dramatic increase in performance is due almost exclusively to the use of buffered file operations.

If you take a closer look at Listing 6.17, you'll notice that the first 30 or so lines of the program are entirely generic—they won't change from one filter program to the next. So, if we wanted to write another filter program, we could copy the first part of CASE.ASM into a new file and then add the code that's specific to the particular filter program we're working on. We don't have to worry about most of the details of program initialization, command-line parsing, or error reporting, because they're all taken care of for us.

Still, I hate trying to remember which part of a program I need to copy, so I took the first part of CASE.ASM and placed it in an include file, FILTER.INC, which is shown in Listing 6.18.

```
 1:   ; Listing 6.18 - FILTER.INC
 2:   ;
 3:   ; FILTER.INC--general-purpose filter shell.
 4:   ;
 5:   ; Contains initialization and control routine for standard
 6:   ; filter programs.
 7:   ;
 8:   ; Should be included at the beginning of the filter program,
 9:   ; as shown.
10:   ;
11:   ; ***************************************************************
12:   ;
13:   ;    ideal
14:   ; include "filter.inc"
15:   ;
16:   ;    DataSeg
17:   ;
18:   ; Include program name & options info and filter-specific
19:   ; routines here.  The last line of the program must read:
20:   ;
21:   ; End Main
22:   ;
23:   ; ***************************************************************
24:   ;
25:   include "macros.inc"
26:   include "dosmacs.inc"
27:
28:      ProgramHeader Small,0100h
29:
30:      CodeSeg
31:
32:   Proc Main
33:      ExeStart                 ; initialize program
34:      GetOptions               ; process the command line
```

```
35:   ;
36:   ; Initialize the input and output files.
37:   ;
38:   InitFile Infile,[ProgOptions.InputFilePtr],16384,\
39:       omRead,smCompat,DoError
40:   InitFile OutFile,[ProgOptions.OutputFilePtr],16384,\
41:       omCreate,faNormal,DoError
42:   call DoFilter          ; do filter processing
43:   jnc @@Done
44: DoError:
45:   DosErrMsg              ; write error message
46:   DosExitProgram 1       ; and exit with error
47: @@Done:
48:   DosCloseFile [InFile.Handle]
49:   DosCloseFile [OutFile.Handle]
50:   DosExitProgram 0       ; exit program
51: Endp Main
```

We can then include this file in our filter programs, as shown in Listing 6.19.

```
 1:   ; Listing 6.19--Using FILTER.INC
 2:   ;
 3:   ; CASE.ASM--Case conversion utility.
 4:   ; Demonstration of the general-purpose filter shell.
 5:   ;
 6:     ideal
 7: include "filter.inc"
 8:
 9:     DataSeg
10:   ;
11:   ; Set up the program description and options information.
12:   ;
13:     ...                  ; rest of CASE.ASM would go here
14:     ...
15:     ...
16:
17:   End Main
```

FILTER.INC only saves about 30 lines of code, but it enables us to forget about the initialization steps so we can worry about the real meat of our programs.

6.6 Shelling Out

Although CASE.EXE is much faster than TRAL.EXE, it's still not as fast as it *could* be if we were to spend the time to hand-optimize it. In most cases, however, the effort we'd have to expend in optimizing the program would hardly be worth the performance gain.

With FILTER.INC and the macros and subroutines that we've developed in this chapter, writing filter programs is almost a snap. If you use these tools as you write filters, you will no longer have to worry about parsing the command line or writing an error handler. File I/O is taken care of, and you're left with the specific problem: the filter-processing routine.

Granted, there's more to assembly language programming than the odd filter program. But filters make up a large part of the programming that I and many other programmers spend their time on. The macros and subroutines we've developed in this chapter can help standardize our filter programs and make them much easier to write.

"Whatcha Got in the Bag, Fred?"

Once again, we've added and changed a lot of library items in this chapter, so let's review the contents of our macro and subroutine libraries.

We haven't made any changes to MACROS.INC in this chapter, but DOSMACS.INC has received a number of additions. The listings that make up the most current DOSMACS.INC file are

Listing 2.21 Constant definitions
Listing 6.2 Macro **ExeStart**
Listing 2.5 Macro **DosCall**
Listing 2.7 Macro **DosExitProgram**
Listing 2.11 Macros **$String** and **zString**
Listing 2.22 Macro **DosOpenFile**
Listing 2.26 Macro **DosCloseFile**
Listing 3.4 Macros **CheckSeg** and **TermString**
Listing 3.5 Macro **WhatType**
Listing 3.9 Macro **CountArgs**
Listing 3.10 Macro **DosDisplayString**
Listing 3.11 Macros **DosReadFile**, **DosWriteFile**, **LenString** and **MakeString**
Listing 4.6 Macro **YesNo**
Listing 4.15 Macro **DosErrMsg**
Listing 6.4 Macros **ProgName**, **Option**, **EndOptions**, and **GetOptions**
Listing 6.7 **FileDef** structure
Listing 6.8 Macro **InitFile**
Listing 6.12 Macro **GetCh**
Listing 6.14 Macros **PutCh** and **FinalWrite**

We've also added two new modules to our MYSTUFF.LIB file. These new modules are

Listing 6.6 PARSEC.ASM
Listing 6.16 BLOCKIO.ASM

And the make file that builds the library, MYSTUFF.MAK, has been modified, as shown, so that it includes the new modules in the library.

```
# MSTUFF.MAK build library MYSTUFF.LIB
#
.asm.obj:
  tasm /m $*
  tlib mystuff -+$*
mystuff.lib: lowertbl.obj yesno.obj errmsg.obj parsec.obj \
  blockio.obj uppertbl.obj swaptbl.obj
```

7

Little Languages

My first programming job was in a bank, maintaining COBOL applications on a PRIME minicomputer. In addition to the COBOL programs, there was a handful of FORTRAN and PL/1 system utilities that I inherited by default—they needed to be fixed and I was willing to play with them. We also had one oddball piece of equipment—a big check reader/sorter that was connected to the PRIME through an RS-232 serial link.

One day my boss instructed me to modify the program that communicated with the reader/sorter so that we could begin offering a new service to some of our bigger customers. About halfway through my first experiments in changing the control program, I wound up debugging the Sorter Control Language (SCL) compiler's job control string and made an amazing discovery. *SCL was actually a set of assembly language macros.* The programs we wrote for the sorter were included in a generic shell, and then assembled and linked with a library of standard routines to produce the final executable program. All of this was done transparently—I thought I was writing programs in "Sorter Control Language," when I was actually writing assembly language macro invocations.

I'll never forget my amazement as I studied the implementation of Sorter Control Language. Whoever had written these macros had the foresight to realize that a little extra effort spent designing a language would be more time efficient than hacking together a special-purpose program each time we wanted to make a minor change to the sorter's behavior.

7.1 The Attraction of Mini Languages

The trend in programming languages continues to be one of generalization, for the simple reason that most problems can be solved using a general purpose programming language. However, there are some problems that require absolute control of the available resources, and there's only one language that can give you that degree of control—assembly language. But assembly language programs, as you well know, are normally difficult to write, debug, and maintain.

What was so amazing about the Sorter Control Language was that it gave me high-level language constructs without the overhead that is normally associated with such languages. In addition, SCL was tailored specifically to controlling the reader/sorter. As a result, the compiled SCL programs were small and fast, but easy to write and maintain. I had the best of both worlds.

Unfortunately (or fortunately, depending on your perspective), you probably don't have a reader/sorter attached to your computer, so duplicating the functions of SCL would be a waste of your time and mine. So, rather than trying to show you how to interface with a particular piece of equipment, this chapter will present a very small general-purpose programming language that's written entirely in assembly language macros.

7.2 Introducing TINY, an Experimental Language

As an experiment in creating little languages with assembly language macros, I've developed TINY—a very minimal and limited-use programming language. I don't expect it to replace BASIC—it wasn't designed for that. It was designed to show you some of the tasks you can perform with assembly language macros.

TINY is something of a cross between Pascal and BASIC. It includes two data types, an assignment statement, a simple conditional structure, one looping construct, and console input and output routines. As I said, it's minimal.

Beginnings

All TINY programs must begin with a **@Program** statement and end with an **@EndProgram** statement. The macros that implement these two keywords are shown in TINY.DEF (Listing 7.1), which also includes some assembler directives that are necessary for TINY programs to assemble correctly.

```
1:    ; Listing 7.1--TINY.DEF
2:    ;
3:    ; TINY.DEF--macros that implement a tiny language.
4:    ;
5:    include "macros.inc"
6:    include "dosmacs.inc"
7:
8:    ; @Program
9:    ; Generate program header and program start address.
10:   ;
11:   Macro @Program
12:     ProgramHeader Small,0100h
13:     CodeSeg
14:     Label ??BeginProgram Near
15:     ExeStart
16:   Endm @Program
17:
18:   ;
19:   ; @EndProgram
20:   ; Generate program startup code and branch to program start.
21:   Macro @EndProgram
22:     DosExitProgram 0
23:     end ??BeginProgram
24:   Endm @Program
```

The **@Program** macro generates the program header, creates a label, **??BeginProgram**, and uses the **ExeStart** macro to generate the .EXE startup code. **EndProgram** generates code to exit to DOS and also generates the assembly language **End** statement.

The smallest possible TINY program, then, would be one that has only the **@Program** and **EndProgram** statements, as shown in Listing 7.2.

```
1:   ; Listing 7.2--Smallest possible TINY program
2:   ;
3:     Ideal
4:   include "tiny.def"
5:
6:     @Program
7:     @EndProgram
```

You can assemble, link, and test this program by creating a file called TEST.ASM that contains Listing 7.2. Then, at the DOS prompt, issue these commands:

```
tasm /l test
tlink test
test
```

The program should do nothing but return you to the DOS prompt. If you're interested in the generated code, take a look at the listing file, TINY.LST.

The only thing I don't like about this setup is that you have to remember a couple of assembler directives in order to get a TINY program running. It's just not *clean*. Sorter Control Language had none of those requirements—the fact of the assembler was completely hidden from the programmer.

We can hide the assembler from the TINY programmer also. All it takes is a little sleight of hand and a very simple batch file. The new TINY.DEF that accomplishes this trick is shown in Listing 7.3.

```
1:   ; Listing 7.3--New TINY.DEF
2:   ;
3:     %NoList
4:   ;
5:   ; TINY.DEF
6:   ;   TINY language definition file. This file contains all
7:   ; of the TINY language macros, and the startup and exit code.
8:   ;
9:   ; Assembly command line:
10:  ;
11:  ;   tasm /m/l/dTinyProg="fname.TNY" tiny.def,fname,fname
12:  ;
13:  ; where fname is replaced by the name of the TINY program to
14:  ; be compiled. This creates fname.OBJ and fname.LST.
15:  ;
16:    ideal
17:  include "macros.inc"
18:  include "dosmacs.inc"
```

```
19:
20:    ;
21:    ; **********************************************************
22:    ; *              Language Definition Macros       .        *
23:    ; **********************************************************
24:    ;
25:
26:    ;
27:    ; @Program
28:    ; Generate program header and program start address.
29:    ;
30:    Macro @Program
31:      ProgramHeader Small,0100h
32:      CodeSeg
33:      Label ??BeginProgram Near
34:      ExeStart
35:    Endm @Program
36:
37:    ;
38:    ; @EndProgram
39:    ; Generate program exit code and End statement.
40:    ;
41:    Macro @EndProgram
42:      DosExitProgram 0
43:      End ??BeginProgram
44:    Endm @Program
45:
46:    ;
47:    ; **********************************************************
48:    ; *              End of Language Definition Macros         *
49:    ; **********************************************************
50:    ;
51:
52:    ;
53:    ; Compile the user's program.
54:    ;
55:      %List
56:    % include TinyProg
57:      %NoList
```

Using this version of TINY.DEF, we can eliminate the assembler directives from our TEST.ASM program, and the smallest possible TINY program becomes a two-liner, as shown in lines 3 and 4 of Listing 7.4.

```
1:    ; Listing 7.4--Smallest possible TINY program
2:    ;
3:      @Program
4:      @EndProgram
```

To see how this works, replace your TINY.DEF file with Listing 7.3 and create a new file called TEST.TNY that contains Listing 7.4. Then, to compile TEST.TNY, issue this command at the DOS prompt:

```
tasm /m/l/dTinyProg="TEST.TNY" tiny.def,test,test
```

This command creates TEST.OBJ and TEST.LST. You can then build TEST.EXE by issuing this command:

```
tlink test
```

at the DOS command line.

How does this work? The magic lies in the command-line argument that reads **/dTinyProg="TEST.TNY"**. This tells the assembler to define a text macro, just as if you had inserted this **EQU** directive in the TINY.DEF file:

```
TinyProg equ <"TEST.TNY">
```

When the assembler encounters the line in TINY.DEF that reads

```
% include TinyProg
```

TinyProg is replaced with its assigned value ("TEST.TNY" in this case), and that file is included.

The only remaining problem is that absurdly long assembler command line, which we can take care of by placing it in a batch file, as shown in Listing 7.5.

```
 1:    rem    Listing 7.5--TINY.BAT
 2:    @echo off
 3:    rem
 4:    rem  TINY.BAT--Compile a TINY program.
 5:    rem
 6:    rem  Usage is TINY filename.
 7:    rem  The filename parameter must not have an extension. All TINY
 8:    rem  programs must have the .TNY extension.
 9:    rem
10:    if "%1%"=="" goto Usage
11:    tasm /m/l/dTinyProg="%1.TNY" tiny.def,%1,%1
12:    if not errorlevel 1 tlink %1
13:    goto AllDone
14:    :Usage
15:    echo Usage is TINY filename
16:    echo The filename parameter must not have an extension.
17:    echo All TINY programs must have the .TNY extension.
18:    :AllDone
```

Now, to compile a TINY program, we simply create a file with the .TNY extension and issue this very simple command:

```
TINY ProgName
```

where **ProgName** is replaced with the name of the program to be compiled. If no errors are encountered, TINY.BAT will assemble and link your TINY program and produce an .EXE file.

TINY Data Types

TINY supports just two data types: **Word** and **String**. As with most structured languages, variables in TINY must be declared before they are used. In TINY, variables may be declared and initialized with the same statement, much like they are in C. For example, all of the following are valid TINY variable declarations:

```
@Word Counter                 ; declare a word variable, Counter
@Word NTimes 5                ; declare a word variable, NTimes,
                              ; and initialize it to 5
@String MyName                ; declare a string variable, MyName
@String Hello <"Hello there"> ; declare a string variable, Hello,
                              ; and give it the value "Hello there"
```

The declaration of word variables is very easy to implement in a macro, as shown by the **@Word** macro in Listing 7.6.

```
 1:   ; Listing 7.6--@Word macro
 2:   ;
 3:   ; @Word VarName,<Value>
 4:   ;
 5:   ; Declares a Word variable, VarName, and optionally initializes
 6:   ; it to Value. If Value is not specified, the variable is
 7:   ; initialized to 0.
 8:   ;
 9:   Macro @Word VarName,Value
10:      ifb <VarName>
11:        Err
12:        Display "Variable name expected"
13:        ExitM
14:      Endif
15:      DataSeg
16:      ifnb <Value>
17:        VarName dw Value
18:      else
19:        VarName dw 0
```

```
20:     Endif
21:     CodeSeg
22:   EndM
```

Constant strings are also fairly easy to implement, as we've seen previously with our **TermString** and **LenString** macros. TINY strings, however, need a little more flexibility than either of these macros provides. All TINY strings, regardless of length, occupy 81 bytes of storage—a length byte and an array of 80 characters. The **@String** macro that declares these strings is shown in Listing 7.7.

```
1:   ; Listing 7.7--@String macro
2:   ;
3:   ; @String VarName,<Value>
4:   ;
5:   Macro @String VarName,Value
6:     Local TheStrLen
7:     ifb <VarName>
8:       Err
9:       Display "Variable name expected"
10:      ExitM
11:    EndIf
12:    DataSeg
13:    ifb <Value>
14:      VarName db 0
15:      db 80 dup (?)
16:    else
17:      VarName db TheStrLen
18:      db Value
19:      TheStrLen = $ - VarName - 1
20:      db 80-TheStrLen dup (?)
21:    Endif
22:    CodeSeg
23:  Endm
```

That's all there is to defining data, but it's far from all we need to do with data types. Just about every construct in the TINY language has to distinguish between the two data types and act accordingly.

7.3 Input and Output

As exciting as looking at the generated code is, it's far more satisfying to see our programs execute and display some real results. So, before we go any further, let's get the output routine working.

We've had a small amount of experience with input and output in our **DosDisplayString**, **DosReadFile**, and **DosWriteFile** macros. **DosDisplayString** is a bit too limited for use in a general-purpose language, so we'll define our

@Write macro using **DosWriteFile**. The first version of **@Write**, shown in Listing 7.8, works only with strings. Take a few moments to look it over.

```
 1:   ; Listing 7.8--@Write macro
 2:   ;
 3:   ; @Write String
 4:   ;
 5:   ; String can be a string literal or a variable name.
 6:   ;
 7:   Macro @Write String
 8:     Local ArgType,TempStr
 9:     quirks
10:     ifb <String>
11:       ideal
12:       Err
13:       Display "Constant or variable name expected"
14:       ExitM
15:     Endif
16:     ideal
17:     WhatType String,ArgType
18:     ;;
19:     ;; If it's a string (ArgType = 0), define the string
20:     ;; before displaying it.
21:     ;;
22:     if ArgType eq 0
23:       @String TempStr,String
24:       xor ch,ch
25:       mov cl,[TempStr]
26:       DosWriteFile StdOut,,<offset TempStr+1>
27:     else
28:       xor ch,ch
29:       mov cl,[String]
30:       DosWriteFile StdOut,,<offset String+1>
31:     Endif
32:   Endm @Write
```

With the addition of **@Write**, we can write TINY programs that actually *do* something—not much, mind you, but we're getting there.

Add Listings 7.6, 7.7, and 7.8 to your TINY.DEF file, right after the **@EndProgram** macro. Your TINY.DEF file should now contain the following macros: **@Program**, **@EndProgram**, **@Word**, **@String**, and **@Write**. Using these macros, we can write our "Hello, world" program in TINY, as shown by the program in Listing 7.9.

```
1:   ; Listing 7.9--HELLO.TNY
2:   ;
3:   @Program
```

```
4:       @Write <"Hello, world">
5:       @Write <"Hi mom">
6:    @EndProgram
```

To test this program, create a new file called HELLO.TNY and enter the code from Listing 7.9. Save the file and compile the program by invoking the TINY batch file with this command line:

```
tiny hello
```

After the program has compiled and linked, you can execute it by entering

```
hello
```

at the DOS prompt.

Oops! The output wasn't quite what was expected. If you did everything right, the program should have displayed:

```
Hello, worldHi mom
```

Fortunately, there's a simple cure for what ails this code. We'll add a new statement, **@WriteLn**, that outputs the argument and then outputs a newline. This new macro is shown in Listing 7.10.

```
 1:    ; Listing 7.10--@WriteLn macro
 2:    ;
 3:    ; @WriteLn TheString
 4:    ;
 5:    Macro @WriteLn TheString
 6:      ;;
 7:      ;; The first time through, we define the string ??CrLf in
 8:      ;; the data segment. The macro is redefined on the first
 9:      ;; pass so that subsequent passes don't attempt to redefine
10:      ;; CrLf.
11:      ;;
12:      DataSeg
13:        ??CrLf db cr,lf
14:      CodeSeg
15:      Quirks
16:      ifnb <TheString>
17:        Ideal
18:        @Write <TheString>
19:      Endif
20:      Ideal
21:      DosWriteFile StdOut,2,<offset ??CrLf>
22:      ;;
23:      ;; First pass through redefines @WriteLn.
24:      ;;
```

```
25:     Macro @WriteLn String
26:        quirks
27:        ifnb <String>
28:          Ideal
29:          @Write <String>
30:        Endif
31:        Ideal
32:        DosWriteFile StdOut,2,<offset ??CrLf>
33:      Endm @WriteLn
34:    Endm @WriteLn
```

Now, if you change the **@Write** statements in HELLO.TNY (Listing 7.9) to **@WriteLn** statements, you'll get two lines of output, as you'd expect.

But **@Write** and **@WriteLn** only work halfway! If we try to output a **@Word** variable, we're going to be very disappointed. Let's tackle that problem next.

Displaying Numbers

Displaying **@Word** variables is a little more difficult, because we have to translate the 2-byte binary representation of a number into a string of characters. That's not too difficult, really, because we can write a subroutine to perform the conversion for us. And having the **@Write** macro determine what type of variable is to be written isn't very difficult, either. The tough part is deciding where to put the subroutine. Let's take a look at the first two problems and then tackle the tough one.

We can use Turbo Assembler's **Size** operator to distinguish between **@String** and **@Word** variables in **@Write**. **Size** will return 1 for **@String** variables and 2 for **@Word** variables. And we can identify numeric constants using our **WhatType** macro. Numeric constants result in a return value of 24h. Because **@Write** isn't the only macro that will need to determine an argument's type, I've created a new macro, **TinyArgType**, that determines what type of argument was passed to it and returns the type and a pointer to the argument. This macro, along with the modified **@Write** macro that uses it, is shown in Listing 7.11.

```
1:    ; Listing 7.11--@Write macro and TinyArgType helper
2:    ;
3:    ; @Write ThisArg
4:    ;
5:    ; ThisArg can be a string or numeric constant, or a variable.
6:    ;
7:    Macro @Write ThisArg
8:       Local ArgType,TempArg
9:       quirks
10:      ifb <ThisArg>
11:         ideal
12:         Err
```

```
13:        Display "Constant or variable name expected"
14:        ExitM
15:     Endif
16:     ideal
17:
18:     TinyArgType <ThisArg>,ArgType,TempArg
19:     if ArgType eq 1
20:        xor ch,ch
21:        mov cl,[TempArg]
22:        DosWriteFile StdOut,,<offset TempArg+1>
23:     else
24:        mov ax,[TempArg]
25:        extrn WriteNumber:Proc
26:        call WriteNumber
27:     Endif
28:  Endm @Write
29:
30:  ;
31:  ; TinyArgType Arg1,AType,TArg
32:  ;
33:  ; Determines type of Arg1 and sets AType and TArg accordingly.
34:  ; AType will be 1 if Arg1 is a @String, 2 if Arg1 is a @Word
35:  ; TArg will point to the argument.
36:  ;
37:  Macro TinyArgType Arg1,AType,TArg
38:     WhatType <Arg1>,AType
39:     if AType eq 2Ah        ;; if it's a TINY variable
40:        AType = Size Arg1    ;; determine variable type
41:        TArg = Arg1
42:     elseif AType eq 0      ;; otherwise, if it's a string constant
43:        @String TArg <Arg1> ;; define the string
44:        AType = 1           ;; and set type to 1
45:     else                   ;; it must be a numeric constant
46:        @Word TArg <Arg1>   ;; so define the constant
47:        AType = 2           ;; and set type to 2
48:     endif
49:  Endm TinyArgType
```

As I said, the subroutine that outputs a number is not very difficult to write. And the logical place for this subroutine is in an object module library along with the other modules that we'll be writing for TINY. The **WriteNumber** subroutine is implemented as an external module in WRITENUM.ASM, which is shown in Listing 7.12.

```
1:   ; Listing 7.12--WRITENUM.ASM
2:   ;
3:   ; WriteNumber subroutine
4:   ;
```

```
 5:    ; Call with AX = number to output.
 6:    ; Formats a number and outputs it to StdOut.
 7:    ;
 8:      ideal
 9:      %NoIncl
10:    include "macros.inc"
11:    include "dosmacs.inc"
12:
13:      model small
14:      DataSeg
15:
16:    NumBuff db 5 dup (?)
17:
18:      CodeSeg
19:    Public WriteNumber
20:    Proc WriteNumber
21:      mov bx,10
22:      mov cx,5
23:      mov si,offset NumBuff+4
24:    @@Loop:
25:      sub dx,dx
26:      div bx
27:      add dl,'0'
28:      mov [si],dl
29:      dec si
30:      loop @@Loop
31:      DosWriteFile StdOut,5,<offset NumBuff>
32:      ret
33:    Endp WriteNumber
34:
35:      End
```

So now we need to build an object module library and to modify TINY.DEF so that it automatically links with this library when a TINY program is compiled.

Listing 7.13 contains TINYLIB.MAK, the file that builds TINYLIB.LIB. This make file is very similar to the MYSTUFF.MAK file that we used in previous chapters.

```
1:    # Listing 7.13--TINYLIB.MAK
2:    #
3:    # TINYLIB.LIB--build library TINYLIB.LIB.
4:    #
5:    .asm.obj:
6:      tasm /m $*
7:      tlib tinylib -+$*
8:
9:    tinylib.lib: writenum.obj
```

Using this make file, we build TINYLIB.LIB by issuing this command:

```
make -ftinylib
```

at the DOS prompt.

The only modification to TINY.DEF is the addition of a single line of code right after the line that includes DOSMACS.INC. The new line should read:

```
includelib "tinylib.lib"
```

Your TINY.DEF file should now contain the full text of Listing 7.3 and the following additional macros: **@Word** (Listing 7.6), **@String** (Listing 7.7), **@WriteLn** (Listing 7.10), and **@Write** (Listing 7.11).

Once you've verified the contents of TINY.DEF and constructed TINYLIB.LIB, compile and test the program shown in Listing 7.14.

```
 1:    ; Listing 7.14--TEST.TNY
 2:    ;
 3:    ; TEST.TNY--a TINY program to test output.
 4:    ;
 5:    @Program
 6:      @Word MyAge 30
 7:      @String Hello <"Hello, world">
 8:
 9:      @WriteLn Hello
10:      @Write <"I'm ">
11:      @Write MyAge
12:      @WriteLn <" years old.">
13:    @EndProgram
```

If everything went as planned, the program should compile and link with no errors, and the program should display

```
Hello, world
I'm 00030 years old.
```

Granted, outputting the number with leading zeros is a bit, shall we say, unrefined, but we've verified that the program works. We can always go back and modify the **WriteNumber** subroutine if we want numbers to be output in a different format.

Input with @Read

After the discussion of **@Write**, I guess you can imagine what the **@Read** macro is going to look like. **@Read** is a fairly straightforward translation of **@Write**, as shown in Listing 7.15, with the major difference being that **@Read** cannot be invoked with a constant argument—the argument *must* be a variable.

```
 1:   ; Listing 7.15--@Read macro
 2:   ;
 3:   ; @Read ThisArg
 4:   ;
 5:   ; ThisArg must be a string variable or a word variable.
 6:   ;
 7:   Macro @Read ThisArg
 8:     Local ArgType,TempStr
 9:     quirks
10:     ifb <ThisArg>
11:       ideal
12:       Err
13:       Display "Variable name expected"
14:       ExitM
15:     Endif
16:     ideal
17:     WhatType ThisArg,ArgType
18:     ;;
19:     ;; If the argument isn't a defined variable, error.
20:     ;;
21:     if (ArgType eq 0) or (ArgType eq 24h)
22:       Err
23:       Display "Variable name expected"
24:       ExitM
25:     else
26:       ;;
27:       ;; It's a defined variable. Determine the type of variable
28:       ;; using the Size operator.
29:       ;;   1--@String variable
30:       ;;   2--@Word variable
31:       ;;
32:       ArgType = Size ThisArg
33:       if ArgType eq 1
34:         DosReadFile StdIn,80,<offset ThisArg+1>
35:         mov [ThisArg],al  ; store number of chars read
36:       else
37:         extrn ReadNumber:Proc
38:         call ReadNumber
39:         mov [ThisArg],ax
40:       Endif
41:     Endif
42:   Endm @Write
```

Add Listing 7.15 to your TINY.DEF file, then create a new file called READNUM.ASM and enter the code shown in Listing 7.16. This is the **ReadNumber** subroutine that we'll be adding to TINYLIB.LIB.

```
 1:   ; Listing 7.16--READNUM.ASM
 2:   ;
 3:   ; ReadNumber subroutine
 4:   ;
 5:   ; Reads a number from StdIn and converts it to a word.
 6:   ; Maximum number length is 5 characters.
 7:   ; Number is converted to a word in AX.
 8:   ;
 9:   ; Overflow and invalid characters are detected, but no
10:   ; action is taken beyond exiting the routine.
11:   ;
12:   ; Returns the number in AX.
13:   ;
14:      ideal
15:      %NoIncl
16:   include "macros.inc"
17:   include "dosmacs.inc"
18:
19:      model small
20:      DataSeg
21:
22:   NumBuff db 7 dup (?)
23:
24:      CodeSeg
25:   Public ReadNumber
26:   Proc ReadNumber
27:      DosReadFile StdIn,5,<Offset NumBuff>
28:      mov di,10
29:      mov cx,7
30:      mov si,offset NumBuff
31:      xor ax,ax
32:   @@Loop:
33:      mov bl,[si]
34:      inc si
35:      IsIn bl,<cr>,@@Done    ; if cr, done
36:      IsDigit bl,,@@Done     ; if not digit, exit
37:      mul di
38:      jo ReadNumber          ; if overflow, exit
39:      sub bl,'0'             ; convert to binary
40:      add al,bl
41:      adc ax,0
42:      loop @@Loop
43:   @@Done:
44:      ret
45:   Endp ReadNumber
46:
47:   End
```

Add READNUM.OBJ to the list of object files in TINYLIB.MAK and rebuild the library. Then compile and test the program shown in Listing 7.17.

```
 1:   ; Listing 7.17--TESTREAD.TNY
 2:   ;
 3:   ; TESTREAD.TNY--a TINY test program.
 4:   ;
 5:   @Program
 6:     @Word YourAge
 7:     @String YourName
 8:
 9:     @Write <"Enter your name ">
10:     @Read YourName
11:     @WriteLn
12:     @Write <"Enter your age ">
13:     @Read YourAge
14:     @WriteLn
15:
16:     @Write <"Hello ">
17:     @WriteLn YourName
18:     @Write <"You're ">
19:     @Write YourAge
20:     @WriteLn <" years old.">
21:   @EndProgram
```

The program's output really isn't what it could be, but that's a very minor complaint compared to what we've accomplished. We can always go back and modify the **@Read** and **@Write** macros and their associated subroutines.

One modification that would be very useful is to allow reading or writing more than a single item on each macro invocation. This change is fairly simple and would be an excellent exercise to test your grasp of the concepts presented thus far.

We now have a programming language with which we can define variables and interact with the user. TINY is still a far cry from a "real" programming language, but you can see it taking shape. Let's continue our discussion with a tour of decision-making constructs.

7.4 Conditionals

Any serious programming language must have some means to make decisions and act on those decisions. TINY is no different. The simplest of TINY's conditional structures is the **@If** statement, which takes the form

```
@If <variable> <condition> <variable>
  ...
  ...
@EndIf
```

Valid conditions are LT (less than), LE (less than or equal to), EQ (equal to), GE (greater than or equal to), GT (greater than), and NE (not equal to). Conditionals can be used on both TINY variable types.

On the surface, processing conditionals looks mighty simple. All you have to do is determine the types of the arguments, generate code to compare them, and then generate the conditional branching instruction represented by the condition passed to the macro. Truthfully, the first two items are fairly easy to implement. But the last item—generating the proper branching instruction—is more difficult than it first appears. Let's see why.

Generating Conditional Branches

For the purpose of our experiments, we're going to use a stripped-down **@If** macro that doesn't do any comparisons—all it does is generate a conditional branch (a **jnz** instruction) to the instruction following the **@EndIf**. Our macro has to keep track of the number of **@If** statements that have been encountered, so that it can generate unique labels for each **@EndIf** statement. Our first try at a usable conditional structure, then, is shown in Listing 7.18.

```
 1:    ; Listing 7.18--First try at conditional processing
 2:    ;
 3:    IfCount = 0              ; initialize If counter
 4:
 5:    Macro @If
 6:       MakeJump jnz,%IfCount
 7:    Endm @If
 8:
 9:    Macro MakeJump JmpType,Arg1
10:       JmpType EndIf&Arg1
11:    Endm MakeJump
12:
13:    Macro @Endif
14:       MakeLabel Endif,%IfCount
15:       IfCount = IfCount + 1
16:    Endm
17:
18:    Macro MakeLabel LblType,Arg1
19:       Label LblType&Arg1 Near
20:    Endm MakeLabel
```

Even as simple as it is, this type of conditional processing can be useful. For example, if you want to make a comparison and execute a section of code only if the two operands are equal, you could write this:

```
cmp al,cr        ; if character is CR
@If
  mov [EOL],1    ; set end-of-line flag
```

```
  @Endif
; continue processing
```

And the generated code would be

```
  cmp al,cr
  jnz EndIf0
  mov [EOL],1
Label EndIf0 Near
```

But we run into problems very quickly when we try to nest **@If** statements. For example, the code fragment shown in Figure 7.1(a), which should expand to the equivalent of Figure 7.1(b), actually produces the code shown in Figure 7.1(c). Why does this happen?

Figure 7.1. Results of nested conditionals

(a)—Nested conditionals

```
  cmp al,cr              ; if character is CR
  @If
    lodsb                ; then get next character
    cmp al,lf            ; if next char is LF
    @If
      mov [EOL],1        ; set end-of-line flag
    @Endif
    dec si               ; otherwise, go back to previous char
  @Endif
```

(b)—Code that should be generated

```
  cmp al,cr
  jnz EndIf0
  lodsb
  cmp al,lf
  jnz EndIf1
  mov [EOL],1
Label EndIf1 Near
  dec si
Label EndIf0 Near
```

(c)—The code that is actually generated

```
  cmp al,cr
  jnz EndIf0
  lodsb
  cmp al,lf
  jnz EndIf0
  mov [EOL],1
Label EndIf0 Near
  dec si
Label EndIf1 Near
```

The problem we encounter is that **IfCount** isn't keeping pace with the **EndIf** labels, and there's not much we can do about it. If we were to increment **IfCount** in the **@If** macro, the **@EndIf** macro would produce duplicate labels. What we need is a stack on which we can store the current value of **IfCount** so that it will be available when the corresponding **@EndIf** is processed.

With a stack, the algorithm for generating branches and **EndIf** labels is very simple, as shown by the following skeleton macros:

```
Macro @If
  Push IfCount
  Generate branch
  Increment IfCount
Endm @If
Macro @EndIf
  Pop LblNo
  Generate label EndIfxx, where xx is replaced by the value of LblNo
Endm @EndIf
```

All we have to do, then, is find some way to implement a stack that can be used at assembly time, which is what the code in Listing 7.19 does.

```
 1:   ; Listing 7.19--Macros that support nested conditionals
 2:   ;
 3:   IfCount = 0              ; initialize If counter
 4:   IfStkPtr = 0             ; and stack pointer
 5:
 6:   ;
 7:   ; @If--Generate a conditional branch.
 8:   ;
 9:   Macro @If
10:     IfStkPtr = IfStkPtr + 1        ;; bump stack pointer
11:     SetIfStk %IfStkPtr,IfCount     ;; push current IfCount on stack
12:     IfCount = IfCount + 1          ;; bump If counter
13:     MakeJump jnz,%IfStkPtr         ;; and generate the branch
14:   Endm @If
15:
16:   ; SetIfStk--"push" a value on the stack.
17:   Macro SetIfStk Num,Value
18:     IfStk&Num = Value
19:   Endm SetIfStk
20:
21:   Macro MakeJump JmpType,Arg1
22:     MakeJump2 JmpType,%IfStk&Arg1
23:   Endm MakeJump
24:
25:   Macro MakeJump2 JmpType,Arg2
26:     JmpType Endif&Arg2
```

```
27:     Endm MakeJump2
28:
29:     ;
30:     ; @EndIf--generate label EndIfxx, where xx is replaced by the
31:     ; value at the top of the stack.
32:     ;
33:     Macro @Endif
34:       MakeLabel %IfStkPtr           ; generate the label
35:       IfStkPtr = IfStkPtr - 1       ; and "pop" value from stack
36:     Endm
37:
38:     Macro MakeLabel Arg1
39:       MakeLabel2 %IfStk&Arg1
40:     Endm MakeLabel
41:
42:     Macro MakeLabel2 Arg2
43:       Label Endif&Arg2 Near
44:     Endm MakeLabel2
```

Using the macros in Listing 7.19, the nested conditionals example of Figure 7.1(a) correctly generates the code shown in Figure 7.1(b).

Adding an @Else Clause

As useful as it is, the conditional structure implemented in Listing 7.19 is still more restrictive than it should be. For example, if we wanted to code an **If...Then...Else** construct, our code would be similar to this:

```
@If
  ;do something
  jmp EndElse
@EndIf
; do something else
Label EndElse Near
```

The problem is that it's too darned easy to forget the line that reads **jmp EndElse**, resulting in a fairly difficult-to-find bug. It would be nice to have an **@Else** clause, so that the preceding code could be rewritten like this:

```
@If
  ;do something
@Else
  ;do something else
@EndIf
```

The code generated by the preceding construct would look something like this:

```
   jnz Else0
   ; do something
   jmp EndIf0
Label Else0 Near
   ; do something else
Label Endif0 Near
```

The only trick to adding an **@Else** clause is the "dangling else" case. If we make the mistake of assuming that every **@If** has a corresponding **@Else**, then a simple **@If** construct like this:

```
@If
   ; do something
@Endif
```

will generate the code

```
   jnz Else0
   ; do something
Label EndIf0 Near
```

which will not assemble correctly, because the label **Else0** is not defined anywhere in the program.

The **@If**, **@Else**, and **@EndIf** macros in Listing 7.20 allow for the "dangling else" case by maintaining a flag that identifies whether an **@Else** clause has been encountered for a particular **@If**. The **@EndIf** macro tests this flag, and if no **@Else** clause was encountered, it generates the **Else** label before generating the **EndIf** label. Here's Listing 7.20; take a few minutes to compare it with Listing 7.19.

```
 1:   ; Listing 7.20--@If, @Else, and @EndIf
 2:   ;
 3:   IfCount = 0
 4:   IfStkPtr = 0
 5:
 6:   ;
 7:   ; @If--Process IF statement.
 8:   ; Currently, perform true code only if Z flag is set.
 9:   ; This will be enhanced to include IF <condition>, where condition
10:   ; is any of the 8088 'jmp' conditions.
11:   ;
12:   Macro @If
13:     IfStkPtr = IfStkPtr + 1          ;; bump the stack pointer
14:     SetStk If,%IfStkPtr,IfCount      ;; push value on stack
15:     SetElseFlag %IfStkPtr,0 ;; clear the ElseFlag for this IF statement
16:     IfCount = IfCount + 1            ;; bump If counter
```

```
17:      MakeJump jnz,Else,If,%IfStkPtr ;; and create the conditional jump
18:    Endm @If
19:
20:    Macro SetStk StkName,Num,Value
21:      &StkName&Stk&Num = Value
22:    Endm SetStk
23:
24:    Macro SetElseFlag Num,Value
25:      ElseFlag&Num = Value
26:    Endm SetElseFlag
27:
28:    Macro MakeJump JmpType,JmpTarget,Targ,Arg1
29:      MakeJump2 JmpType,JmpTarget,%&Targ&Stk&Arg1
30:    Endm MakeJump
31:
32:    Macro MakeJump2 JmpType,JmpTarget,Arg2
33:      JmpType JmpTarget&Arg2
34:    Endm MakeJump2
35:
36:    ;
37:    ; @Else--process @Else statement.
38:    ;
39:    Macro @Else
40:      MakeJump jmp,Endif,If,%IfStkPtr ;; generate the branch around the Else
41:      MakeLabel Else,IfStk,%IfStkPtr ;; generate label for the Else code
42:      SetElseFlag %IfStkPtr,1 ;; and set the Else flag for this condition
43:    Endm @Else
44:
45:    ;
46:    ; @Endif--process @Endif statement.
47:    ;
48:    Macro @Endif
49:      CheckElseLbl %IfStkPtr    ;; generate Else label if required (that is,
50:                                ;; if no @Else was used in this statement)
51:      MakeLabel Endif,IfStk,%IfStkPtr ;; generate the Endif label
52:      IfStkPtr = IfStkPtr - 1 ;; and bump to previous IfStk array item
53:    Endm
54:
55:    Macro CheckElseLbl Arg1
56:      if ElseFlag&Arg1 eq 0 ;; if Else label hasn't been defined yet
57:        MakeLabel Else,IfStk,%IfStkPtr ;; generate the label
58:      endif
59:    Endm CheckElseLbl
60:
61:    Macro MakeLabel LblType,StkPtr,Arg1
62:      MakeLabel2 LblType,%&StkPtr&Arg1
63:    Endm MakeLabel
64:
```

```
65:    Macro MakeLabel2 LblType,Arg2
66:      Label LblType&Arg2 Near
67:    Endm MakeLabel2
```

We now have macros that will generate the conditional branches and labels required for **If...Then...Else** processing. Believe it or not, that was the hard part. The second half of the problem—implementing the comparisons—is a bit easier.

Comparing TINY Values

We'll tackle **@Word** variables first, because there are assembly language instructions that will compare two words. Comparing **@String** variables is going to require another subroutine, which isn't very difficult to write, but we need to get the basic form of our final **@If** macro before we tackle it.

For starters, we'll restrict our comparisons to **@Word** variables. The **@Compare** macro in Listing 7.21 accepts a conditional statement and generates code to compare the two variables.

```
 1:    ; Listing 7.21--Skeleton @Compare macro
 2:    ;
 3:    Macro @Compare Arg1,Condition,Arg2
 4:      Local CFlag
 5:      ;; Check for arguments
 6:      ifb <Arg1>
 7:        Err
 8:        Display "Variable name expected"
 9:        Exitm
10:      endif
11:      ifb <Arg2>
12:        Err
13:        Display "Variable name expected"
14:        Exitm
15:      endif
16:      ;;
17:      ;; Check for condition.
18:      ;;
19:      CFlag = 0
20:      irp tCond,<LT,LE,EQ,GE,GT,NE>
21:        ifidni <Condition>,<TCond>
22:          CFlag = 1
23:          ExitM
24:        endif
25:      endm
26:      if CFlag eq 0
27:        Err
28:        Display "Invalid condition"
```

```
29:        Exitm
30:      endif
31:
32:      ;; Generate comparison code.
33:      mov ax,[Arg1]
34:      cmp ax,[Arg2]
35:    Endm @Compare
```

The **@Compare** macro in Listing 7.21 is not very complex at all. It verifies
that the macro has been invoked with two variables and a valid condition, then
generates a comparison. Using this macro, the following TINY code fragment:

```
@Word HisAge 30
@Word HerAge 28

@Compare HisAge LT HerAge
```

will generate this assembly language code:

```
    DataSeg
  HisAge dw 30
  HerAge dw 28
    CodeSeg
  mov ax,[HisAge]
  cmp ax,[HerAge]
```

But that's not all there is to it. TINY programs can use constants and strings
as well as **@Word** variables, and these other data types can be used in conditional tests. Our **@Compare** macro must be able to identify each variable or
constant type and generate the proper code in all circumstances.

When we implemented **@Write**, we created a helper macro called
TinyArgType that can distinguish among the different variable types. The
version of **@Compare** shown in Listing 7.22 uses this same macro to determine
the data type of each of the arguments, and then determines whether the
arguments can be compared. If the arguments are not type compatible, an error
message is issued and no code is generated.

```
 1:   ; Listing 7.22--Complete @Compare macro
 2:   ;
 3:   Macro @Compare Arg1,Condition,Arg2
 4:     Local CFlag,AType1,AType2,TArg1,TArg2
 5:     ;;
 6:     ;; Check for arguments.
 7:     ;;
 8:     ifb <Arg1>
 9:       Err
10:       Display "Constant or variable name expected"
```

```
11:        Exitm
12:      endif
13:      ifb <Arg2>
14:        Err
15:        Display "Constant or variable name expected"
16:        Exitm
17:      endif
18:      ;;
19:      ;; Check for condition.
20:      ;;
21:      CFlag = 0
22:      irp tCond,<LT,LE,EQ,GE,GT,NE>
23:        ifidni <Condition>,<TCond>
24:          CFlag = 1
25:          ExitM
26:        endif
27:      endm
28:      if CFlag eq 0
29:        Err
30:        Display "Invalid condition"
31:        Exitm
32:      endif
33:
34:      ;; Determine type of first argument.
35:      ;;
36:      WhatType Arg1,AType1
37:      if AType1 eq 2Ah        ; if it's a variable
38:        AType1 = Size Arg1    ; determine variable type
39:        TArg1 = Arg1
40:      elseif AType1 eq 0      ; otherwise, if it's a string constant
41:        @String TArg1 <Arg1>; define the string
42:        AType1 = 1            ; and set type to 1
43:      else                    ; it must be a numeric constant
44:        @Word TArg1 <Arg1>   ; so define the constant
45:        AType1 = 2            ; and set type to 2
46:      endif
47:
48:      ;;
49:      ;; Determine type of second argument.
50:      WhatType Arg2,AType2
51:      If AType2 eq 2Ah
52:        AType2 = Size Arg2
53:        TArg2 = Arg2
54:      elseif AType2 eq 0
55:        @String TArg2 <Arg2>
56:        AType2 = 1
57:      else
58:        @Word TArg2 <Arg2>
```

```
59:        AType2 = 2
60:     endif
61:
62:     ;;
63:     ;; Compare argument types. If they're incompatible,
64:     ;; issue an error message and exit.
65:     ;;
66:
67:     If AType1 ne AType2
68:        Err
69:        Display "Incompatible variable types in comparison"
70:        ExitM
71:     endif
72:
73:     ;;
74:     ;; Generate the proper comparison code. @String comparisons
75:     ;; call the StrCmp subroutine. @Word comparisons are
76:     ;; generated in-line.
77:     ;;
78:
79:     If AType1 eq 1
80:        ;; Set up variables and call string comparison routine.
81:        push ds
82:        pop es
83:        mov si,offset TArg1
84:        mov di,offset TArg2
85:        extrn StrCmp:Proc
86:        call StrCmp
87:     else
88:        mov ax,[TArg1]
89:        cmp ax,[TArg2]
90:     Endif
91:  Endm @Compare
```

@Compare will now identify argument types and generate the proper comparison code based on the parameters that are passed to it. All we have left to do is make **@If** generate the branching instruction that corresponds to the condition passed to it, and we've got a working **If...Then...Else** structure.

Putting It All Together

The conditional branching instructions generated by **@If** are the *complement* of the conditions passed in the **Condition** parameter. For example, this TINY statement:

```
@If MyAge eq 30
```

must generate a **jne** instruction, as shown:

```
  DataSeg
@Word ??0002 30
  CodeSeg
mov ax,[MyAge]
cmp ax,[??0002]
jne EndIf0
```

The final version of our **@If** macro is a combination of Listing 7.20 and the **@Compare** macro in Listing 7.22, with a few instructions thrown in to glue the pieces together. This final **@If** macro is shown in Listing 7.23, along with the **@Else** and **@EndIf** macros that work along with it.

```
 1:   ; Listing 7.23--@If, @Else, and @EndIf
 2:   ;
 3:   IfCount = 0
 4:   IfStkPtr = 0
 5:
 6:   Macro @If Arg1,Condition,Arg2
 7:     Local CFlag,AType1,AType2,TArg1,TArg2
 8:     ;;
 9:     ;; Check for arguments.
10:     ;;
11:     ifb <Arg1>
12:       Err
13:       Display "Constant or variable name expected"
14:       Exitm
15:     endif
16:     ifb <Arg2>
17:       Err
18:       Display "Constant or variable name expected"
19:       Exitm
20:     endif
21:     ;;
22:     ;; Check for condition.
23:     ;;
24:     CFlag = 0
25:     irp tCond,<LT,LE,EQ,GE,GT,NE>
26:       ifidni <Condition>,<TCond>
27:         CFlag = 1
28:         ExitM
29:       endif
30:     endm
31:     if CFlag eq 0
32:       Err
33:       Display "Invalid condition"
```

```
34:        Exitm
35:    endif
36:
37:    TinyArgType <Arg1>,AType1,TArg1        ;; determine type of Arg1
38:    TinyArgType <Arg2>,AType2,TArg2        ;; determine type of Arg2
39:
40:    ;;
41:    ;; Compare argument types. If they're incompatible,
42:    ;; issue an error message and exit.
43:    ;;
44:
45:    If AType1 ne AType2
46:       Err
47:       Display "Incompatible variable types in comparison"
48:       ExitM
49:    endif
50:
51:    ;;
52:    ;; Generate the proper comparison code. @String comparisons
53:    ;; call the StrCmp subroutine. @Word comparisons are
54:    ;; generated in-line.
55:    ;;
56:
57:    If AType1 eq 1
58:       ;; Set up variables and call string comparison routine.
59:       push ds
60:       pop es
61:       mov si,offset TArg1
62:       mov di,offset TArg2
63:       extrn StrCmp:Proc
64:       call StrCmp
65:    else
66:       mov ax,[TArg1]
67:       cmp ax,[TArg2]
68:    Endif
69:
70:    ;;
71:    ;; Now generate the required branching instruction.
72:    ;;
73:
74:    IfStkPtr = IfStkPtr + 1        ;; bump the stack pointer
75:    SetStk If,%IfStkPtr,IfCount    ;; push value on stack
76:    SetElseFlag %IfStkPtr,0 ;; clear the ElseFlag for this IF statement
77:    IfCount = IfCount + 1          ;; bump If counter
78:
79:    ifidni <Condition>,<LT>
80:       MakeJump jnb,Else,If,%IfStkPtr
81:    elseifidni <Condition>,<LE>
```

```
82:        MakeJump jnbe,Else,If,%IfStkPtr
83:     elseifidni <Condition>,<EQ>
84:        MakeJump jne,Else,If,%IfStkPtr
85:     elseifidni <Condition>,<GE>
86:        MakeJump jnae,Else,If,%IfStkPtr
87:     elseifidni <Condition>,<GT>
88:        MakeJump jna,Else,If,%IfStkPtr
89:     elseifidni <Condition>,<NE>
90:        MakeJump je,Else,If,%IfStkPtr
91:     endif
92:
93:     Endm @If
94:
95:     Macro SetStk StkName,Num,Value
96:        &StkName&Stk&Num = Value
97:     Endm SetStk
98:
99:     Macro SetElseFlag Num,Value
100:       ElseFlag&Num = Value
101:    Endm SetElseFlag
102:
103:    Macro MakeJump JmpType,JmpTarget,Targ,Arg1
104:       MakeJump2 JmpType,JmpTarget,%&Targ&Stk&Arg1
105:    Endm MakeJump
106:
107:    Macro MakeJump2 JmpType,JmpTarget,Arg2
108:       JmpType JmpTarget&Arg2
109:    Endm MakeJump2
110:
111:    ;
112:    ; @Else--process @Else statement.
113:    ;
114:    Macro @Else
115:       MakeJump jmp,Endif,If,%IfStkPtr ;; generate the branch around
116:                                       ;; the Else
117:       MakeLabel Else,IfStk,%IfStkPtr  ;; generate label for the
118:                                       ;; Else code
119:       SetElseFlag %IfStkPtr,1         ;; and set the Else flag for
120:                                       ;; this condition
121:    Endm @Else
122:
123:    ;
124:    ; @Endif--process @Endif statement.
125:    ;
126:    Macro @Endif
127:       CheckElseLbl %IfStkPtr  ;; generate Else label if required
128:                    ;; (that is, if no @Else was used in this statement)
129:       MakeLabel Endif,IfStk,%IfStkPtr  ;; generate the Endif label
```

```
130:        IfStkPtr = IfStkPtr - 1 ;; and bump to previous IfStk array item
131:    Endm
132:
133:    Macro CheckElseLbl Arg1
134:      if ElseFlag&Arg1 eq 0      ;; if Else label hasn't been defined yet
135:        MakeLabel Else,IfStk,%IfStkPtr ;; generate the label
136:      endif
137:    Endm CheckElseLbl
138:
139:    Macro MakeLabel LblType,StkPtr,Arg1
140:      MakeLabel2 LblType,%%StkPtr&Arg1
141:    Endm MakeLabel
142:
143:    Macro MakeLabel2 LblType,Arg2
144:      Label LblType&Arg2 Near
145:    Endm MakeLabel2
```

Comparing Strings

Before we look at a sample program that uses our new conditional branching instructions, let's add the **StrCmp** subroutine to our TINYLIB library. Listing 7.24 holds the entire source of the STRCMP.ASM file, which compares two TINY strings.

```
 1:   ; Listing 7.24--STRCMP.ASM
 2:   ;
 3:   ; STRCMP.ASM--String comparison for TINY.
 4:   ;
 5:   ; Call with DS:SI pointing to first string.
 6:   ;            ES:DI points to second string.
 7:   ;
 8:   ; Returns (x == don't care).
 9:   ;   Carry   Zero
10:   ;    Flag    Flag    Meaning
11:   ;   ------------------------
12:   ;    1       0       String1 < String2
13:   ;    x       1       String1 = String2
14:   ;    0       0       String1 > String2
15:   ;
16:      Ideal
17:      model small
18:      CodeSeg
19:   Public StrCmp
20:   Proc StrCmp
21:      lodsb                    ; length of string1 in AL
22:      mov ah,[es:di]           ; length of string2 in AH
23:      inc di
```

```
24:        mov cl,al               ; if string 1
25:        cmp cl,ah               ; is longer than string2
26:        jb @@Around
27:        mov cl,ah               ; use length of string2
28:     @@Around:
29:        xor ch,ch
30:        repe cmpsb              ; compare the strings
31:        jne @@Done              ; if strings not equal to this point
32:                                ; we're done
33:        cmp al,ah               ; otherwise, compare lengths
34:     @@Done:
35:        ret
36:     Endp StrCmp
37:
38:        End
```

Create a new file called STRCMP.ASM from the code in Listing 7.25. Then, edit TINYLIB.MAK and add **strcmp.obj** to the list of files that make up TINYLIB.LIB. Save the file and rebuild the library using MAKE.

To test our conditional structures, create a new file called IFTEST.TNY and enter the code shown in Listing 7.25.

```
 1:     ; Listing 7.25--IFTEST.TNY
 2:     ;
 3:     ; IFTEST.TNY--a test of TINY conditional structures.
 4:     ;
 5:     @Program
 6:        @String YourName
 7:        @Word YourAge
 8:        @Word MyAge 30
 9:     ;
10:     ; Get name and age.
11:     ;
12:        @Write "Enter your name "
13:        @Read YourName
14:        @WriteLn
15:        @Write "How old are you? "
16:        @Read YourAge
17:     ;
18:     ; Display greeting.
19:     ;
20:        @Write "Hello "
21:        @WriteLn YourName
22:        @Write "I see you are "
23:        @If YourAge gt MyAge
24:          @Write "older than"
25:        @Else
26:          @If YourAge lt MyAge
```

```
27:        @Write "younger than"
28:      @Else
29:        @Write "the same age as"
30:      @Endif
31:    @EndIf
32:    @WriteLn " I am."
33:  @EndProgram
```

Compile and link the program, and then run it by issuing the command:

```
iftest
```

at the DOS prompt. The program will ask you for your name and age, then tell you if you are older than, younger than, or the same age as I am.

With the addition of conditional structures, TINY is almost a real language—minimal, but real. All it requires is the addition of an assignment statement, arithmetic functions, and a looping construct. We'll look at assignments and arithmetic functions in the next section.

7.5 Assignment Statements and Arithmetic Functions

TINY assignment statements are very similar to assembly language assignment statements. For example, to assign the value 5 to the assembly language variable **ItemCount**, we would use this instruction:

```
mov [ItemCount],5
```

In TINY, we replace the **mov** instruction with the **@Assign** keyword, like this:

```
@Assign ItemCount 5
```

There are two basic differences between TINY **@Assign** statements and assembly language **mov** statements. First of all, in TINY, we can assign strings with a single statement, like this:

```
@Assign Hello <"Hello, world.">
```

assuming, of course, that **Hello** is a **@String** variable. In assembly language, this particular construct requires many lines of code to set up the index registers and copy each byte of the string using **movsb**.

The other major difference is that TINY variables can be directly assigned, as shown here:

```
@Assign SaveItemCount ItemCount
```

whereas in assembly language, we'd have to use a register for a temporary storage place. For example, the TINY code just shown would require these two assembly language statements:

```
mov ax,[ItemCount]
mov [SaveItemCount],ax
```

Arithmetic functions are also similar to their assembly language counterparts, but there is one other major difference. The TINY arithmetic functions accept a third parameter—a destination—which specifies where the result of an operation should be stored. For example, if we wanted to add 5 to the value of **ItemCount** and store the result in a variable called **CountPlus5**, the assembly language code would look something like this:

```
mov ax,[ItemCount]
add ax,5
mov [CountPlus5],ax
```

In TINY, we can accomplish the same thing with this single line of code:

```
@Add ItemCount 5 CountPlus5
```

which is equivalent in function to this C statement:

```
CountPlus5 = ItemCount + 5;
```

Neither assignment statements nor arithmetic functions are terribly difficult to implement in macros. Let's see how, starting with assignment statements.

Assigning TINY Values

The **@Assign** macro is really quite simple, compared to what we've already done. It's very similar to the **@Compare** macro that we used in the last section. Other than the generated code, the biggest difference between the two macros is that **@Assign** must ensure that the first parameter passed to it is a TINY variable. This extra bit of checking is easily handled by the **WhatType** macro, as shown in Listing 7.26.

```
1:    ; Listing 7.26--@Assign macro
2:    ;
3:    ; @Assign Arg1,Arg2.
4:    ;   Arg1 must be a TINY variable.
5:    ;   Arg2 can be a variable or a constant.
6:    ;   Incompatible argument types cause an error message.
7:
```

```
 8:    Macro @Assign Arg1,Arg2
 9:      Local AType1,AType2,TArg1,TArg2
10:      ;;
11:      ;; Check for arguments.
12:      ;;
13:      ifb <Arg1>
14:        Err
15:        Display "Variable name expected"
16:        Exitm
17:      endif
18:      ifb <Arg2>
19:        Err
20:        Display "Constant or variable name expected"
21:        Exitm
22:      endif
23:
24:      WhatType <Arg1>,AType1         ;; determine type of Arg1
25:      if AType1 ne 2Ah               ;; if it's not a TINY variable
26:        Err                          ;; display error message
27:        Display "Variable name expected"
28:        ExitM                        ;; and exit macro
29:      endif
30:
31:      TinyArgType <Arg1>,AType1,TArg1       ;; determine type of Arg1
32:      TinyArgType <Arg2>,AType2,TArg2       ;; determine type of Arg2
33:
34:      ;;
35:      ;; Compare argument types. If they're incompatible,
36:      ;; issue an error message and exit.
37:      ;;
38:
39:      If AType1 ne AType2
40:        Err
41:        Display "Incompatible variable types in assignment"
42:        ExitM
43:      endif
44:
45:      ;;
46:      ;; Generate the proper assignment code.
47:      ;;
48:      If AType1 eq 1
49:        push ds
50:        pop es
51:        mov si,offset TArg2
52:        mov di,offset TArg1
53:        mov cl,[TArg2]
54:        xor ch,ch
55:        rep movsb
```

```
56:      else
57:        mov ax,[TArg2]
58:        mov [TArg1],ax
59:      Endif
60:    Endm @Assign
```

Notice that assigning strings doesn't require an external subroutine. If we really wanted to save code bytes, we could make an external routine, but the small savings really isn't worth the trouble.

TINY Arithmetic Functions

As I said, **@Assign** wasn't too terribly difficult. Arithmetic functions are quite similar to **@Assign**, with the addition of a possible third parameter. As with **@Assign**, the arithmetic functions must ensure that the first parameter is a variable name. In addition, these functions must also ensure that the third parameter, if present, is also a variable name.

With the exception of the actual code generated, all of the TINY arithmetic instructions are identical. So, it would make sense to write a helper macro that performs all of the variable checking. The individual arithmetic functions, then, are very simple, as illustrated by the **@Add** macro in Listing 7.27.

```
1:    ; Listing 7.27--@Add macro
2:    ;
3:    ; @Add Arg1 Arg2 [Dest].
4:    ;
5:    Macro @Add Arg1,Arg2,Dest
6:      Local AType,TArg2
7:
8:      VarCheck Arg1,Arg2,Dest,AType,TArg2
9:      ;;
10:     ;; If AType is 0, there was an error in
11:     ;; the parameters, so exit the program.
12:     ;;
13:     If AType eq 0
14:       ExitM
15:     else
16:       mov ax,[Arg1]
17:       add ax,[TArg2]
18:       ifnb <Dest>
19:         mov [Dest],ax
20:       else
21:         mov [Arg1],ax
22:       endif
23:     endif
24:   Endm @Add
```

The **@Add** macro uses a macro called **@VarCheck** to verify the variable types. We'll get to **VarCheck** shortly.

If you examine the **@Add** macro, you'll see that there is only one line of code that will change for each of the arithmetic functions. For example, to make the **@Add** macro into a **@Sub** macro, all we have to do is change the line that reads:

```
add ax,[TArg2]
```

into

```
sub ax,[TArg2]
```

The **@Rem** (remainder) instruction will require two lines of code, but that's easily handled by a macro. If we apply the principles that we learned when we implemented the **MakeShiftRot** macro, we can save ourselves quite a bit of trouble, as shown in Listing 7.28, which implements all of the TINY arithmetic functions.

```
 1:    ; Listing 7.28--TINY arithmetic functions
 2:    ;
 3:    ; @Add Arg1 Arg2 [Dest]
 4:    ; @Sub Arg1 Arg2 [Dest]
 5:    ; @Mul Arg1 Arg2 [Dest]
 6:    ; @Div Arg1 Arg2 [Dest]
 7:    ; @Rem Arg1 Arg2 [Dest]
 8:    ;
 9:
10:    Macro TinyRem Arg1
11:      div [Arg1]
12:      mov ax,dx              ;; move remainder to AX
13:    Endm TinyRem
14:
15:    ;
16:    ; TinyArithFcn--generate a TINY arithmetic function.
17:    ;
18:    Macro TinyArithFcn FcnName,Inst
19:      Macro FcnName Arg1,Arg2,Dest
20:        Local AType,TempArg
21:        VarCheck Arg1,Arg2,Dest,AType,TempArg
22:        ;;
23:        ;; If AType is 0, there was an error in
24:        ;; the parameters, so exit the program.
25:        ;;
26:        If AType eq 0
27:          ExitM
```

```
28:        else
29:          mov ax,[Arg1]
30:          Inst                 ;; macro-dependent instruction(s)
31:          ifnb <Dest>
32:            mov [Dest],ax
33:          else
34:            mov [Arg1],ax
35:          endif
36:        endif
37:      Endm FcnName
38:    Endm TinyArithFcn
39:
40:    TinyArithFcn @Add,<add ax,[TempArg]>
41:    TinyArithFcn @Sub,<sub ax,[TempArg]>
42:    TinyArithFcn @Mul,<mul [TempArg]>
43:    TinyArithFcn @Div,<div [TempArg]>
44:    TinyArithFcn @Rem,<TinyRem TempArg>
```

The only thing left to implement is the **VarCheck** macro, which performs all of the parameter checking for the arithmetic functions. **VarCheck** ensures that each of the parameters is a **@Word** and that the first parameter (and the optional third parameter) are defined variables. If all of the parameters check out, **VarCheck** will return with the **AType** parameter set to 1. If any error occurs, **VarCheck** will issue an error message and return with **AType** set to 0. This processing is very similar to that done by the **Assign** macro, as you can see by Listing 7.29.

```
1:    ; Listing 7.29--VarCheck macro
2:    ;
3:    Macro VarCheck Arg1,Arg2,Dest,AType,TArg2
4:      Local AType1,AType2,TArg1,TDest,DType
5:      ;;
6:      ;; Check for arguments.
7:      ;;
8:      ifb <Arg1>
9:        Err
10:        Display "Variable name expected"
11:        Exitm
12:      endif
13:      ifb <Arg2>
14:        Err
15:        Display "Constant or variable name expected"
16:        Exitm
17:      endif
18:
19:      WhatType <Arg1>,AType1          ;; determine type of Arg1
20:      if AType1 ne 2Ah                ;; if it's not a TINY variable
```

```
21:        Err                          ;; display error message
22:        Display "Variable name expected"
23:        ExitM                        ;; and exit macro
24:     endif
25:
26:     TinyArgType <Arg1>,AType1,TArg1 ;; determine type of Arg1
27:     TinyArgType <Arg2>,AType2,TArg2 ;; determine type of Arg2
28:
29:     ifnb <Dest>                      ;; if Dest specified,
30:       WhatType <Dest>,DType          ;; determine type of Dest
31:       if DType ne 2Ah                ;; if it's not a TINY variable
32:         Err                          ;; display error message
33:         Display "Variable name expected"
34:         ExitM                        ;; and exit program
35:       endif
36:       TinyArgType <Dest>,DType,TDest
37:     else
38:       DType = 2                      ;; otherwise, just set it
39:     endif
40:
41:     if (AType1 ne 2) or (AType2 ne 2) or (DType ne 2)
42:       Err
43:       Display "All arguments must be of type @Word"
44:       AType = 0
45:     Else
46:       AType = 1
47:     Endif
48:   Endm VarCheck
```

Now we have a real programming language. It's primitive, sure, but we can write programs that actually *do* something. For example, the TINY program shown in Listing 7.30 prompts for your name and age, and then tells you how much younger or older you are than I am.

```
 1:  ; Listing 7.30--AGE.TNY
 2:  ;
 3:  ; AGE.TNY--a test of TINY arithmetic functions.
 4:  ;
 5:  @Program
 6:     @String YourName
 7:     @Word YourAge
 8:     @Word MyAge 30
 9:     @Word Work
10:  ;
11:  ; Get name and age.
12:  ;
13:     @Write "Enter your name "
14:     @Read YourName
```

```
15:     @WriteLn
16:     @Write "How old are you? "
17:     @Read YourAge
18:   ;
19:   ; Display greeting.
20:   ;
21:     @Write "Hello "
22:     @WriteLn YourName
23:     @Write "I see you are "
24:     @If YourAge gt MyAge
25:       @Sub YourAge MyAge Work
26:       @Write Work
27:       @Write " years older than"
28:     @Else
29:       @If YourAge lt MyAge
30:         @Sub MyAge YourAge Work
31:         @Write Work
32:         @Write " years younger than"
33:       @Else
34:         @Write "the same age as"
35:       @Endif
36:     @EndIf
37:     @WriteLn " I am."
38:   @EndProgram
```

We've got one other construct to cover before we wrap up our discussion of TINY. Currently, TINY is a one-way language. Execution starts at the top of the program and continues to the end with only simple conditionals to break the program flow. In order to get any but the simplest work done, our language really needs a looping construct. Fortunately, adding such a construct is fairly simple, especially since we've already done most of the hard work.

7.6 TINY Loops

Looping in TINY is accomplished with the **@While** statement. TINY **@While** loops work in much the same way as **while** loops work in Pascal, C, or BASIC. The function of a TINY **@While** loop can be loosely described by this pseudocode:

```
Top:
  if condition is met
    perform statements between @While and @EndWhile
    goto top
  endif
```

We've already got a conditional structure, **@If**, so processing the condition is no great problem. The only difficulty lies in keeping track of the **@While** statements so that nested looping constructs are supported. We discussed nesting problems when we implemented **@If**, and **@While** will use the same format. There aren't really any new concepts to introduce, so let's just take a look at the implementation of **@While** and **@EndWhile** in Listing 7.31.

```
 1:    ; Listing 7.31--@While, @EndWhile, @Break
 2:    ;
 3:    WhileCount = 0
 4:    WhileStkPtr = 0
 5:
 6:    Macro @While Arg1,Condition,Arg2
 7:      WhileStkPtr = WhileStkPtr + 1
 8:      SetStk While,%WhileStkPtr,WhileCount
 9:      MakeLabel While,WhileStk,%WhileStkPtr
10:      WhileCount = WhileCount + 1
11:      @If <Arg1> <Condition> <Arg2>
12:    Endm @While
13:
14:    Macro @EndWhile
15:      MakeJump jmp,While,While,%WhileStkPtr
16:      MakeLabel EndWhile,WhileStk,%WhileStkPtr
17:      WhileStkPtr = WhileStkPtr - 1
18:      @Endif
19:    Endm @EndWhile
20:
21:    Macro @Break
22:      MakeJump jmp,EndWhile,While,%WhileStkPtr
23:    Endm @Break
```

The **@While**, **@EndWhile**, and **@Break** macros make heavy use of the helper macros that were introduced with the **@If** structure.

The program in Listing 7.32, WHILETST.TNY, illustrates the use of **@While** loops in a simple program.

```
 1:    ; Listing 7.32--WHILETST.TNY
 2:    ;
 3:    ; WHILETST.TNY--illustrate the use of @While.
 4:    ;
 5:    @Program
 6:      @Word Mine 0
 7:      @Word Yours
 8:      @While Mine lt 10
 9:        @Add Mine 1
10:        @WriteLn Mine
11:        @Assign Yours Mine
12:        @While Yours gt 0
13:          @Write " "
14:          @WriteLn Yours
```

```
15:            @Sub Yours 1
16:          @EndWhile
17:          @If Mine gt 3
18:             @Break
19:          @EndIf
20:      @EndWhile
21:  @EndProgram
```

When executed, this program will produce the following output:

```
00001
   00001
00002
   00002
   00001
00003
   00003
   00002
   00001
00004
   00004
   00003
   00002
   00001
```

7.7 TINY Enhancements

That's as far as we'll take TINY. As primitive as it is, the language can be used for programs that do real work. And we could easily make it even more useful by adding features. I've experimented with several extensions to the language and have been pleased with the results. Let me share with you some of the additions that I've experimented with.

@Goto Statement

One of the most useful additions to the TINY language would be an unconditional branching statement similar to the BASIC **GOTO** statement. There are several cases in which this construct would come in handy. A situation that comes readily to mind is in complex conditionals.

Because TINY conditionals cannot use the boolean operators **and**, **or**, and **not**, writing complex conditionals is a fairly painful process. For example, this Pascal conditional statement:

```
If (NumFlag = 1) and (EndOfLine = False) Then
  WriteLn ('OK');
```

```
else
  WriteLn ('Not OK');
```

is translated into the following TINY statements:

```
@If NumFlag eq 1
  @If EndOfLine eq False
    @WriteLn "OK"
  @Else
    @WriteLn "Not OK"
  @EndIf
@Else
  @WriteLn "Not OK"
@EndIf
```

If we were to add a **@Goto** statement to TINY, we could rewrite the previous code so that it looks like this:

```
  @If NumFlag eq 1
    @If EndOfLine eq False
      @WriteLn "OK"
    @Else
      @Goto NotOk
    @EndIf
  @Else
@Label NotOk
    @WriteLn "Not OK"
  @EndIf
```

which is still more cumbersome than the Pascal syntax but more efficient in terms of code size than the current TINY syntax.

@ElseIf and @Switch

TINY's conditional structure is very primitive and would benefit from any enhancements that we could make. Adding an **@ElseIf** statement would enable us to turn this TINY code fragment:

```
@If Count eq 1
  ; Do this.
@Else
  @If Count eq 0
    ; Do that.
  @Else
    ; Do the other thing.
  @EndIf
@EndIf
```

into this, which I consider more readable:

```
@If Count eq 1
  ; Do this.
@ElseIf Count eq 2
  ; Do that.
@Else
  ; Do the other thing.
@EndIf
```

Similarly, a **@Switch** statement would make long strings of **@If** statements easier to write and understand, and would also generate slightly more efficient code. Using **@Switch**, the preceding code would become

```
@Switch Count
  @Case 1
    ; do this
  @Case 2
    ; do that
  @Else
    ; do the other thing
@EndSwitch
```

The addition of **@ElseIf** and **@Switch** is more involved than adding **@Goto**, but still not terribly difficult. If you attempt these enhancements, you will find that most of the "guts" can be found in the code that implements **@If**, **@Else**, and **@EndIf**.

More Looping Structures: @Repeat and @For

In most programming languages, all looping structures are modifications of the **while** construct. If you use the basic **@While** structure of TINY, you can implement Pascal-like **@For** and **@Repeat** loops.

Again, these modifications, although involved, should present no great difficulty if you understand the concepts that have been presented in this book.

Using Assembly Language Instructions

You have probably noticed that nothing in the TINY language prevents you from interspersing assembly language instructions in your TINY programs. For example, the TINY program below writes asterisks on the screen until a key is pressed.

```
@Program
  @Word KeyFlag 0 ; flag is set to 1 when key is pressed
```

```
    @While KeyFlag eq 0
      @Write "*"
      mov ah,1
      int 16h     ; use BIOS to see whether a key is available
      jz NoKey
      @Assign KeyFlag 1
Label NoKey Near
    @EndWhile
@EndProgram
```

As long as your sequence of assembly language instructions ends with the current segment pointer pointing to the code segment, you can use any assembly language instructions you like inside your TINY programs.

This ability to intermix assembly language instructions and TINY statements brings about an interesting possible use for an enhanced **@If** structure. If you were to modify the **@If** macro so that it recognized register names and 8086 flag conditions, you could use the macro in your everyday assembly language programs.

For example, with an enhanced **@If** statement, you could turn this assembly language code:

```
GetKey:      ; wait for key press
  mov ah,1
  int 16h
  jz GetKey
```

into this:

```
@While Z      ; wait for key press
  mov ah,1
  int 16h
@EndWhile
```

This is a *very* useful enhancement that provides high-level language syntax to assembly language programmers *at no cost in code efficiency.*

That's just a sample of the possible additions you can make to the TINY language. For the most part, any high-level language construct can be duplicated using macros. I've experimented with procedures and functions, formatted I/O, and even modem interfacing with TINY-like languages, and I've been very pleased with the results.

7.8 Wrapping It Up

I pointed out at the beginning of this chapter that I don't expect TINY to replace BASIC, Pascal, or C as an all-purpose programming language. The point is that you can implement a rudimentary language using assembly language macros. I have found this ability useful in two situations, the first of which I mentioned at the beginning of the chapter—designing a special-purpose language for controlling an oddball piece of equipment.

I have also used macros in developing new compiled languages. It's much easier to create a macro that implements a large portion of a construct than it is to develop a parsing routine and code generator that will implement the entire thing. When I'm developing a language that will be used in a product, the first experiments are coded in assembly language macros. This enables me to concentrate on getting the constructs' syntax down without having to recode a parser or lexical analyzer every time I make a small change in the language. Once I'm satisfied with the syntax of the language, I can build the customized parser.

If you've compiled the example programs presented in this chapter, you have noticed that TINY programs take longer to compile than do "normal" assembly language programs. Short of rewriting the assembler, there's not much we can do to increase the compile speed. However, as I pointed out in Chapter 1, the extra time the programs take to compile will be more than made up for by the time you save in writing your programs.

The next time you need to interface with a special-purpose piece of equipment, or if you need a small language for an application you're writing, consider implementing the language using assembly language macros. I think you'll find that your development time is shortened and that your finished programs are faster and smaller than equivalent programs written in a higher-level language. And with the major control constructs already implemented by TINY, developing the new language is a simple matter of adding the application-specific macros.

Building TINY.DEF and TINYLIB.LIB

The files that make up the TINY system are the definitions file, TINY.DEF, and the library file, TINYLIB.LIB. TINYLIB.LIB only contains three modules. They are

Listing 7.12 WRITENUM.ASM
Listing 7.16 READNUM.ASM
Listing 7.24 STRCMP.ASM

The file that tells MAKE how to build TINYLIB is called TINYLIB.MAK. Its contents are shown in Listing 7.33.

```
1:   # Listing 7.33--TINYLIB.MAK
2:   #
3:   # TINYLIB.LIB--build library TINYLIB.LIB.
```

```
4:    #
5:    .asm.obj:
6:      tasm /m $*
7:      tlib tinylib -+$*
8:
9:    tinylib.lib: writenum.obj readnum.obj strcmp.obj
```

Finally, the file that contains all of the TINY definitions is called TINY.DEF. Instructions for building TINY.DEF are shown in Listing 7.34.

```
1:    ; Listing 7.34--Building TINY.DEF
2:    ;
3:      %NoList
4:    ;
5:    ; TINY.DEF
6:    ;   TINY language definition file. This file contains all
7:    ; of the TINY language macros.
8:    ;
9:    ; Assembly command line:
10:   ;   tasm /m/l/dTinyProg="fname.TNY" tiny.def,fname,fname
11:   ;
12:   ; where <fname> is replaced by the name of the TINY program to
13:   ; be compiled. This will create fname.OBJ and fname.LST.
14:   ;
15:     ideal
16:   include "macros.inc"
17:   include "dosmacs.inc"
18:   includelib "tinylib.lib"
19:
20:   ;
21:   ; ********************************************************
22:   ; *              Language Definition Macros              *
23:   ; ********************************************************
24:   ;
25:
26:   ;
27:   ; @Program
28:   ; Generate program header and program start address.
29:   ;
30:   Macro @Program
31:     ProgramHeader Small,0100h
32:     CodeSeg
33:     Label ??BeginProgram Near
34:     ExeStart
35:   Endm @Program
36:
37:   ;
38:   ; @EndProgram
```

```
39:    ; Generate program exit code and End statement.
40:    ;
41:    Macro @EndProgram
42:      DosExitProgram 0
43:      End ??BeginProgram
44:    Endm @Program
45:
46:    Include the following listings:
47:
48:    Listing 7.6      ; @Word
49:    Listing 7.7      ; @String
50:    Listing 7.10     ; @WriteLn
51:    Listing 7.11     ; @Write
52:    Listing 7.15     ; @Read
53:    Listing 7.16     ; @If, @Else, @EndIf
54:    Listing 7.27     ; @Assign
55:    Listing 7.29     ; Arithmetic functions
56:    Listing 7.30     ; VarCheck (used by 7.29)
57:    Listing 7.32     ; @While, @EndWhile, @Break
58:
59:    ;
60:    ; Compile the user's program.
61:    ;
62:      %List
63:    include TinyProg
64:      %NoList
```

8

Version-Specific Information

All of the macros in the preceding chapters have been tested with (and work fine with) Ideal mode in all versions (1.0 through 3.0) of Turbo Assembler. The MASM-compatible code on the listings diskette has also been tested with all versions of Turbo Assembler. As written, the code will not assemble with any version of Microsoft Assembler, for reasons that I will point out in this chapter.

Since I began working on this book, both Microsoft and Borland have released new assemblers: Microsoft Macro Assembler 6.0 and Borland Turbo Assembler 3.0. Some of the features of these new assemblers come in very handy when you work with macros. In addition, several of the new features of MASM 6.0 are of interest even if you're not using macros in your programs.

8.1 TASM 3.0 New Features

Three new macro-specific features were included in Turbo Assembler version 3.0. They are the **GOTO** directive, the **WHILE** directive, and argument typing. Let's take a quick look at each one.

Tags and the GOTO Directive

The **GOTO** macro directive works just like a **GOTO** statement in BASIC—it transfers control from the current line to the line that contains the specified tag symbol. For example, the following macro will display "Hello, world" only if the variable **Flag** is equal to 1:

```
Macro Greeting Flag
  if Flag ne 1
    goto DontGreet
  endif
  display "Hello, world"
:DontGreet
Endm Greeting
```

Notice that the tag symbol, **DontGreet**, must start with a colon and occupy the entire macro line.

I haven't had to use **GOTO** very much, but then, I've never had it to use until just recently. Every time I've used **GOTO**, it has been within a complex conditional structure. For example, consider the following macro, which expects **Arg1** to be nonblank and **Arg2** to be greater than 0:

```
Macro ThisMac Arg1,Arg2
  ifnb <Arg1>
    if Arg2 gt 0
      Display "Proper calling sequence"
    else
```

```
      Display "Improper calling sequence"
    endif
  else
    Display "Improper calling sequence"
  endif
Endm ThisMac
```

Using **GOTO**, macro **ThisMac** can be rewritten as shown:

```
Macro ThisMac Arg1,Arg2
  ifnb <Arg1>
    if Arg2 gt 0
      Display "Proper calling sequence"
      Goto Around
    endif
  endif
  Display "Improper calling sequence"
:Around
Endm ThisMac
```

The benefits of **GOTO** are difficult to show with such a small example—you have to use some imagination. Suppose we replaced the **Display** statement in the previous example with 100 assembly language instructions. Which of the macros would you rather write?

Be very careful, though, where you place the target of your **GOTO** directive. Placing it within a conditional or within a **REPT** or **WHILE** block will cause an error. For example, the **GOTO** target in the following macro is in the middle of a REPT loop:

```
Macro TestMac
  goto Around
  rept 2
:Around
    Display "This is a test"
  endm
Endm TestMac
```

When this macro is invoked, the **GOTO** directive transfers control to the middle of the **REPT** block—bypassing the **REPT** directive. When the assembler encounters the **ENDM** directive that ends the **REPT** block, it thinks the macro is ended. Then it encounters the line that reads

```
Endm TestMac
```

and issues this error message:

```
**Error** test.ASM(13) TESTMAC(6) Can't use this outside macro
```

Be careful also of infinite loops. With **GOTO**, it's quite possible to build a macro that never exits. If this happens, the assembler could very well go off into Never Never Land and not tell you that it ran out of memory. Be careful when you use **GOTO** to jump backward in your macros.

The WHILE Directive

The macro **WHILE** directive works just like a Pascal or C **while** statement—it repeats a block of statements while a condition is true. The syntax, as shown here, is very similar to the syntax of the **REPT** directive:

```
WHILE expression
  macro body
ENDM
```

I've found **WHILE** to be very useful when generating tables or performing other tasks that require a counting variable. For example, we used **REPT** to generate the lowercase conversion table in Listing 3.13 because that was the only looping structure we had. If we had known about the **WHILE** directive, we could have written this:

```
; Generate the lowercase conversion table.
Char = 0
While Char le 256
  if (Char ge 'A') and (Char le 'Z')
    db Char or 20h
  else
    db Char
  endif
  Char = Char + 1
endm
```

Using **WHILE** doesn't save any lines of code, true, but it does seem more understandable to me.

Remember, though, that **WHILE** can be used for more than just counting loops. For example, consider the following macro that generates up to 10 **DISPLAY** statements, depending on the value of the argument passed to it:

```
Macro TestMac Arg1
  While Arg1 lt 10
    Display "Hello"
    Arg1 = Arg1 + 1
  Endm
Endm TestMac
```

Duplicating this macro using **REPT** is possible, but messy, as shown:

```
Macro TestMac Arg1
  rept 10
    if Arg1 ge 10
      exitm
    else
      Display "Hello"
      Arg1 = Arg1 + 1
    endif
  Endm
Endm TestMac
```

I don't know about you, but I'd rather use the **WHILE** directive for things like this.

As with **GOTO**, you must be careful when using **WHILE**, lest you code an infinite loop. Make sure that your conditional expression can evaluate to false, or include some other way for the loop to end—either with **EXITM** or **GOTO**.

Argument Typing

One of the most common errors that programmers make when using macros is forgetting to pass an argument. If the macro that is being invoked does not have sufficient argument checking, failure to pass an argument can cause some very strange errors during assembly. Fortunately, TASM 3.0 provides two argument types that help lessen the consequences of making this type of error.

You may recall the following code fragment from our **IsIn** macro (Listing 5.7). This is typical of the code that we must write in order to ensure that a macro is invoked with the proper arguments:

```
Macro IsIn Reg,Values,YesBranch,NoBranch
  Local Done,Counter
  ifb <Reg>
    err
    Display "<Reg> parameter required in macro IsIn"
    exitm
  elseifb <Values>
    err
    Display "<Values> parameter required in macro IsIn"
    exitm
  endif
  . . .
  . . .
Endm IsIn
```

The new argument typing directives provided by TASM 3.0 eliminate the need to do this type of argument checking. If we define the macro argument as required (with **Req**), the assembler will perform the argument checking for us:

```
Macro IsIn Reg:Req,Values:Req,YesBranch,NoBranch
  Local Done,Counter
  . . .
  . . .
Endm IsIn
```

With this macro definition, the macro invocation

```
IsIn al,,IsThere,NotThere
```

will produce an error message similar to the following:

```
**Error** test.ASM(10) Macro argument is required
```

Many times, we want to have the value of a macro argument default to some known value if the argument is not specified in the macro invocation. For example, in our **ProgramHeader** macro (Listing 2.2, reproduced here), the default memory model is **Small**, and the default stack size is **0100H**:

```
Macro ProgramHeader ModelName,StackSize
  %PushLCtl
  %Macs
  Jumps
  ifnb <ModelName>
    Model ModelName
  else
    Model Small      ; default to SMALL model
  endif
  ifnb <StackSize>
    Stack StackSize
  else
    Stack 100h     ; default stack size is 0100h
  endif
  %PopLCtl
Endm ProgramHeader
```

With TASM 3.0, we can give a macro argument a default value simply by specifying the default value when we define the macro. This is done by using the **:=** argument typing directive, as shown:

```
Macro ProgramHeader ModelName:=<Small>,StackSize:=<0100h>
  %PushLCtl
  %Macs
```

```
   %Masm51
   Jumps
   Model ModelName
   Stack StackSize
   %PopLCtl
Endm ProgramHeader
```

If we were to invoke the above macro with this statement:

```
ProgramHeader
```

the assembler would produce the following directives:

```
Jumps
Model Small
Stack 0100h
```

We can still override the defaults by specifying the arguments when the macro is invoked. For example, if we needed a larger stack, we could invoke the macro with this statement:

```
ProgramHeader ,0800h
```

and the assembler would correctly generate a **Stack 0800h** directive.

Two other argument types, **VARARG** and **REST**, determine how the assembler treats extra arguments passed to macros. The first, **VARARG**, causes the macro to interpret the last argument and everything following it as a comma-separated list of values. Angle brackets and commas are added to ensure this interpretation. For example, a very early version of macro **IsIn** simply set the flags and branched to the end of the macro. This version of **IsIn** was very simple, as shown:

```
Macro IsIn Reg,Values
  Local Done
  irp V,<Values>
    cmp <Reg>,V
    jz Done
  endm
Done:
Endm IsIn
```

The macro was invoked in much the same way as the new **IsIn** macro, but there were no branching parameters. For example, this macro invocation:

```
IsIn al,<' ',',',tab,cr>
```

would produce this code:

```
  cmp al,' '
  jz Done
  cmp al,','
  jz Done
  cmp al,tab
  jz Done
  cmp al,cr
  jz Done
Done:
```

Using **VARARG**, it is not necessary to enclose the second argument to **IsIn** in angle brackets. If the macro definition were changed to

```
Macro IsIn Reg,Values:Vararg
```

then the following macro invocation would also produce the code just shown:

```
IsIn al,' ',',',tab,cr
```

The **REST** argument type is similar to **VARARG**, but subtly different. Whereas **VARARG** treats extra text as a comma-separated list of values, **REST** treats it as raw text—no commas or angle brackets are added. To see how these two interpretations differ, consider a very simple macro that defines a text string 1 byte at a time. This macro, **DefStr**, is shown here:

```
Macro DefStr Str:Vararg
  irpc Chr,<Str>
    db '&Chr&'
  endm
endm DefStr
```

When **DefStr** is invoked with the following statement (notice that there are spaces between the letters):

```
DefStr H E L L O
```

the macro generates the following code:

```
db 'H'
db ','
db 'E'
db ','
db 'L'
db ','
db 'L'
```

```
db ','
db '0'
```

No matter how many spaces we put between the characters, the macro will generate the preceding code. Why? Because **VARARG** causes the assembler to treat extra arguments as a comma-separated list of values. Extra white space is condensed and commas are placed between the arguments. This interpretation produces the same result as if we had invoked the macro with this statement:

```
DefStr <H,E,L,L,O>
```

If we were to change the macro definition so that the **Str** argument has the **REST** type, as shown here:

```
Macro DefStr Str:Rest
```

and then invoke it as previously shown, the result would be this code:

```
db 'H'
db ' '
db 'E'
db ' '
db 'L'
db ' '
db 'L'
db ' '
db '0'
```

REST causes extra arguments to be treated as raw text. In this case, the arguments are interpreted as though we had typed this:

```
DefStr <H E L L 0>
```

8.2 Using the MASM Mode Code

Although the discussions and code examples in the preceding chapters have been specific to Turbo Assembler Ideal mode, most of the information in this book is applicable to Turbo Assembler's MASM compatibility mode, Microsoft Assembler, and most Microsoft-compatible assemblers. There are a few syntax differences, though, that can be confusing if they sneak up on you.

MASM Mode Macro Definitions

The most basic difference between Ideal mode macros and MASM mode macros is in the macro definition. As you recall, an Ideal mode macro takes this form:

```
Macro MacroName [Arguments]
  macro body
Endm MacroName
```

MASM mode macros use a slightly different syntax. The macro name comes before the **Macro** directive, and the macro name cannot be given after the **EndM** directive. So, a MASM mode macro takes this form:

```
MacroName Macro [Arguments]
  macro body
Endm
```

If you get confused and try to use an Ideal mode macro definition in a MASM mode program, the assembler will issue an "Illegal Instruction" error.

The MASM mode syntax for the **Proc** and **Struc** directives is reversed as well. For example, a MASM mode procedure is defined like this:

```
ProcName Proc
  ; body of procedure
ProcName EndP
```

Similarly, a MASM mode structure looks like this:

```
StrucName Struc
  ; structure definitions
StrucName Ends
```

SymType Versus .TYPE

Beyond those very elementary syntatic changes, most Ideal mode code is MASM mode compatible. There are some other differences, which you can see by comparing the two versions of the code that are supplied on the listings diskette. The most significant of these is the MASM mode use of the **.TYPE** directive in place of **SymType**, because **SymType** is recognized only in Ideal mode.

8.3 Other Assemblers

Try as I might, I was unable to completely avoid the use of TASM-specific features in the MASM mode code. In several places, I've used TASM-specific listing directives (**%NoIncl**, **%PushLCtl**, and **%PopLCtl**), and the **Masm51** directive is required in order to use some of the assembler's features, most notably continuation lines and the **InStr** operator. Two other TASM-specific features, though, were absolutely necessary in order to get the code to work properly.

Automatic Jump Sizing

If you've worked with Microsoft Assembler versions prior to 6.0, you're more than likely familiar with the "Jump out of range by 3 byte(s)" error that the assembler spits out when you code a conditional jump whose offset is not within the proper range. For example, this code fragment:

```
    .code
There:
  db 127 dup (?)
  jnz There
```

will produce the following error message when assembled with MASM 5.1:

```
error A2053: Jump out of range by 1 byte(s)
```

Turbo Assembler has the ability (enabled by inserting a **Jumps** directive in your code) to automatically change the preceding code to the following, which is what you would have written anyway if you had known that your jump was going to be out of range:

```
    .code
There:
  db 127 dup (?)
  jz Around
  jmp There
Around:
```

This feature is called *automatic jump sizing* and was pioneered (as near as I can tell) by SLR System's OPTASM optimizing assembler. It works like this: If the assembler determines that the offset is not within the 1-byte range of the conditional jump instructions, the assembler substitutes the longer "jump around a jump" code shown earlier.

Some of the sample programs on the listings diskette, and *all* of the macros that accept branching parameters, require automatic jump sizing to be enabled. If your assembler supports automatic jump sizing, be sure that it is enabled.

If your assembler does not support this feature, at least one of the filter subroutines will not assemble correctly as it is currently written. Furthermore, your branching parameters to **IsIn**, **IsRange**, **GetCh**, and many of the other macros will be restricted to 1-byte offsets. You could conceivably rewrite these macros so that they produce the longer "jump around a jump" code by default, but you'd be much better off to spend the money on one of the newer assemblers.

QUIRKS Mode

When we were enhancing our **DosDisplayString** macro in Chapter 3, we discussed a construct that Turbo Assembler is unable to handle unless the **QUIRKS** mode is enabled. To recap, if the assembler encounters an **ifb**, **ifnb**, or other macro conditional whose argument contains characters after the first right angle bracket, the assembler outputs an "Extra characters on line" error.

For example, the following macro accepts a single parameter and reports whether the parameter is blank:

```
TestParam Macro Param
  ifb <Param>
    %Out "Blank parameter"
  else
    %Out "Parameter passed"
  endif
EndM
```

If this macro is invoked with an argument that contains nested angle brackets, like this:

```
TestParam <Hello, <"Hello, world">>
```

the assembler will output this error message:

```
**Error** test.ASM(13) TESTPARAM(1) Extra characters on line
```

If, however, we place a **QUIRKS** directive somewhere in the source before we invoke **TestParam**, TASM will ignore the "extra character" on the line, and the program will assemble correctly.

The mandatory use of **QUIRKS** mode for this particular construct causes two problems. First of all, the code cannot be assembled with MASM unless you first remove all of the **QUIRKS** directives from the code. Secondly, there isn't a **NOQUIRKS** directive. The only way that I know of to turn off **QUIRKS** is to go into **Ideal** mode and then back to **MASM** mode.

Fortunately, both of these problems can be overcome with the use of macros. In the MASM mode code on the listings diskette, you'll notice that I've included a **NoQuirks** macro that looks like this:

```
NoQuirks Macro
  Ideal
  Masm
Endm
```

I use this macro in place of the **Ideal** directives within conditional expressions in the macros that need it.

Using Other Assemblers

In order to assemble the example programs with MASM, OPTASM, or other assemblers, you'll have to identify each of the Turbo Assembler-specific directives that I've used and disable them using text equates. For example, the following text equates disable the **Locals**, **Masm**, **Ideal**, **Quirks**, and **%NoIncl** directives:

```
; Disable TASM-specific directives
Locals equ <>
Masm equ <>
Ideal equ <>
Quirks equ <>
%NoIncl equ <>
```

There are other TASM-specific directives used in the code on the listings diskette. They must all be disabled as shown in order to use the code with other assemblers.

Unfortunately, some assemblers do not correctly handle some of the constructs that our macros use. For example, MASM version 5.1 cannot correctly assemble our redefined shift and rotate instructions. It appears that MASM 5.1 does not correctly **Purge** the macro definition, causing it to go into an infinite loop—which causes a stack overflow.

There are several other incompatibilities that I discovered while I was attempting to make these macros usable with Microsoft Assembler. After struggling with the conversion for several days, MASM's inability to correctly handle the **MakeShiftRot** and **ShiftRot** macros finally convinced me to abandon the project. As a result, the macros on the listings diskette have not been tested with anything other than Turbo Assembler.

8.4 MASM 6.0 New Features

You may wonder, after reading the previous section, why I've chosen to discuss MASM 6.0. Actually, after my experience with MASM 5.1, I did seriously consider omitting any discussion at all of any version of MASM. But Microsoft Assembler version 6.0 is a completely new product that has very little at all in common with MASM 5.1. In addition, version 6.0 provides some additional macro directives that, unless I miss my guess, will be included in the next version of Turbo Assembler.

Tags, GOTO, WHILE, and Argument Typing

As far as I've been able to determine, the **GOTO** and **WHILE** directives in MASM 6.0 work exactly as they do in TASM 3.0, as do the three argument typing directives: **REQ**, **VARARG**, and **:=**. The other argument typing directive supported by TASM 3.0, **REST**, is not supported by MASM 6.0.

For more information on using these directives, refer to the section on TASM 3.0 at the beginning of this chapter.

FOR, FORC, REPEAT

In what appears to be an attempt at making assembly language programming a bit less of a "black art," Microsoft has renamed the **IRP**, **IRPC**, and **REPT** directives. The **FOR** directive replaces **IRP**, **FORC** replaces **IRPC**, and **REPEAT** replaces **REPT**.

I thought long and hard about this one, and seriously considered writing a nasty letter to Microsoft, complaining about that company's changes to the language. After all, **FOR** is just too simple and easy to remember. We assembly language programmers need obscure things like **IRPC** to keep us interested.

After thinking about it for a while, though, I decided that Microsoft was right. **FORC** *is* easier to remember than **IRPC**. So I added these three text equates to my MACROS.INC file:

```
for equ <irp>
forc equ <irpc>
repeat equ <rept>
```

TEXTEQU

In older versions of MASM, using the **EQU** directive was a crapshoot. You never knew whether you were going to end up with a constant or a text equate. There are rules to follow that will predict the outcome of a particular use of **EQU**, but the rules are pretty darned complicated and rife with exceptions, restrictions, and phase-of-the-moon irregularities. Rather than try to memorize the rules, I did the simplest thing I could think of: All of my text equates are bracketed, and my constants are defined using the **=** operator.

MASM 6.0 introduces the **TEXTEQU** operator, which *always* defines a text equate. Furthermore, labels defined with **TEXTEQU** can be redefined, just like labels defined with **=** can be redefined.

TEXTEQU is still a bit weird, though, in that *sometimes* it evaluates an expression when the label is defined, and other times it evaluates the expression when the label is used. Fortunately, there is one very simple rule that determines when the expression is evaluated. If the expression is bracketed, like this:

```
Msg TextEqu <Some text>
```

then the expression is evaluated when the label **Msg** is encountered in the source file. If the expression is not bracketed, the assembler attempts to evaluate it immediately. If we were to write this text equate:

```
Msg TextEqu Some text
```

the assembler would attempt to evaluate the expression **Some text**, and report that the symbol **Some** is not defined.

All in all, though, **TEXTEQU** is more powerful and more consistent than **EQU**. I recommend that you use **TEXTEQU** for defining your text equates and **=** to define constants. Let **EQU** die.

Macro Functions

Macro functions—macros that return a value—are positively the *slickest* addition to MASM 6.0. If they aren't available in the next version of Turbo Assembler, I will seriously consider changing assemblers once again. Let me show you what's so slick about macro functions.

Consider, for example, a simple macro that multiplies two numbers and returns the result. Using the techniques that you learned in Chapter 3 when we developed the **WhatType** and **CheckSeg** macros, we might write this macro like this:

```
MulMac Macro Arg1, Arg2, Result
  Result = (Arg1 * Arg2)
Endm
```

Now, if we invoked this macro with this statement:

```
MulMac 3, 5, TheAnswer
```

the generated code would be

```
TheAnswer = (3 * 5)
```

Using this technique is all right, but it strikes me as something of a kludge. If you're familiar with Pascal, you'll probably draw the parallel of using a **VAR** procedure parameter to return a value, rather than using a function. It's just not *clean*.

With MASM 6.0, macros can be used to return values—just like functions in Pascal or C. And it's really simple to do. For example, our **MulMac** macro written as a macro function looks like this:

```
MulMac Macro Arg1, Arg2
  exitm <(Arg1 * Arg2)>
Endm
```

Now, if we want to define a label using this macro, we simply write:

```
TheAnswer = MulMac (3, 5)
```

The result is the same, but macro functions just look so much *cleaner.*

Of course, nobody would write a macro function to multiply two numbers. But imagine how much cleaner some of our macros would look if we turned **CheckSeg** and **WhatType** into macro functions.

High-Level Language Structures

Probably the second slickest enhancement to MASM 6.0 is the addition of high-level language structures. These structures provide assembly language programmers with high-level **If...Then...Else** processing and looping constructs, at no cost in code efficiency. This addition to the assembly language makes it much easier to write loops and conditionals.

Consider, for example, a very simple assembly language conditional statement, in which you want to branch if the value in the AX register is less than 10. An experienced assembly language programmer would have no problem writing the following code to accomplish this task:

```
  cmp ax,10      ; if AX < 10
  jc LessThan10  ; branch
  ; Otherwise, do something else.
LessThan10:
```

But a beginner is very likely to interpret the flags incorrectly and code a **jnc** rather than a **jc**.

With MASM 6.0's new conditional structures, this is no longer a problem. Why? Because we can now write a high-level conditional statement that the assembler interprets. For example, the example just shown would be written like this:

```
.if ax < 10
  ; Do "less than 10" processing.
.else
  ; Do "greater / equal 10" processing.
.endif
```

The code that MASM will generate from the preceding construct will look like this:

```
  cmp ax,000Ah
  jae GreaterEqual10
  ; Do less than 10 processing.
```

```
    jmp Done
GreaterEqual10:
  ; Do "greater / equal 10" processing.
Done:
```

Using the new conditional structures is certainly easier than trying to remember whether you want to write a **jc** or a **jnc**.

In addition to the new conditional structures, MASM 6.0 added three high-level looping structures:

- **.WHILE** and **.ENDW**
- **.REPEAT** and **.UNTIL**
- **.REPEAT** and **.UNTILCXZ**

As with the conditional structures, these loops work much like their counterparts in Pascal or C.

As an example, consider a code fragment that skips forward to the first nonspace character in a string. Using traditional assembly language syntax, you would write something like this:

```
SkipLoop:
  lodsb
  cmp al, ' '
  jz SkipLoop
```

Using the new looping constructs of MASM 6.0, your code would become a bit more readable, as you can see here:

```
.Repeat
  lodsb
.Until (al != ' ')
```

Most of the time, the high-level language structures will generate code that's just as good as what an experienced assembly language programmer would write. That being the case, you should use these new constructs whenever you can. You may encounter some cases where you can outcode the assembler, but those cases will be few and far between. In the vast majority of cases, you're better off letting the assembler worry about the details.

The Listings Diskette

The listings diskette contains all of the macros and subroutines that we've developed over the course of this book. There are two subdirectories on the diskette—one for the Ideal mode code and one for the MASM mode code. Each of the subdirectories contains the following files, whose descriptions follow their names:

BLOCKIO.ASM
ReadBuffer and **WriteBuffer** subroutines from Chapter 6. Called by the **GetCh**, **PutCh**, and **FinalWrite** macros. Used in constructing MYSTUFF.LIB.

CASE.ASM
Also from Chapter 6. This program is a demonstration of the general purpose filter shell.

DOSMACS.INC
This file contains all of the DOS access macros developed throughout the book. See Appendix B for a full list of the macros found in this file.

ERRMSG.ASM
DosDispErrMsg and **DosDispErrMsg1** procedures from Chapter 4. Used in conjunction with the **DosErrMsg** macro. Used in constructing MYSTUFF.LIB.

FILTER.INC
General filter program include file described in Chapter 6. This included file handles the initialization that is common to all filter programs.

LOWERTBL.ASM

Definition of lowercase conversion table described in Chapter 4. Used in conjunction with the **ToLower** macro. Used in constructing MYSTUFF.LIB.

MACROS.INC

This file contains all of the general-purpose macros used in the book. See Appendix B for a full list of the macros found in this file.

MYSTUFF.MAK

MAKE file for constructing the object module library, MYSTUFF.LIB.

PARSEC.ASM

Command-line parsing subroutine defined in Chapter 6. Called by the **GetOptions** macro. Used in constructing MYSTUFF.LIB.

READNUM.ASM

TINY subroutine that reads a number from standard input. Used in constructing TINYLIB.LIB

SF2.ASM

Super Filter 2 is a more useful demonstration of the general purpose filter shell that was too large to fit into Chapter 6. A description of this program can be found in Appendix C.

STRCMP.ASM

TINY string comparison subroutine. Used in constructing TINYLIB.LIB.

SWAPTBL.ASM

Definition of case-swap conversion table described in Chapter 4. Used in constructing MYSTUFF.LIB.

TINY.BAT

Batch file for compiling and linking TINY programs.

TINY.DEF

Header file for TINY programs that includes all macros and other definitions required for compiling TINY programs. See Chapter 7 for a full list of the macros found in this file.

TINYLIB.MAK

Make file for constructing the object module library, TINYLIB.LIB.

TRAL.ASM

The original TRAL program described in Chapter 3. This program uses no macros and is included as an example of programming without the use of macros.

TRALM.ASM

The final version of TRAL from Chapter 3.

UPPERTBL.ASM

Definition of uppercase conversion table described in Chapter 4. Used in constructing MYSTUFF.LIB.

WHILETST.TNY

A TINY test program from Chapter 7.

WRITENUM.ASM

TINY's **WriteNumber** subroutine. Used in constructing TINYLIB.LIB.

YESNO.ASM

GetYesNo subroutine from Chapter 4. Called by the **YesNo** macro. Used in constructing MYSTUFF.LIB.

Copying the Listings Diskette

To copy the listings files onto your hard disk, place the listings diskette in your diskette drive (either A: or B:), and enter the following command at the DOS prompt:

```
XCOPY A:*.* C:\MACROS /S/E
```

You can replace the source drive (A:) with the drive letter that contains the listings diskette. You may also change the destination drive letter and path. When XCOPY has finished copying the files, the MACROS directory on your hard disk will contain two subdirectories—one named IDEAL and one named MASM, which contain the Ideal mode and MASM mode code, respectively.

Contents of Macro Include Files

This appendix lists the constants, structures, and macros that are defined in MACROS.INC and DOSMACS.INC. The contents of the TINY.DEF file are discussed in Chapter 7.

Constant Definitions

The following constants are defined in DOSMACS.INC.

```
bs  = 08h              ; ASCII backspace
tab = 09h              ; ASCII vertical tab
lf  = 0ah              ; ASCII line feed
ff  = 0ch              ; ASCII form feed
cr  = 0dh              ; ASCII carriage return
eof = 1ah              ; DOS end-of-file character
Escape = 1bh           ; ASCII escape character

; Standard file handles
StdIn  = 0             ; Standard input device
StdOut = 1             ; Standard output device
StdErr = 2             ; Standard error device
StdAux = 3             ; Standard auxiliary device
StdPrn = 4             ; Standard list device

; File open modes
omRead   = 0           ; Read only
omWrite  = 1           ; Write only
omRW     = 2           ; Read/write
omCreate = 3           ; Create new file
```

```
; File sharing modes
smCompat    = 0         ; Compatibility mode
smDenyRW    = 10h       ; Read/write access denied
smDenyWrite = 20h       ; Write access denied
smDenyRead  = 30h       ; Read access denied
smAllowAll  = 40h       ; Full access permitted
smPrivate   = 80h       ; Private to current process

; File Attributes
faNormal   = 00h        ; Normal file
faReadOnly = 01h        ; Read-only
faHidden   = 02h        ; Hidden file
faSystem   = 04h        ; System file
faVolume   = 08h        ; Volume label
faDirec    = 10h        ; Directory
faArchive  = 20h        ; Archive
```

CPU Identification Macros

These text macros, defined in MACROS.INC, identify the processor for which code is being generated.

```
Cpu86   equ <1 and @Cpu>
Cpu186  equ <2 and @Cpu>
Cpu286  equ <4 and @Cpu>
Cpu386  equ <8 and @Cpu>
Cpu486  equ <10h and @Cpu>
CpuPriv equ <80h and @Cpu>
Cpu87   equ <0100h and @Cpu>
Cpu287  equ <0400h and @Cpu>
Cpu387  equ <0800h and @Cpu>
```

Macro Definitions

This section gives a brief description of each macro that is included in the MACROS.INC and DOSMACS.INC files on the listings diskette. The format of each macro description is shown by this example:

Macro NiceDay Time,Weather

Determine how well you will do at the fishing hole, depending on the weather conditions and the time you roll out of bed.

Defined in: FISH.INC

Parameters:

Time   Time (in 24-hour format) that your fishing buddies come to get you out of bed.

<Weather>   Expected weather conditions. If not specified, the macro assumes that it will be cold and cloudy.

Note that the **Weather** parameter is optional. In the following macro descriptions, all macro parameters that are optional will be enclosed in angle brackets.

Character Identification Macros

Macro IsAlpha Reg,YesBranch,NoBranch
Set the Z flag if the character in the specified register or memory location is an alpha character (A-Z or a-z), and branch to the appropriate location if requested.

Defined in: MACROS.INC

Parameters:

Reg	The register or memory location to test.
<YesBranch>	Location to branch to if the character is in range.
<NoBranch>	Location to branch to if the character is not in range.

Macro IsDigit Reg,YesBranch,NoBranch
Set the Z flag if the character in the specified register or memory location is a digit (0-9) and branch to the appropriate location if requested.

Defined in: MACROS.INC

Parameters:

Reg	The register or memory location to test.
<YesBranch>	Location to branch to if the character is in range.
<NoBranch>	Location to branch to if the character is not in range.

Macro IsLower Reg,YesBranch,NoBranch
Set the Z flag if the value in the specified register or memory location is a lowercase alpha character (a-z), and optionally branch to the appropriate location.

Defined in: MACROS.INC

Parameters:

Reg	The register or memory location to test.
<YesBranch>	Location to branch to if the character is in range.
<NoBranch>	Location to branch to if the character is not in range.

Macro IsUpper Reg,YesBranch,NoBranch
Set the Z flag if the value in the specified register or memory location is an uppercase alpha character (A-Z), and optionally branch to the appropriate location.

322 ▲ *Macro Magic with Turbo Assembler*

Defined in: MACROS.INC

Parameters:

Reg	The register or memory location to test.
<YesBranch>	Location to branch to if the character is in range.
<NoBranch>	Location to branch to if the character is not in range.

Character Conversion Macros

Macro CaseSwap Reg,UseXlat,LoadBX

If the character in the specified register or memory location is an alpha character (A-Z or a-z), swap the case of the character, optionally using the case-swap conversion table defined in SWAPTBL.ASM.

Defined in: MACROS.INC

Parameters:

Reg	Register or memory location to convert.
<UseXlat>	If nonblank, this parameter causes the macro to use the case-swap conversion table.
<LoadBX>	If nonblank, this parameter causes the macro to load the BX register with the address of the case-swap conversion table.

Macro ToLower Reg,UseXlat,LoadBX

If the character in the specified register or memory location is an uppercase alpha character (A-Z), convert the character to lowercase, optionally using the lowercase conversion table defined in LOWERTBL.ASM.

Defined in: MACROS.INC

Parameters:

Reg	Register or memory location to convert.
<UseXlat>	If nonblank, this parameter causes the macro to use the lowercase conversion table.
<LoadBX>	If nonblank, this parameter causes the macro to load the BX register with the address of the lowercase conversion table.

Macro ToUpper Reg,UseXlat,LoadBX

If the character in the specified register or memory location is a lowercase alpha character (a-z), then convert the character to uppercase, optionally using the uppercase conversion table defined in UPPERTBL.ASM.

Defined in: MACROS.INC

Parameters:

Reg	Register or memory location to convert.
\<UseXlat\>	If nonblank, this parameter causes the macro to use the upper-case conversion table.
\<LoadBX\>	If nonblank, this parameter causes the macro to load the BX register with the address of the uppercase conversion table.

Value Selection and Identification Macros

Macro IsGreater Reg,Val,YesBranch,NoBranch

Set the Z flag if the value in the specified register or memory location is greater than the value specified by the **Val** parameter and optionally branch to the appropriate location.

Defined in: MACROS.INC

Parameters:

Reg	The register or memory location to test.
Val	The value to test against.
\<YesBranch\>	The location to branch to if the value specified by **Reg** is greater than the value specified by **Val**.
\<NoBranch\>	The location to branch to if the value specified by **Reg** is less than or equal to the value specified by **Val**.

Macro IsGreaterEqual Reg,Val,YesBranch,NoBranch

Set the Z flag if the value in the specified register or memory location is greater than or equal to the value specified by the **Val** parameter, and optionally branch to the appropriate location.

Defined in: MACROS.INC

Parameters:

Reg	The register or memory location to test.
Val	The value to test against.
\<YesBranch\>	The location to branch to if the value specified by **Reg** is greater than or equal to the value specified by **Val**.
\<NoBranch\>	The location to branch to if the value specified by **Reg** is less than the value specified by **Val**.

Macro IsIn Reg,Values,YesBranch,NoBranch

Set the Z flag if the value in the specified register or memory location is equal to one of the values in the comma-separated list, **Values**, and optionally branch to the appropriate location.

Defined in: MACROS.INC

Parameters:

Reg	The register or memory location to test.
Values	The values to test against.
<YesBranch>	The location to branch to if the value specified by **Reg** is equal to one of the values in the **Values** list.
<NoBranch>	The location to branch to if the value specified by **Reg** is not equal to one of the values in the **Values** list.

Macro IsLess Reg,Val,YesBranch,NoBranch

Set the Z flag if the value in the specified register or memory location is less than the value specified by the **Val** parameter, and optionally branch to the appropriate location.

Defined in: MACROS.INC

Parameters:

Reg	The register or memory location to test.
Val	The value to test against.
<YesBranch>	The location to branch to if the value specified by **Reg** is less than the value specified by **Val**.
<NoBranch>	The location to branch to if the value specified by **Reg** is greater than or equal to the value specified by **Val**.

Macro IsLessEqual Reg,Val,YesBranch,NoBranch

Set the Z flag if the value in the specified register or memory location is less than or equal to the value specified by the **Val** parameter, and optionally branch to the appropriate location.

Defined in: MACROS.INC

Parameters:

Reg	The register or memory location to test.
Val	The value to test against.
<YesBranch>	The location to branch to if the value specified by **Reg** is less than or equal to the value specified by **Val**.
<NoBranch>	The location to branch to if the value specified by **Reg** is greater than the value specified by **Val**.

Macro IsRange Reg,Lower,Upper,YesBranch,NoBranch

Set the Z flag if the value in the specified register or memory location falls within the range of the **Lower** and **Upper** bounds, inclusive, and optionally branch to the appropriate location.

Defined in: MACROS.INC

Parameters:

Reg	The register or memory location to test.
\<Lower\>	The lower-bound of the range.
\<Upper\>	The upper-bound of the range.
\<YesBranch\>	The location to branch to if the value specified by **Reg** is within range.
\<NoBranch\>	The location to branch to if the value specified by **Reg** is not within range.

Note that the **Lower** and **Upper** parameters are optional, but at least one of these two parameters must be passed to the macro. Passing only one of the parameters results in code that is equivalent to one of the conditional branching macros above. For example, eliminating the **Upper** parameter, as in:

```
IsRange al,100,,LE100,GT100
```

produces the same result as would this invocation of **IsLessEqual**:

```
IsLessEqual al,100,LE100,GT100
```

Utility Macros

Macro ExeStart

Generate .EXE startup code that sets up the segment registers, resizes the allocated memory block, and adjusts the stack so that it can be accessed with the DS register.

Defined in: DOSMACS.INC

Parameters:

None

Macro ProgramHeader ModelName,StackSize

Set the memory model and stack size for the program.

Defined in: MACROS.INC

Parameters:

\<ModelName\>	The memory model to use for this program. If not specified, the memory model defaults to **Small**.
\<StackSize\>	Size of stack to use for this program. If not specified, the stack size will default to 256 bytes.

Macro PopCheck

Determine whether the number of registers **POP**ped matches the number of registers **PUSH**ed and issue an error message if not.

Defined in: MACROS.INC

Parameters:

   None

Macro PopRegs RegList

Pop one or more registers from the stack, decrementing the **PushCount** variable once for each register popped.

Defined in: MACROS.INC

Parameters:

   RegList   Comma-separated list of registers to be popped.

Macro PushRegs RegList

Push one or more registers onto the stack, incrementing the **PushCount** variable once for each register pushed.

Defined in: MACROS.INC

Parameters:

   RegList   Comma-separated list of registers to be pushed.

Macro YesNo StringDef,YesBranch,NoBranch

Display a prompt on the screen and wait for a Yes or No answer from the keyboard. Optionally branch to the appropriate location.

Defined in: MACROS.INC

Parameters:

   <StringDef>   String to display on screen. If not specified, the string addressed by DS:DX will be displayed.

   <YesBranch>   Location to branch to if the user enters a Yes answer.

   <NoBranch>   Location to branch to if the user enters a No answer.

DOS Access Macros

Macro DosCall Fcn

Perform the INT 21h function specified by the **Fcn** parameter.

Defined in: DOSMACS.INC

Parameters:

<Fcn>   INT 21h function to perform. If not specified, the value in the AH register determines the DOS function that will be performed.

Macro DosCloseFile Handle,ErrJmp,ErrMsg

Close the file specified by the **Handle** parameter, optionally displaying an error message and/or branching if an error occurs while the file is being closed.

Defined in: DOSMACS.INC

Parameters:

<Handle>   The file handle to close. If not specified, the handle value in the BX register will be used.

<ErrJmp>   The location to branch to if an error occurs while closing the file.

<ErrMsg>   The message to display if an error occurs.

Macro DosDisplayString StringDef

Display the specified string on the standard output device.

Defined in: DOSMACS.INC

Parameters:

<StringDef>   The string to be displayed. If not specified, the string addressed by DS:DX will be displayed.

Macro DosErrMsg String,Arg2

Display the DOS error message corresponding to the value in the AX register, optionally defining and displaying a preliminary message prior to the DOS error message.

Defined in: DOSMACS.INC

Parameters:

<String>   A string literal or the label name of the string to be displayed.

<Arg2>   A string literal to be defined and displayed.

If the first argument is a string literal, that string will be displayed. If the first argument is a label name and the second argument is blank, the string defined by the label name will be displayed. If the second argument is nonblank, the string will be defined and then displayed.

Macro DosExitProgram ReturnCode

Terminate the program via INT 21h function 4Ch, optionally setting the return value.

Defined in: DOSMACS.INC

Parameters:

    <ReturnCode>   The exit code of the program. If not specified, the value in the AL register will be used.

Macro DosOpenFile FileName,OpenMode,ShareMode,Handle,ErrJmp,ErrMsg

Open a file with the specified attributes, storing the handle and optionally branching on error.

Defined in: DOSMACS.INC

Parameters:

    <FileName>   The name of the file to be opened. This can be a fully qualified pathname. If not specified, the name addressed by DS:DX will be used.

    <OpenMode>   One of the file open modes defined in DOSMACS.INC. If not specified, the value in the AL register will be used.

    <ShareMode>   For existing files, the file-sharing mode. If not specified, the value in AL will be used.

            For new files, the file attributes. If not specified, the value in CX will be used.

    <Handle>   The memory location in which to store the returned file handle.

    <ErrJmp>   The location to branch to if an error occurs when opening the file.

    <ErrMsg>   The message to be displayed if an error occurs when opening the file.

Macro DosReadFile Handle,NumChar,Buffer,EofJmp,ErrJmp,ErrMsg

Read a number of bytes from a file into a buffer, optionally branching and/or displaying a message on end of file or error.

Defined in: DOSMACS.INC

Parameters:

    <Handle>   The file handle of a previously opened file. If not specified, the value in the BX register will be used.

    <NumChar>   The number of characters to read. If not specified, the value in the CX register will be used.

    <Buffer>   The address of the buffer in which to store the data. If not specified, the buffer addressed by DS:DX will be used.

<EofJmp>	Address to branch to if end-of-file is reached.
<ErrJmp>	Address to branch to if an error occurs.
<ErrMsg>	Message to display if an error occurs.

Macro DosWriteFile Handle,NumChar,Buffer,ErrJmp,ErrMsg,FullMsg

Write a number of bytes from a buffer to a file, optionally branching and/or displaying a message if an error occurs.

Defined in: DOSMACS.INC

Parameters:

<Handle>	The file handle of a previously opened file. If not specified, the value in the BX register will be used.
<NumChar>	The number of characters to read. If not specified, the value in the CX register will be used.
<Buffer>	The address of the buffer in which to store the data. If not specified, the buffer addressed by DS:DX will be used.
<ErrJmp>	Address to branch to if an error occurs.
<ErrMsg>	Message to display if an error occurs.
<FullMsg>	Message to display if a disk-full condition occurs.

Data Definition Macros

Macro $String LblName,String

Define a dollar sign-terminated string with the specified label name.

Defined in: DOSMACS.INC

Parameters:

| <LblName> | The label name to assign to this string. |
| String | The text string to define. |

Macro LenString Name,String

Define a text string with an associated length word.

Defined in: DOSMACS.INC

Parameters:

| <Name> | Label name to assign to this string. If specified, this macro will define two labels: the requested label, which defines the string, and a label with the **Len** suffix, which defines the string length. |
| String | The string to define. |

Macro TermString LblName,String,Terminator
Define a string with a terminating character.

Defined in: MACROS.INC

Parameters:

    <LblName>   Name to assign to this string.

    String   The string to define.

    Terminator   The character that terminates the string definition.

This macro is normally used as a "helper" macro by macros such as **$String** and **zString**.

Macro zString LblName,String
Define a zero-terminated (ASCIIZ) string.

Defined in: MACROS.INC

Parameters:

    <LblName>   Name to assign to this string.

    String   The string to define.

Extended Syntax Shift and Rotate Instructions

The following macros are defined at compile time when the MACROS.INC file is included into the source program.

Macro shl Reg,Num,UseCL
Macro shr Reg,Num,UseCl
Macro sal Reg,Num,UseCl
Macro sar Reg,Num,UseCl
Macro rcl Reg,Num,UseCl
Macro rcr Reg,Num,UseCl
Macro rol Reg,Num,UseCl
Macro ror Reg,Num,UseCl

Shift or rotate (depending on the macro) the specified register or memory location the number of places specified by the **Num** parameter, optionally using the CL register to hold the shift count.

Defined in: MACROS.INC

Parameters:

    Reg   The register or memory location on which to perform the operation.

    <Num>   The number of places to shift or rotate. If not specified, 1 is used. If **Num** is CL, the value is shifted (or rotated) the number of times specified in the CL register.

        `<UseCL>`   If nonblank, this parameter causes the macro to load the CL register with the **Num** value and generate a **shl reg,cl** form of the instruction.

If 80186 instructions are enabled, this macro will generate the extended form of the instruction, if appropriate.

Filter Shell Structures and Macros

See Chapter 5 for more information on how to use the general-purpose filter shell.

Structure Definitions

The following structure definitions are used by the general-purpose filter routines.

```
;
; Options record structure used by ParseCommandLine
;
Struc OptRec
  ProgNameAddr  dw ?    ; pointer to program name
  ProgDescAddr  dw ?    ; pointer to program description
  UsageInfoAddr dw ?    ; pointer to additional usage info
  OptTableAddr  dw ?    ; pointer to options table
  PostProcess   dw ?    ; pointer to options post-processing routine
  InputFilePtr  dw 0    ; pointer to input file name
  OutputFilePtr dw 0    ; pointer to output file name
Ends OptRec

; File definition structure
;
Struc FileDef
  BuffSize dw ?    ; File buffer size
  FNamePtr dw 0    ; pointer to filename string
  Handle   dw 0    ; file handle
  BuffSeg  dw 0    ; buffer starting segment
  BuffPtr  dw 0    ; current position in buffer
  NChars   dw 0    ; Number of characters in buffer
                   ; (input files only)
Ends FileDef
```

Macro EndOptions PPRtn

Build the **Options** structure and the options pointer table.

Defined in: DOSMACS.INC

Parameters:

    `<PPRtn>`   Pointer to the options postprocessing routine.

Macro FinalWrite LblName,StoreDi
Write the final partial buffer to output before the output file is closed.

Defined in: DOSMACS.INC

Parameters:

LblName   Base name of file that was previously initialized using the **InitFile** macro.

<StoreDi>   If nonblank, this parameter causes the macro to store DI to the file structure **BuffPtr** variable.

Macro GetCh LblName,EofJmp,ErrJmp,LoadSi
Read a character from a file into the AL register, optionally branching on end-of-file and/or error.

Defined in: DOSMACS.INC

Parameters:

LblName   Base name of file that was previously initialized using the **InitFile** macro.

<EofJmp>   Location to branch to if end-of-file encountered.

<ErrJmp>   Location to branch to if an error occurs in reading a character.

<LoadSi>   If nonblank, this parameter causes the macro to reload the SI register from the file structure **BuffPtr** variable each time a character is read.

Macro GetOptions
Call the **ParseCommandLine** subroutine to read file names and program options from the command line.

Defined in: DOSMACS.INC

Parameters:

    NONE

Macro InitFile LblName,FName,BuffSize,OpenMode,ShareMode,ErrExit
Initialize a file for buffered input or output.

Defined in: DOSMACS.INC

Parameters:

LblName   The base name of the file. This is the name that the other I/O macros will use to refer to this file.

FName   Address of an ASCIIZ filename string.

BuffSize	Size of the I/O buffer to use for this file. This value must be at least 1 and can be as large as 0FFFFh.
OpenMode	**omRead**, **omWrite**, or **omCreate**.
ShareMode	For existing files, the file-sharing mode. If not specified, the value in AL will be used.
	For new files, the file attributes.
<ErrExit>	Location to branch to if an error occurs during file initialization.

This macro performs all required file initialization, including definition and initialization of a **FileDef** structure in the data segment, allocating memory for the buffer, and opening the file.

Macro Option OptChar,Descrip
Define one program option.

Defined in: DOSMACS.INC

Parameters:

OptChar	The character used to specify this option. The option character must be an alpha character. Case is not significant.
Descrip	A string that briefly describes the option.

Macro ProgName Name,Desc
Define the program name and a short description of the program's function.

Defined in: DOSMACS.INC

Parameters:

Name	The program name.
Desc	A short (one-line) description of the program's function.

Macro PutCh LblName,ErrJmp,LoadDi
Write one character from the AL register to a file, optionally branching on error.

Defined in: DOSMACS.INC

Parameters:

LblName	Base name of file that was previously initialized using the **InitFile** macro.
<ErrJmp>	Location to branch to if an error occurs in writing a character.
<LoadDi>	If nonblank, this parameter causes the macro to re-load the DI register from the file structure **BuffPtr** variable each time a character is written.

"Helper" Macros

The following macros, which are defined in the include files, are not intended for use by the programmer. Rather, they are included as "helper" macros for use by the other macros in the include files.

Macro CheckSeg Cur,Target,Directive,YesNo	DOSMACS.INC
Macro CountArgs ArgList	DOSMACS.INC
Macro MakeShiftRot Inst	MACROS.INC
Macro MakeString StringDef	DOSMACS.INC
Macro ShiftRot Inst,Reg,Num,UseCL	MACROS.INC
Macro WhatType Arg1,Arg2	DOSMACS.INC

The Super Filter Program

In addition to the macros and programs that are described in this book's chapters, the listings diskette also contains SF2.ASM, a "Super Filter" program that provides a more detailed example of using the general purpose filter shell.

Super Filter: An Introduction

SF2 is a relatively simple, but very useful, filter program that enables you to do global search and replace functions on any type of file. In addition, SF2 will perform the same case conversions that CASE.EXE (from Chapter 6) is capable of and will also strip the high bit from the characters in a text file, if requested. Let's take a look at the options that SF2 accepts, and then I'll give you a few examples of its use.

As with our other filter programs, the SF2 command-line takes this form:

```
SF2 [{/|-}options] [infile [outfile]]
```

If SF2 is invoked without options, or if the /? option is given on the command line, this information message will be displayed:

```
SF2: Super Filter 2

Usage: SF2 [{/|-}options] [infile [outfile]]

Valid options
  ? - displays this help message
  h - Strip high bits in file
  i - Ignore case in comparisons
  l - Convert all alpha characters to lower-case
```

```
r - Replacement string
s - Search string
u - Convert all alpha characters to upper-case
x - Swap case of all alpha characters

The /l, /u, and /x options are mutually exclusive.
If infile is not specified, STDIN is used
If outfile is not specified, STDOUT is used
```

Most of the options that SF2 accepts are similar to the options that CASE.EXE accepts. The **/h**, **/i**, **/l**, **/u**, and **/x** options are all "flag" options. The **/r** and **/s** options, however, must be followed by a string, the format of which is very important.

As an example, suppose you wanted to search a file for all occurrences of the string "Hello" and replace them with the string "GoodBye." The SF2 command line in this case would be

```
SF2 infile outfile /sHello /rGoodBye
```

Note that the options can occur before or after the filenames on the command line. This is true of all programs that use the **ParseCommandLine** subroutine.

The preceding example is the most common use of SF2—replacing one word with another. But there are times when you might want to replace more than one word. For example, suppose you wanted to replace all occurrences of "Hello, world" with "Hi Mom!." In this case, the search and replacement strings that you pass to SF2 will have to be quoted, like this:

```
SF2 infile outfile /s"Hello, world" /r"Hi Mom!"
```

SF2 can be used for more than just text substitutions. In fact, the reason I wrote SF2 was that I needed a program that would make changes to binary files—something that my text editor doesn't like to do. Consider, for example, the problem of porting text files from an MS-DOS system to a Unix system. Most DOS text editors terminate lines with a carriage return/line feed pair. But Unix systems use only the line feed. Using SF2, you can make short work of changing the end-of-line markers, like this:

```
SF2 infile outfile /s$0d$0a /r$0a
```

which will convert all of the CR/LF pairs in the file into LF characters.

The **$** character begins a two-character hexadecimal constant. The ability to specify the hexadecimal value of a character is useful for more than just control characters. DOS, for example, treats any occurrence of the < character as input redirection. If you want to use < in your search or replacement string, you'll have to specify the hexadecimal value of the character ($3C in this case).

One other character, the "escape" character, plays a special role in SF2 strings. In SF2, the "escape" character is the backslash, \. When this character is given on the command line, the next character is taken literally. This enables you to use quotes or dollar signs in your search and replacement strings. So, if you wanted to change all occurrences of the dollar sign with a right angle bracket, your SF2 command line would look like this:

```
SF2 infile outfile /s\$ /r$3E
```

Space limitations prevent me from listing the program. I suggest, however, that you study the code on the listings diskette because it provides some additional information on how to use the filter routines. In particular, the search and replacement strings processing illustrates how an option processing routine can read information from the command line.

SF2 is one of those programs that you don't use every day, but when you need it, you *really* need it. Keep it in mind; I think you'll find it useful in many situations.

Macro Quick Reference

The following pages are a "Quick Reference" to the macros and subroutines developed throughout the course of the book, and which are included on the listings diskette. The first section lists all of the macros in alphabetic order, along with the listing number and the macro library file that contains the macro. The second section groups the macros loosely by function. The final section lists the contents of each of the subroutine libraries.

Macros Listed Alphabetically By Macro Name

Macro Name	Listing Number	Filename
$String	2-11	DOSMACS.INC
CaseSwap	4-12	MACROS.INC
CheckSeg	3-4	DOSMACS.INC
CountArgs	3-9	DOSMACS.INC
Cpu186	5-9	MACROS.INC
Cpu286	5-9	MACROS.INC
Cpu287	5-9	MACROS.INC
Cpu386	5-9	MACROS.INC
Cpu387	5-9	MACROS.INC
Cpu486	5-9	MACROS.INC
Cpu86	5-9	MACROS.INC
Cpu87	5-9	MACROS.INC
CpuPriv	5-9	MACROS.INC
DosCall	2-5	DOSMACS.INC
DosCloseFile	2-26	DOSMACS.INC
DosDisplayString	3-10	DOSMACS.INC
DosErrMsg	4-15	DOSMACS.INC
DosExitProgram	2-7	DOSMACS.INC
DosOpenFile	2-22	DOSMACS.INC
DosReadFile	3-11	DOSMACS.INC
DosWriteFile	3-11	DOSMACS.INC
EndOptions	6-4	DOSMACS.INC
ExeStart	6-2	DOSMACS.INC
FileDef	6-7	DOSMACS.INC
FinalWrite	6-14	DOSMACS.INC
GetCh	6-12	DOSMACS.INC
GetOptions	6-4	DOSMACS.INC
InitFile	6-8	DOSMACS.INC
IsAlpha	5-2	MACROS.INC
IsDigit	5-2	MACROS.INC
IsGreater	5-4	MACROS.INC
IsGreaterEqual	5-4	MACROS.INC
IsIn	5-7	MACROS.INC
IsLess	5-4	MACROS.INC
IsLessEqual	5-4	MACROS.INC
IsLower	5-2	MACROS.INC
IsRange	5-5	MACROS.INC
IsUpper	5-2	MACROS.INC
LenString	3-11	DOSMACS.INC
MakeShiftRot	5-13	MACROS.INC
MakeString	3-11	DOSMACS.INC
Option	6-4	DOSMACS.INC
PopCheck	1-15	MACROS.INC

Macro Name	Listing Number	Filename
PopRegs	1-15	MACROS.INC
ProgName	6-4	DOSMACS.INC
ProgramHeader	2-2	MACROS.INC
PushRegs	1-15	MACROS.INC
PutCh	6-14	DOSMACS.INC
rcl	5-14	MACROS.INC
rcr	5-14	MACROS.INC
rol	5-14	MACROS.INC
ror	5-14	MACROS.INC
sal	5-14	MACROS.INC
sar	5-14	MACROS.INC
ShiftRot	5-11	MACROS.INC
shl	5-14	MACROS.INC
shr	5-14	MACROS.INC
TermString	3-4	DOSMACS.INC
ToLower	4-12	MACROS.INC
ToUpper	4-8	MACROS.INC
WhatType	3-5	DOSMACS.INC
YesNo	4-6	DOSMACS.INC
zString	2-11	DOSMACS.INC

Macros Listed by Function

Data Definition

Macro Name	Listing Number	Filename
$String	2-11	DOSMACS.INC
zString	2-11	DOSMACS.INC
LenString	3-11	DOSMACS.INC
TermString	3-4	DOSMACS.INC

DOS Access

Macro Name	Listing Number	Filename
DosCall	2-5	DOSMACS.INC
DosCloseFile	2-26	DOSMACS.INC
DosDisplayString	3-10	DOSMACS.INC
DosErrMsg	4-15	DOSMACS.INC
DosExitProgram	2-7	DOSMACS.INC
DosOpenFile	2-22	DOSMACS.INC
DosReadFile	3-11	DOSMACS.INC
DosWriteFile	3-11	DOSMACS.INC

Block File Operations

Macro Name	Listing Number	Filename
FileDef	6-7	DOSMACS.INC
FinalWrite	6-14	DOSMACS.INC
GetCh	6-12	DOSMACS.INC
InitFile	6-8	DOSMACS.INC
PutCh	6-14	DOSMACS.INC

Filter Options Definition

Macro Name	Listing Number	Filename
EndOptions	6-4	DOSMACS.INC
GetOptions	6-4	DOSMACS.INC
Option	6-4	DOSMACS.INC

Value Identification and Conversion

Macro Name	Listing Number	Filename
CaseSwap	4-12	MACROS.INC
IsAlpha	5-2	MACROS.INC
IsDigit	5-2	MACROS.INC
IsGreater	5-4	MACROS.INC
IsGreaterEqual	5-4	MACROS.INC
IsIn	5-7	MACROS.INC
IsLess	5-4	MACROS.INC
IsLessEqual	5-4	MACROS.INC
IsLower	5-2	MACROS.INC
IsRange	5-5	MACROS.INC
IsUpper	5-2	MACROS.INC
ToLower	4-12	MACROS.INC
ToUpper	4-8	MACROS.INC
YesNo	4-6	DOSMACS.INC

CPU Identification Macros

Macro Name	Listing Number	Filename
Cpu186	5-9	MACROS.INC
Cpu286	5-9	MACROS.INC
Cpu287	5-9	MACROS.INC
Cpu386	5-9	MACROS.INC
Cpu387	5-9	MACROS.INC
Cpu486	5-9	MACROS.INC
Cpu86	5-9	MACROS.INC
Cpu87	5-9	MACROS.INC
CpuPriv	5-9	MACROS.INC

General-Purpose Macros

Macro Name	Listing Number	Filename
ExeStart	6-2	DOSMACS.INC
PopCheck	1-15	MACROS.INC
PopRegs	1-15	MACROS.INC
ProgName	6-4	DOSMACS.INC
ProgramHeader	2-2	MACROS.INC
PushRegs	1-15	MACROS.INC
rcl	5-14	MACROS.INC
rcr	5-14	MACROS.INC
rol	5-14	MACROS.INC
ror	5-14	MACROS.INC
sal	5-14	MACROS.INC
sar	5-14	MACROS.INC
shl	5-14	MACROS.INC
shr	5-14	MACROS.INC

Helper Macros Used by Other Macros

Macro Name	Listing Number	Filename
CheckSeg	3-4	DOSMACS.INC
CountArgs	3-9	DOSMACS.INC
MakeShiftRot	5-13	MACROS.INC
MakeString	3-11	DOSMACS.INC
ShiftRot	5-11	MACROS.INC
WhatType	3-5	DOSMACS.INC

TINY Macros

Macro Name	Listing Number	Filename
@Add	7-28	TINY.DEF
@Assign	7-26	TINY.DEF
@Break	7-31	TINY.DEF
@Div	7-28	TINY.DEF
@Else	7-23	TINY.DEF
@EndIf	7-23	TINY.DEF
@EndProgram	7-1	TINY.DEF
@EndWhile	7-31	TINY.DEF
@If	7-23	TINY.DEF
@Mul	7-28	TINY.DEF
@Program	7-1	TINY.DEF
@Read	7-15	TINY.DEF
@Rem	7-28	TINY.DEF
@String	7-7	TINY.DEF
@Sub	7-28	TINY.DEF

TINY Macros (continued)

Macro Name	Listing Number	Filename
@While	7-31	TINY.DEF
@Word	7-6	TINY.DEF
@Write	7-11	TINY.DEF
@WriteLn	7-10	TINY.DEF
CheckElseLbl	7-23	TINY.DEF
MakeJump	7-23	TINY.DEF
MakeJump2	7-23	TINY.DEF
MakeLabel	7-23	TINY.DEF
MakeLabel2	7-23	TINY.DEF
SetElseFlag	7-23	TINY.DEF
SetStk	7-23	TINY.DEF
TinyArgType	7-11	TINY.DEF
TinyArithFcn	7-28	TINY.DEF
TinyRem	7-28	TINY.DEF
VarCheck	7-28	TINY.DEF

Subroutine Libraries

MYSTUFF.LIB

External Name	Listing Number	Filename
??CsTable	4-14	SWAPTBL.ASM
??LcTable	4-7	LOWERTBL.ASM
??UcTable	4-13	UPPERTBL.ASM
DosDispErrMsg	4-16	ERRMSG.ASM
DosDispInfoMsg	4-16	ERRMSG.ASM
GetYesNo	4-5	YESNO.ASM
ParseCommandLine	6-6	PARSEC.ASM
ReadBuffer	6-16	BLOCKIO.ASM
WriteBuffer	6-16	BLOCKIO.ASM

TINYLIB.LIB

External Name	Listing Number	Filename
ReadNumber	7-16	READNUM.ASM
StrCmp	7-24	STRCMP.ASM
WriteNumber	7-12	WRITENUM.ASM

Index

V

values
   lists of, 181-185

X

xlat, 109-114